USS
MARYLAND
(BB-46)

TURNER PUBLISHING COMPANY
412 Broadway, P.O. Box 3101
Paducah, KY 42002-3101
Phone: 502-443-0121

Feature Article: Selected excerpts from the self-
published limited first edition book, *"Memoirs"
Of The Crew Of The Battleship, USS Maryland,
BB46* © 1990 by Fred R. Vreeken, all rights
reserved, used by permission of the author.
Original Naval action photos in "Memoirs"
section by ship photographer, William Chase.

Turner Publishing Company Staff:
Publishing Consultant: Keith R. Steele
Project Assistant: John Mark Jackson

Library of Congress Catalog
Card No: 97-61566
ISBN 978-1-63026-950-0
Additional copies may be purchased from
Turner Publishing Company.

Cover: USS Maryland (BB-46) photo
submitted by Walter J. Mycka.

Rear endsheet and left front endsheet photos
submitted by Walter J. Mycka.
Front right top endsheet photo submitted
by Harold O. Swanson.
Front right bottom endsheet photo submitted
by T.E. Hannon.

TABLE OF CONTENTS

Dedication 4

Publisher's Message 5

History 7

Memoirs: USS Maryland BB-46 14

Special Stories 55

Veterans 71

Roster 91

Index 95

DEDICATION

This book which is being written on the history of the USS *Maryland* (BB-46) is dedicated with gratitude to those sailors who lost their lives on that day which we shall never forget, Pearl Harbor, December 7, 1941, and also to those who lost their lives in subsequent battles with the enemy in the South Pacific during the years 1943 through 1945.

There was much confusion at the time of this unforgettable attack on Pearl Harbor. The name of one sailor, *Warren H. McCutcheon, S2c*, was not included in the records as having been killed on that fateful day. Unfortunately his family was not notified for several months.

This incident was researched and verified by several members of the USS Maryland (BB-46) Veterans Association who were on board at the time and witnessed the attack that killed McCutcheon.

These shipmates gave their lives in action with the enemy.

Other Shipmates Killed At Pearl Harbor December 7, 1941:

Brier, Claire R., MM2c, USN
Ginn, James B. LT (jg), USN

Crow, Howard D. Ens., USNR
Lutz, Carroll F., S1c, USN

Saipan June 22, 1944 (Torpedo Attack)

Bone, Freddie R., S2c, USNR

Woodridge, Robert M., S1c, USNR

Leyte Gulf Nov. 29, 1944

Alcock, Harold B., BM2c, USNR
Dunn, Robert A., SK3c, USN
Goldstein, Morris, S1c, USN
Hilton, Carl C., F2c, USNR
Johnson, Leroy A., Y2c, USN
Kester, Robert E., HA2c, USNR
Lamb, Fargust E., HA2c, USNR
Mangold, Jack E., F1c, USNR
Markshausen, Robert T., FC3c, USNR
Newman, Victor D., SF2c, USNR
Nopen, Irwin G., GM3c, USN
Overstreet, Rufus M., Jr., S2c, USNR
Riley, Layton F., BM1c, USN
Sturgeon, Raymond W., S1c, USN
Thomas, Glenn C., S2c, USNR
Williams, Vernon R., S2c, USNR

Cripes, Kenneth, MUS2c, USNR
Evans, Charles E., CTC, USN
Hathcox, William M, HA1c, USNR
Hoffman, Charles J., F1c, USNR
Kendrick, Stonewall J., S2c, USN
Kukon, Thomas E., S2c, USNR
Lucas, Jack S., S1c, USNR
Manly, Pete C., HA2c, USNR
Milligan, Lloyd T., S1c, USNR
Niss, Rudolph R., EM1c, USNR
O'Rourke, Henery J., S1c, USNR
Peacock, "J." "R.", S1c, USNR
Ryman, Gordon O., S1c, USNR
Thau, Melvin (n), S1c, USN
Voyles, Hollice L., Y2c, USN
Zoller, Vernon (n), CBM, USN

Okinawa April 7, 1945

Andrews, Rex W., GM3c, USNR
Chambers, "C." "H.", S2c, USNR
Gates, Eugene W., S1c, USN
Hargrove, Roy P., S1c, USNR
Hill, Lawrence L., S1c, USNR
Langford, Leslie G., S2c, USNR
Medaris, Jack E., S1c, USNR
Scott, Harold A., COX, USN
White, Clyde T., BM2c, USN

Cedillo, Luis Z., S1c, USNR
Conwill, "J." "A.", S2c, USNR
Gist, James W., S1c, USNR
Harrington, James D., S2c, USNR
Land, Arnold L., S1c, USNR
Lanning, Harold M., S2c, USNR
Noel, William O., COX, USN
Seagraves, Edward H., GM2c, USNR

These young men of the USS *Maryland* (BB-46) gave their lives in the fight for freedom. They should be truly remembered.

Eternal rest grant unto them and let perpetual light shine upon them,
and may they rest in peace . . . Amen

PUBLISHER'S MESSAGE

Dave Turner, President - Turner Publishing Company

Among the most famous battleships in the history of the US Navy, the USS *Maryland* (BB-46) is certainly one of the most respected. From her commissioning on July 21, 1921 and her brave service throughout World War II to surviving the attack on Battleship Row at Pearl Harbor to her final decommissioning in April 1947, the USS *Maryland* traveled the world in the name of freedom.

This book is dedicated to those of you who proudly served aboard the USS *Maryland* defending those persecuted by aggression. It was you, the veterans, who selflessly gave yourselves, heart and soul, and risked you lives. It was you, who through your actions, created the history of the USS *Maryland* that is held in such high esteem today.

I would like to thank all of you who submitted your photographs, personal experience stories and biographies to be included in this history book. I would like to personally thank Mr. Dick Beaman, President of the USS *Maryland* BB-46 Veterans Association, for his efforts in making this volume possible. Appreciation goes to Walter Mycka, Wayne Ring and Ed Davis for their help at various stages of the project. Also, I would like to thank Mr. Fred Vreekan for providing his revised manuscript, *Memoirs*, that is featured in this publication. Finally, I would like to thank Mr. Keith Steele, publishing consultant, whose dedication to publishing Naval history helped make this book possible.

Dave Turner
President, Turner Publishing Company

USS Maryland (BB-46)
History

A different view of the capsized Oklahoma and the Maryland at Pearl Harbor with the West Virginia burning fiercely to the right. The upper level of smoke is from the exploding and burning of the Arizona. (Courtesy of Walter J. Mycka)

8

Official History of the
USS *Maryland* (BB-46)

Maryland has logged enough nautical miles to take her many times around the world. In 1921, shortly after her commissioning, the ship was assigned as flagship of Admiral Hilary P. Jones. She continued as flagship until 1923, when the flag was shifted to USS *Pennsylvania*. During this time the battleship made her first visit to a foreign port when she had the honor of carrying Honorable Charles Evans Hughes, then Secretary of State, to Brazil as representative of the President on the occasion of the Brazilian Centennial Exposition. Here the *Maryland* played host to representatives of every Navy in the world. In the same year, 1922, the aircraft catapult of the *Maryland* type was perfected. From this forward step in the progress of sea warfare, *Maryland* named the paper published by the ship's complement, *The Catapult*.

For twenty years *Fighting Mary* patrolled the seas, the cream of the Navy's battleship fleet, always in readiness to match her skill and strength with any contestants. During this time the ship prepared for any possible warfare, never knowing that when the inevitable hour arrived it would be the sudden and unceremonious death and destruction of 7 December 1941 at Pearl Harbor.

It was a fairly quiet Sunday morning on 7 December, and some of the crew were getting ready for liberty at 0900, others were finishing breakfast. Back from battle maneuvers with the *Maryland* were other battleships moored along Ford Island. Alongside to port was the *Oklahoma* with lines and gangway connecting the two ships. Ahead was moored the battleship *California* and astern were the *Tennessee* and the *West Virginia* moored together with the *Nevada* and *Arizona* moored farther astern. These were the battleships along "Battleship Row."

Considerable excitement and noise attracted the attention of men below decks who come topsides to find that the cause for the distant noise was machine-gun fire and bombs dropping. Suddenly, dive bombers with unusual insignia on the wings roared over in a low-level attack. Thundering explosions jolted the outboard battleships and the boatswain's mate of the watch piped the word "Away fire and rescue party" and the bugler blew general quarters.

The anti-aircraft batteries sprung into action as more low flying bombers appeared. Many men were climbing aboard from the badly listing *Oklahoma,* and though covered with oil and badly shaken, they pitched in to assist the men on the guns. Shortly thereafter the *Oklahoma* sunk with her mast in the muddy bottom of Pearl Harbor and her starboard hull bulged out of the water with keel and propeller shaft in clear view. The ships astern were obscured from view by oil flames and great clouds of black smoke.

After a lull in the attack, bombing planes roared in again toward "battleship row" to hammer the inboard ships which torpedoes could not reach—*Maryland, Tennessee* and *Arizona.* One bomb landed on the forecastle; another swerved under water piercing the ship's side to explode in the storerooms which were promptly flooded. Late in the morning the attack ended and many of the crew formed fire-fighting parties to help the nearby ships which were more critically damaged. Tapping from within the hull of the overturned *Oklahoma* prompted the men to cut holes in the skin of the ship to release many of the trapped men.

"Fighting Mary" had taken a beating but had not fared as badly as some of the other battleships. Two officers and two men of the *Maryland* were killed. The other men aboard the battleship were filled with suppressed excitement, curiosity and anger as they waited in vain for the Japs to return. Throughout the attack the men had shown fine spirit as they went about their tasks efficiently and quickly.

The Japs boasted that the *Maryland* was on the bottom, permanently sunk in the mud, never to rise again, never to fight again. What the Japs did not know was that the *Maryland* pulled into Puget Sound Navy Yard twenty-three days later for battle damage repairs. Of the five ships "sunk" in the raid which started the war, *Maryland* was the second to arrive at Bremerton, Washington. *Tennessee* was a day ahead of her—and the race to repair these two ships for return to the fleet was a race against time.

In a very commendable effort, *Maryland* received damage repairs, new rifles, new fighting equipment and an overhaul which was to make her a better ship than ever before through two and a half years of fighting. When she left the Puget Sound Navy Yard, the battleship was the first ship damaged at Pearl Harbor to return to the wars from a United States yard. Numerous cruises from West Coast ports, including one toward the Christmas Islands, were made before the ship was sent out near Midway in June 1942.

There was a grave threat of the Japanese invading the Hawaiian Islands and a large Japanese fleet with many transports was heading east. *Maryland* served as a stopper in the advance of the Japs in which their forces were defeated in this most decisive battle of the Pacific War—The Battle of Midway. The *Maryland* stood by awaiting call from the forward forces until the danger was over after which she was routed to San Francisco.

Several weeks later Battleship Divisions 2, 3, and 4, which included *Maryland,* departed the West Coast together for a westward cruise. Directed to proceed to Pearl Harbor, the old battleships entered port in grand style for it was the first time these battleships entered the harbor enmasse since the attack of 7 December 1941. With officers and enlisted men at division parade in their whites, the ships made a very impressive entry; an entry in which they were fully repaired and ready for war.

Maryland with other ships, departed southward for the forward area in the first part of November. King Neptune and his Royal Court came aboard on 12 November 1942 to administer initiations upon the pollywogs when the ship crossed the equator. Along with the *Colorado, Maryland* steamed to the Fiji Islands as sentinels and a menace to the Japanese who might have landed on Samoa or the Fiji Islands, thereby cutting off the lifelines to Australia. Several times during their sentinel duty, there were hints of Japanese task forces in the area and the ships steamed out to search the seas.

In the middle of February 1943, as advances were being made by our forces in the Solomon Islands, the *Maryland* and *Colorado* moved as two major pieces in a chess game to the New Hebrides. The flies and intolerable heat at Efate were strong allies of the Japanese and made the six and one-half months stay at this "tropical paradise" anything but pleasant.

The next stop, Espiritu Santo, with its steamy heat and heavy rains, made a generous contribution to the discomfort of the crew before *Maryland* and *Colorado* stood out of Aore Harbor in August and set course for Pearl Harbor. During the five weeks in the shipyard there, many 40mm anti-aircraft guns were installed on the decks and foremast as a protection against the enemy air raids anticipated in future operations. Returning to the staging area at Efate Island, *Maryland* joined a large task force and departed for Tarawa Atoll in the Gilbert Islands on 12 November 1943.

"Old Mary" was the flagship of the entire operation, carrying aboard

The crew on the upturned hull of the Oklahoma buring holes through the hull to permit rescue of the men trapped inside. One of the Oklahoma launches is in the foreground. The Maryland is in the backround. (Courtesy of Walter J. Mycka)

Vice Admiral H.W. Hill, Commander of the Fifth Amphibious Group, with his staff. Also aboard with his staff during this operation was General "Howling Mad" Smith, commanding the Marine landing forces, including Colonel Carlson of Carlson's Raiders. In the early morning of 20 November, as the ships approached their objective, Batio Island in the Tarawa Atoll, *"Fighting Mary"* had her first chance to roar in defiance as her big guns took the offensive. At 0500 a shore battery on the southwestern point of Betio Island opened fire on her. *Maryland* at once took up the fight and silenced the battery in five salvos. An hour later she commenced her scheduled bombardment.

Moving up close to shore to draw enemy fire and thus locate the camouflaged batteries, *Maryland* guns each spoke with an authoritative flash and a roar. Main and secondary batteries hammered without mercy at Japanese gun emplacements, control stations, pillboxes, and anything Japanese within reach. Approaching the beach at 0900, the first wave of Marines landed and some units fought their way to the airstrip. The second and third waves of landing forces met heavy opposition and many were killed by a murderous cross-fire of machine guns which covered the beaches.

Maryland's guns wiped out several of these harassing positions and waited call fire from the observation planes which were following the progress of the assault. Flying over the installations, the *Maryland* planes radioed first hand reports on the movements and attacked machine-gun nests and other positions with hand grenades and machine guns. During the action the Japs retaliated by seriously puncturing the plane and wounding the radioman.

That night bitter fighting raged on the island and at their battle stations on the *Maryland,* sailors watched the occasional flashes of flame throwers and artillery. After three days of supporting and call fire from the beach, *Maryland* left for the island of Apamama to guard a landing of Marines there. The only resistance on this islet was a group of about 30 Japanese most of whom formally committed hara-kari. Two prisoners were taken aboard *Maryland* and on 7 December, the ship left Apamama for Pearl Harbor. The Navy and "Fighting Mary" had completed the first phase of the long uphill struggle to prove the invincibility of the United States even after the disaster at Pearl Harbor.

A short trip to San Francisco to effect repairs was completed in time for *Maryland* to depart on 13 January 1944 to proceed to Lahaina Roads in the Hawaiian Islands where Task Group 53 was assembling. Two days of loading ammunition, refueling, and provisioning, prepared the ships to get under way for the coming operation in the Marshall Islands. These islands were well protected with secret installations of the Japanese. They were low, narrow, coral formations, studded with islets that enclosed the lagoons. Kwajalein, the world's largest atoll was the very hub of the Jap fortifications.

In the dark of the night on 30 January, *Maryland* maneuvered toward her objective; Roi Island in the Kwajalein Atoll. In the predawn hours as the ship drew in closer, great fires could be seen lighting up the clouds of smoke on shore. A raid of carrier planes had just pounded the island to helped soften resistance. At sunrise a part of the Northern Support Group, including the *Maryland, Santa Fe, Biloxi* and *Indianapolis* commenced firing at their predetermined targets. The big guns roared with flashes of fire and billows of smoke. Suddenly a Jap pillbox would disappear, counter battery fire would be silenced or a Jap position would be obscured from view by an explosion and emerge from the drifting smoke a pile a rubble. *Maryland* fired until she split the liners in the guns of turret No. 1; she gave the Japs everything she had.

The performance of the fire support ships weakened the Japanese defenses to the extent that the casualties during landing operations were among the lightest experienced in amphibious warfare in the Pacific thus far. On the second day, *"Mary"* helped protect the assault waves by maintaining intense fire with all batteries only a few hundred yards ahead of the advancing troops. Following the successful invasion Vice Admiral Connally came aboard with his staff, making *Maryland* his flagship. For over two weeks after the landings, the ship provided many of the smaller vessels with provisions and fuel before departing for Pearl Harbor with a task unit of several small carriers and destroyers on 15 February 1944.

Steaming back to the Navy Yard at Bremerton, Washington, she acquired new guns and a general overhaul.

Her guns once again readied for battle, *Maryland* steamed westward to participate in the biggest campaign of the Pacific War yet attempted-Saipan. Enroute sailors on the ship heard the suave voice of "Tokyo Rose" blandly announce that the garrison and air groups of Saipan were eagerly awaiting the arrival of the American forces. Again it was the job of *"Mary"* to help prepare the way for the invasion.

The thundering guns of the battleship pointed toward Saipan on the morning of 14 June 1944, quickly silencing two coast defense guns in a brief duel. The planes directed the ship's firing to choice targets on the shore and the shells blasted gun positions, ammunition dumps, small boats, storage tanks, blockhouses and buildings in the town of Garapan. The town of Tanapag, which had been thick with troublesome snipers was leveled with the bombarding of the ships. The invasion of 17 June was successful and *Maryland* stood by for call fire in support of the ground forces.

At dusk on 22 June, the ships were anchored off the southeast coast of Saipan when a Jap plane came in low over the Saipan hills to avoid radar detection. The twin-engine bomber was heard as it zoomed in a sharp bank and appeared over the bow of the *Pennsylvania* which was anchored to port of the *Maryland.* The plane suddenly headed for the battleships, crossed the bow of the *Pennsylvania,* dropped a torpedo and flew into the dusk just as an explosion jolted the *Maryland.*

A torpedo had ripped into the port bow opening a gaping hole in the ship's hull. Aviation gasoline vapors spread rapidly into nearby compartments but miraculously, no explosion resulted. It soon became apparent that one bulkhead forward of the collision bulkhead firmly separated the rest of the ship from the sea. Ship's repair parties quickly brought the damage under control and *Maryland* weighed anchor and proceeded to Eniwetok with two escorting destroyers. The ship was directed to Pearl Harbor for repairs at the Navy Yard. Burial services were held for the two men who lost their lives in the explosion and at reduced speed, *Maryland* ploughed her way into Pearl Harbor.

Departing Pearl Harbor on 13 August 1944 with a large task group, *Maryland* set course for the Solomon Islands. The ships anchored in Purvis Bay off Florida Island and remained there for about two weeks before getting underway for the Palau Islands on 6 September. Under Vice Admiral J.B. Oldendorf, the task groups approached Peleliu and Anguar Islands in the early morning of 12 September (D-minus 3-day). It was well known routine for the guns of *Maryland* to bombard the shore installations and gun positions preparatory to an invasion. The greatest difficulty in this operation was locating the extremely well camouflaged gun positions and other targets. With the hot shells from the ships arching overhead, the underwater demolition teams worked at their dangerous task of clearing the approaches to the beaches for the landing craft. The biggest danger to the ships during this operation was from small boats loaded with explosives. Remaining until the last of the month, *Maryland,* with several other large ships, set course for Manus in the Admiralty Islands.

At anchor in Seeadler Harbor, Manus, from the first of the month, *Maryland,* as part of the Seventh Fleet under Admiral Kincaid, sortied to sea on 12 October, Task Group 77.2, which was the gunfire and covering force for the initial landings of the Philippines at Leyte, was composed of five battleships, numerous cruisers and several destroyer divisions. With paravanes streaming, and the ships in column to avoid mines, they steamed into Leyte Gulf in the early morning of 18 October.

Minesweepers had been at work the day before clearing as much as possible in an inadequate amount of time. While entering, two mines were encountered by the fleet. *California's* paravanes surfaced one which was sunk by rifle fire and the other was marked with flags to warn the ships to steer clear.

Taking her place off Red and White beaches, early the next morning *"Fighting Mary"* commenced bombarding for the landing which took place at 1000 on the 20th. With beaches well secured, the ships performed the remainder of their mission by guarding the sea approaches to Leyte Gulf.

During the succeeding days the ships underwent increasingly heavy Jap air raids during which a new lesson in Japanese "diplomacy" was introduced—the Kamikaze or suicide dive. It was an indication that the Japs were getting desperate in their attempt to stem the tide of American advance in the Pacific.

Several days after the beginning of the invasion of the Philippines, the U.S. Navy's submarines in the South China Sea radioed what they had just seen through their periscopes. The pagoda structures of five Japanese battleships were leading a large force toward San Bernardino Strait, north of Leyte. About the same time, long-range scout planes had sighted another large force headed by four aircraft carriers from Singapore, rounding northern Luzon. It was apparent that the battleship force planned to sink the transports and combatant ships in Leyte Gulf while the carrier force hoped to blast the decks of Admiral Halsey's carriers while the planes were out on a strike.

Submarines sank and damaged several of the Japanese ships during their approach while the U.S. carrier force severely damaged the battleship force and headed north. In the evening of 24 October, the ships of the Seventh Fleet prepared for the impending battle. Since a night action was expected, the ship's scouting planes were flown to the southern beach where they were tied up to the stern of an LST. Along the battle line guarding the entrance to Leyte Gulf at Surigao Strait, were five of the old battleships which the Japs had thought were sunk at Pearl Harbor: *California, Tennessee, Pennsylvania, West Virginia* and *Maryland.*

The cloak of darkness enshrouded the Japanese fleet as it slipped through the blackness of the early morning of the 25th. Ahead of them lay the PT boats waiting to ambush. As the huge dark forms of the Japanese ships swept by the narrows the torpedo boats attacked successfully, scoring several hits. The Japanese ships forged ahead to be met by the torpedoes of the destroyers who reported "torpedoes away" and rejoined the formation. The Jap ships still came on.

Several miles ahead, Vice Admiral Olendorf's cruisers and battleships waited in perfect formation, cunningly waiting for the enemy force to come within range. The Japanese battleships *Fuso* and *Yamashiro,* with their screen, steamed unwaveringly into the narrow, 12-miles pass; into the trap. The thundering guns of the U.S. Navy's cruisers and old battleships laid down a semi-circular mass of fire, slowing down the formation and setting the leading Jap ships on fire. Both *Fuso* and *Yamashiro* were sunk, while the other ships hesitated . . . then turned and fled from the insalubrious narrows. Only a bare remnant of the original force escaped, trailing oil behind them through the Mindanao Sea. Here the Navy planes pounded them with a hail of bombs.

Admiral Olendorf's ships were prevented from pursuing the beaten Japanese force by the threat of the other Japanese surface force to the north. This force similarly met disaster from the bombing of U.S. carrier-bases planes and was forced to turn and run in ignominious defeat.

As a sentinel, *"Mary"* stood guard at the mouth of the straits until 28 October to keep the enemy away from the amphibious forces. A trip to the Admiralty Islands to take on ammunition and refuel brought the battleship back to the Leyte area by 16 November 1944, where she protected the beaches, transports and amphibious craft against enemy attack. The fanatical suicide attacks mounted in their fury and the attacks on transport ships was diverted to a heavy concentration on the combat ships in the gulf. Incessant attacks kept the crew at battle stations much of the time and the Japs sneaked in as many as 18 raids in a single day. For thirteen days the fleet went through one of the worst air barrages of the Pacific war during which time many ships were damaged. In one of the raids *"Mary"* maneuvered to avoid the torpedo of a plane which had just been "splashed".

November 29 dawned much the same as the previous ones, with air alerts and men hurrying to their battle stations. Shortly after sunset Japanese planes were reported in the vicinity and the anti-aircraft guns flashed angrily from the ships. One plane suddenly commenced a dive on the cruiser *Denver,* changed his mind and pulled out of the dive to disappear momentarily in the clouds. Skirting around the barrage of gunfire, the plane spotted *"Fighting Mary"* through a hole in the clouds and came down in a screaming dive to crash between turrets one and two.

The bomb pierced the forecastle, main and armored decks and ripped a hole in the four-inch steel. Everything close by was demolished in the area around the forecastle. Bulkheads were torn open, lockers smashed, plumbing, lighting and ventilation ducts in the adjoining compartment were ruined as the ship caught on fire. Thick, acrid smoke hampered the firefighting and repair parties while most of the crew remained at battle stations for the ship was now a neon-lighted target for subsequent attacks.

The fire was promptly put out and the damage localized, although there were many casualties. Only a few men survived the tremendous concussion in the nearby vicinity of the explosion and they were seriously burned. Thirty-one men were killed with one officer and 29 men injured. All the injured were quickly and efficiently cared for in spite of the severe damage to the medical department. The operating room, pharmacy, offices, laboratory and wards were demolished or ruined, but battle dressing stations in various parts of the ship were set up in anticipation of just such a disaster.

Three days later, *Maryland* left Leyte Gulf in company with two badly damaged destroyers. The oppressive heat, persistent air raids and the recent disaster and loss of shipmates, left the crew in pretty low spirits. But there was more work and more fighting to do and spirits perked up as the ship returned to Pearl Harbor for repairs and recuperation.

Her repairs completed *"Fighting Mary"* slipped through the channel at Pearl Harbor and set her course westward again to anchor off Ulithi on 16 March 1945. Here ships of the Fifth Fleet were gathering for the gigantic operation of Okinawa. In the early morning of 21 March, *Maryland* sortied with other ships to take her place in the huge disposition of ships which were to provide gunfire in support of the largest amphibious operation the world has ever known. Officer in tactical command was Rear Admiral M.L. Deyo with his flag in the *Tennessee.*

General Quarters was sounded on the morning of 25 March as the ships of the bombardment force approached their assigned sectors. The big guns of *Maryland* were assigned the job of knocking out shore batteries, pillboxes, and other targets of opportunity. The main purpose was to support a diversionary landing on the southeast coast of Okinawa to distract the enemy's attention from the main invasion force on the west coast.

Air raids were not long in coming. One of *Maryland's* radar picket destroyers, USS *Luce,* was badly hit by a kamikaze and was sinking. The nearest destroyer, went over to rescue the crew and was also attacked by a kamikaze plane.

While plastering enemy positions up and down the west coast of Okinawa on 3 April, an urgent message was radioed to *Maryland* to proceed to the west coast of the island. There she was ordered to combat shore batteries which had been uncovered by the 8" guns of the cruiser *Minneapolis.* So it was that the 16" guns of *"Fighting Mary"* set out upon another major assignment. Needless to say, the old battleship kept alive the traditional excellence which had sailed the seas with her for so many years. The enemy guns were completely destroyed with six four-gun salvos.

Captain Wilson, skipper of the ship had this to say, "That was one of the bigger moments of my career, to see our guns perform so excellently. After the shooting was over, I received a message from the skipper of *Minneapolis* that really made me swell with pride." The message went something like this, "Nice going! I see that the old guns are as good as ever. My peashooters couldn't even touch those guns." This is just another incident that made the ship what she was in the eyes of the rest of the fleet.

After the invasion, *Maryland* stood by with the rest of the support task force, awaiting calls from the beach for main battery fire. Long hours were spent at general quarters and the anti-aircraft batteries were in "Condition 1" most of the time. The huge mass of ships off Bolo Point were given an unmerciful pounding, every day ships went to the bottom and every day the Japanese scored. In spite of all the danger and the vicious air assaults, the fleet still stood by.

Maryland was not destined to come through this operation unscathed. On 7 April the crew had been up early in the morning for an air alert and more alerts kept all hands at their battle station during the afternoon. Just before dusk, a number of the ships were on a northerly course to intercept an enemy raiding force which was headed for Okinawa. At 1849, a Japanese kamikaze plane swooped down and crashed his plane with its 500-pound bomb into the top of turret III on the starboard side. The plane burst into flame, the bomb exploded and the 20mm mounts on turret III were demolished. All but one of the men manning these mounts were blown from their stations. Great flames lit up the entire scene to the ships nearby. In the macabre glare could be seen debris and dead and wounded men. The heat of the flames exploded 20mm shells and the flying fragments burned and wounded other men at stations in the mainmast and on the quarterdeck.

The next day the more severely injured men were put aboard a patrol craft for transfer to the hospital ship USS *Comfort*. There were a total of 53 casualties, with ten dead, six missing, 19 seriously injured and 18 moderately injured. Although *Maryland* remained at Okinawa for one week after the damage pumping out salvo after salvo, the damaged turret III, though usable, was held silent. The gallant seventeen men who stood by their guns on top of the turret until the enemy plane exploded in their midst, had made the supreme sacrifice.

After seven more days of call fire, air raids and suspense, *"Fighting Mary"* left the forward area for Guam and Pearl Harbor. While enroute, a message was received with the good news that the ship would go into the Navy Yard at Bremerton, Washington. On the day victory was proclaimed in Europe, the ship arrived at Bremerton.

At the Navy Yard in Puget Sound, the damaged turret was repaired and *"Old Mary"* was decked out with the latest thing in electronic equipment, new secondary battery guns and for the first time the crew had bunks to sleep in instead of the cots or hammocks. In August, just as the improved *Maryland* left Bremerton for tests and training runs off the coast of California, Japan surrendered, ending the war. The termination of hostilities brought a complete change in plans for the venerable battleship. She became part of the Magic Carpet operation, one of the large number of US Navy ships assigned to bring veterans back home from the forward areas.

With her Magic Carpet duties ended, *Maryland* was placed out of commission in reserve on 3 April 1947, as part of the Bremerton Group, Pacific Reserve Fleet. To the newer ships *"Old Mary"* has passed on the torch of glorious naval tradition in the hope that it will always burn brightly as it did for *Maryland*.

USS *Maryland* earned seven battle stars for operations listed below:
American Area Campaign Medal

1. Asiatic-Pacific Campaign Medal:
2. 1 Star/Pearl Harbor-Midway: 7 Dec 1941
3. 1 Star/Gilbert Islands Operation: 13 Nov - 8 Dec 1943
4. 1 Star/Marshall Islands Operation:
   Occupation of Kwajalein and Majuro Islands 28 Jan 1944 - 8 Feb 1944
5. 1 Star/Marianas Operation:
   Capture and occupation of Saipan - 11 June - 10 Aug 1944
6. 1 Star/Western Caroline Islands Operations:
   Capture and occupation of southern Palau Island - 6 Sep - 14 Oct 1944
7. 1 Star/Leyte Operation:
   Leyte Landings - 1 Oct - 29 Nov 1944
8. 1 Star/Okinawa Gunto Operation:
   Assault and occupation of Okinawa Gunto - 24 Mar - 30 June 1945

World War II Victory Medal

List of Commanding Officers

Capt. C.F. Preston, USN	21 July 1921 - 1 March 1922
Capt. D.F. Sellers, USN	1 March 1922 - 10 May 1923
Capt. F.H. Clark, USN	10 May 1923 - 9 June 1925
Capt. T.T. Craven, USN	9 June 1925 - 24 May 1927
Capt. J.V. Klemann, USN	24 May 1927 - 6 September 1928
Capt. V.A. Kimberly, USN	6 September 1928 - 16 May 1930
Capt. J.K. Taussig, USN	16 May 1930 - 3 February 1931
Capt. R. Morris, USN	3 February 1931 - 21 December 1932
Capt. L.B. Porterfield, USN	21 December 1932 - 1 March 1934
Capt. D.C. Bingham, USN	1 March 1934 - 27 July 1935
Capt. G.S. Bryan, USN	27 July 1935 - 20 June 1936
Capt. L.P. Davis, USN	20 June 1936 - 16 December 1937
Capt. W.A. Glassford, USN	16 December 1937 - 31 March 1939
Capt. G.C. Logan, USN	31 March 1939 - 28 September 1940
Capt. E.W. McKee, USN	28 September 1940 - 21 November 1941
Capt. D.C. Godwin, USN	21 November 1941 - 14 January 1943
Capt. C.H. Jones, USN	14 January 1943 - 15 December 1943
Capt. H. J. Ray, USN	15 December 1943 - 30 December 1944
Capt. J.D. Wilson, USN	30 December 1944 - 1 December 1945
Capt. B.W. Decker, USN	1 December 1945 - March 1946

Original Statistics

Length Over-All:	624'
Extreme Beam:	97'6"
Normal Displacement:	
Tons:	32,600
Mean Draft:	30'6"
Design Speed;	21
Design Complement:	
Officers:	58
Enlisted:	1022
Armament:	
Main:	(8) 16"/45
Secondary	(12) 5"/51
	(8) 3"/50
Torpedo Tubes:	(2) 21" subm.
Armor:	
Maximum Thickness:	18"

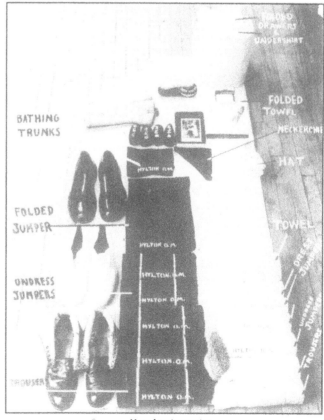

Navy bag inspection.

MEMOIRS:
USS *Maryland*, BB-46
By Fred R. Vreeken

Note: The following section contains selected excerpts from the self published limited first edition book, "MEMOIRS" Of The Crew Of The Battleship, USS *Maryland*, BB-46 © 1990 by Fred R. Vreeken, All rights reserved. Original Naval Action photos by ship photographer, William Chase.

The Peaceful Years ...1921-1941...

The keel of the battleship USS *Maryland*, BB-46, was laid down April 24, 1917, by the Newport News Ship Building Company, Newport News, Virginia, at a time when a new breed of tyrants began to emerge. President Wilson declared in his war message to Congress, "The world must be made safe for democracy," as war prostrated Europe proved sterile ground for the growth of democracy and producing instead a new Tyranny of totalitarianism.

In Russia, on October, 1917, the Communists had already seized power from the constitutional Kerensky Government. The strutting Benito Mussolini formed his Fascist party in 1919. By 1922, his black-shirted bullies had so threatened the Government, that by 1922 he was able to become an absolute dictator! The German Nazi party was also formed in 1919. Totalitarianism opposed everything that true Freedom and Democracy stood for.

The USS *Maryland*, BB-46, was launched March 20, 1920, and commissioned July 21, 1921. Captain C.F. Preston, was first in command, at a time of great concern with the events of the world outside. Brig. General William (Billy) Mitchell, sank four obsolete American Battleships, (including the USS Alabama), from the air, in a futile campaign to convince the economy minded American Government, and conservative military men, that our nation needed a strong air force. But for America, in the safety and freedom of a different hemisphere, politicians were complacent. Emphasis was placed on a strong Naval Force , to protect our shores... We were at peace, ... yet with our maneuverable Navy, carried a big stick!

The USS *Maryland*, the first battleship of her class, was the most formidable battleship in the world and would soon be followed by her sister ships, the USS *Colorado* and the USS *West Virginia*.

It was no wonder that the men who served aboard the USS *Maryland* in a relatively peaceful hemisphere in he 1920's and 30's felt that magnificent pride!

She was the king of the seas! — A dreadnought to be feared and looked upon with awe. The men who walked her decks and felt her disciplined strength, stood prepared to defend America from any enemy at any time and any where, in any ocean of the World!

For those who served aboard the USS *Maryland*, BB-46 during this era, it would remain for them a proud experience, during the remainder of their lives.

The USS *Maryland*, BB-46 Held Many Honors In Naval History:
- The FIRST American Battleship to carry and fire 16 inch guns.
- The FIRST American Battleship to carry and catapult aircraft from her decks.
- The FIRST American Battleship of her class.
- The FIRST American Battleship to rejoin the fleet after Pearl Harbor.
- The FIRST American Battleship to carry and launch torpedoes.
- The ONLY American Battleship to be equipped with a unique German made range finder.
- The most powerful battleship in the world, when commissioned, July 21, 1921.
- The flagship of the American Fleet.
- Selected for President Elect Hoover's good will tour to Latin America, in 1928.
- Participated in seven major battles in the Pacific area during WWII.
- Damaged by bombs, torpedoes and Japanese Kamikaze suicide aircraft on four different occasions.
- Suffered 121 World War II combat casualties.
- Returned thousands of combat troops home during "Magic Carpet" duty.

The Peacetime Navy

Little has been written about the pre-war peacetime navy. It really matters not when a man served aboard the USS *Maryland*, BB-46, because every man shared the same pride and everlasting fond memories of this grand lady, — "The Queen Of The Seas".

Indeed, it is interesting to taste the spirit of the "Roaring Twenties", the devastating depression which followed, and when the Navy was a haven for many souls who made themselves a good life, learned new skills, discipline, vocations, not to mention unforgettable adventure and travel! It had always been and always will be, a cherished and memorable experience for all of those who served their Country well, aboard this grand lady of the sea.

The stories of peacetime service gives the reader an opportunity to partake of the many interesting adventures, combined with humorous and often mischievous side of a carefree sailor's life. (Some which required censorship!)

We especially honor those who served aboard the USS *Maryland* just after she was commissioned in 1921. Only a very few souls have survived. The oldest living survivor today, is 100 years old! His name is Russell J. Bitting. We hope that you will enjoy his comments of Navy life during the time he served, from August 2, 1921 to March 28, 1925. It depicts naval life and experiences of long ago not often found in text books. The memories they have recorded herein, will last as long as we able to preserve them.

You will discover as we progress through these "Memoirs", that from time to time, many structural changes and improvements had taken place, which have kept the USS *Maryland*, BB-46 outfitted with heavier armor, increased firepower, sophisticated electronics and radar tracking systems.

Fred R. Vreeken, author, when serving aboard the USS Maryland during WW II. (Courtesy of Fred R. Vreeken)

From left to right, Harry Moyce, BM2/c, Ralph Hallman, (visitor), F. Williams, CM2/C, Russell J. Bitting, GM3/c, George Walt, (visitor). Visiting ship at San Pedro, California.

The capsized Oklahoma. (Courtesy of Fred R. Vreeken)

The Memoirs of Russell J. Bitting, GM 3/C

Born March 23, 1904. Served Aug. 2, 1921 - Mar. 28, 1925 (Oldest living survivor)

The Flagship USS *Maryland*, BB-46 departed from berth eight, North River, New York at 3 PM, Friday, August 18, 1922, past the Battery into the Ambrose Channel. There, the Battleship USS *Nevada* joined with us, to represent the United States, on the one Hundredth Anniversary of Brazilian Independence.

The USS *Maryland* was the pride of the navy at this time, with a new type seaplane catapult and sixteen inch guns .... The most powerful warship in the entire world!

The Initiation As Shellbacks
By Russell "Dutch" Bitting

On August 29th, 1922, when we crossed the equator, Rear Admiral Williams greeted "His Royal Highness", King Neptune aboard. I was rather nervous concerning the charges which were made against me, but it turned out I didn't have as many as some of the others did? I got a good dunking though. Seaman 1/C Egen in our Torpedo Division and I had to walk through the center line on forward deck. The shellbacks, (ie, those who have crossed the equator before, having received their traditional initiations), gave us some good whacks with canvas clubs! It did sting some, and I tell you, we really scrambled through there!

It was a wonderful sight to enter the beautiful harbor of Rio De Janiero, Brazil. It is said to be one of the most beautiful harbors in the world. We had some fine liberties there, which included visits to Sugar Loaf Mountain by cable car, viewing the panorama of the city below and partaking of life in the city itself.

Animals and Pets Kept Aboard
By Russell "Dutch" Bitting

Animals of various kinds, (dogs, cats, monkeys, parrots, etc.) were allowed aboard ship during a period in the peacetime navy. Coming back from Rio De Janiero, we had the then Secretary of State Evan Hughes and his wife aboard, as well as Representative Porter of Illinois. I had a few words of conversation with them on the boat deck. They were curious about the parrot I had obtained in Rio, and had asked me questions about him ... and the keeping of animals aboard ship? We were individually responsible for taking care of them.

The Memoirs of W.E. "Pete" Peterson, FC1C
Served Sept. 1928- March, 1937

Only a few of our surviving *Maryland* Veterans, remember the persons we had aboard during the late 1920's. There were two dogs, (breed unknown), whose names were "Cinco" and "Peso". They had the run of the crew's quarters. It wasn't unusual to wake up in the morning to find a dog sleeping with you!

Nick Carte and Cox, "F" Division, had a beautiful large macaw parrot, that sat on a wooden "T" above *the trash can*. On numerous occasions it had chewed through the perch and fell into his droppings in the trash can! Remedy? Nick gave it a bath in the midship's wash room!

One of our Marines, had a cheetah that lived in an old ice cream freezer in the Marine 5 inch gun casement. The cheetah was very tame, and didn't protest being led around on a leash..

Two monkeys that had the freedom of the topside — One jumped overboard from the after mast, and I can't remember what happened to the hell happened other one?

The Memoirs of James E. Fox, S 2/C
Born Feb. 20, 1912 Served December 1929 to Dec. 1931

Trinidad, was a British Island of 1,864 Sq. Miles, in the Atlantic Ocean off of the coast of Venezuela. It is now part of the independent state of Trinidad and Tobago. It was really a very interesting port of call.

On our visit, we discovered that there was a natural asphalt lake there. We were taken to visit this lake on a small train. We also understood that the asphalt from this lake was exported from Trinidad to the United States.

We traveled on this train through places where there were some natives tribes. The men wore metal rings around their necks. Each one had eight to ten rings on their fingers. Soon we arrived at a lake, where we enjoyed the food and some beer. All in all, it was interesting and enjoyable.

Getting Acquainted With The "Holy Stone"

Every Friday, we "Holy Stoned" the deck! Using a brick shaped pumice with a hole in the center of it, a handle was placed into the hole and held in position while standing. The "Holy Stone", as it is called, was then vigorously too and fro with the grain of our teakwood deck planks, which were about four inches wide, and four inches deep. Tar was placed between each plank, thus allowing the planks to shift forwards and backwards with the movement of the ship. The salt water bleached the deck planks white. The decks were maintained so clean, that a man could sit or lay on the deck in his white uniform and never get them soiled nor spotted.

My battle station at that time was a pointer in a 16 " gun turret ... A pointer fires the projectile on command. When these huge guns were fired, they recoiled right over our heads. The concussion on the outside surface would blow the hats right off of a persons head.

On one humorous occasion in Washington, there were signs on some of the lawns which read, "Sailors and Dogs — Keep Off The Lawns!"

The Day of Infamy, Pearl Harbor, December 1941

The Surprise Attack At Pearl Harbor

America will never forget it's lesson learned from that day of the infamous attack on Pearl Harbor in the early morning hours of Sunday, December 7th, 1941, by the Japanese. It was a time of great concern and unpreparedness. Even while unsuspecting Japanese envoys came to Washington to talk of peace assurances, Japanese aircraft carriers and battle fleet were nearing their objective — The destruction of the American Fleet, and the military installations at the great naval base in Pearl Harbor Hawaii. (The American Fleet was the only threat against the Japanese plan to dominate the pacific arena).

Though their deed was a dastardly one, it was bold and extremely effective! It resulted in the achievement of all of Japan's initial military and naval objectives .... However, they didn't count on the tremendous, fighting mad, patriotic zeal of the American people! They were willing to make any sacrifice, in order to defend their rights, freedoms, and way of life! Perhaps the Japanese surprise attack at Pearl Harbor, though effective from a military point of view, may have brought about the very catalyst which would lead to their downfall! It had cemented the iron will of all Americans to join together in a patriotic realization the world had never witnessed! America's way of life had been threatened! We had never lost a war! We were a champion of peace and an example of progress to the nations of the world ... and we would have our revenge!

How could we ever forget December 7, 1941 —That "Day of Infamy!"

Where was Pearl Harbor? With the lack of communications in those days, many Americans hadn't the vaguest idea, that a great naval base even existed so far into the Pacific? Communications over a half century ago, were certainly not what they are today! We lived in an entirely different environment. Having learned an important lesson, America is now determined to never let her guard down again!

The Typical American Scene—December 1941

In 1941, Communications were primarily limited to radio stations and newspapers. We didn't know what smog was? There were no freeways. Model "A" Fords were still popular. The newest vehicles still had running boards, and by today's standards, were built like great monolithic mastodons! Gas was only 10 or 11 cents per gallon and was pumped from a long cylindrical glass tube, with each gallon measurement appearing thereon. The fuel was gravity drawn through a rubber hose and handle. A station attendant would fill your tank for you, wash your windows and check your oil levels as part of the service, at no charge! No refreshments were sold, except perhaps a Coca Cola container, filled with ice! The Coke was only a nickel! Newspapers were sold by kids on street corners, who screamed out the headlines. The Los Angeles Herald and Examiner newspaper were only five cents each. The Daily News, was only three cents, and you could buy a huge, rich, thick malted milk of any flavor for the same nickel!

It was a time when America was only just recovering from the great depression. Ah, yes, the early forties were times of great simplicity and unity, when life moved at a slow and easy pace.

It was early morning, December 7th, 1941, when all radio stations were suddenly interrupted to announce that the Japanese had bombed Pearl Harbor! Everyone's ears were glued to their radios, soaking up the drama.

Recruiting stations across the Nation were immediately bombarded with angry patriotic volunteers, incensed at the audacity of Japan to strike a dastardly surprise blow like this! Our national pride was hurt and we were eager to even the score! Our Country immediately solidified into a fighting mad hornet's nest!

Pearl Harbor was a terrible disaster. There were real fears that the Japanese would attempt a landing there, or even bombard America's Pacific coastline cities.

The next morning, all across the nation, there were long lines of angry young American men at the recruiting stations, eager to volunteer for military service. They wanted revenge and retaliation at the Japanese! There was a certain spirit of excitement and adventure about it all. The "glamour" of war did strange things to many fine young men. They would soon find out, all to soon that the glamour would fade into the night, only to turn into a wild nightmare of death and destruction. There would be a big price to pay for heroism, and many, — too many, would have to pay that awful price...

The Memoirs of Charles G. Forselles, SC 1/C, Dec. 7, 1941
Served 1941-1944

It is rare, to find one individual who had served in all three branches of the military service. I was one of those individuals. With all of these experiences, the most lasting and memorable moments in my life occurred

during my first enlistment while I had served aboard the Battleship USS *Maryland*, BB-46.

I was 17, when I enlisted in the United States Navy. Before my enlistment, I worked eight months for a farmer, who paid me $35.00 per month. I never dared to leave the farm, nor even cashed any of the checks he gave me. One day, I went with him to Antasberg and bought myself a pair of new trousers, a shirt, and a pair of shoes. When I saw myself in a mirror, I was surprised at how much I had grown? I had even developed muscles! Imagining that I might also look well in a navy uniform, I decided to enlist! It would be a new adventure and experience.

Since I was under enlistment age, I was required to contact my mother for written permission, which she reluctantly provided. I managed to pass all of the examinations, for military service, and was accepted on April 2, 1941. After rigid training at San Diego, California, I was assigned to the Battleship USS *Maryland*, BB-46.

The First Taste of Battle — December 7, 1941
By Charles G. Forselles, SC, 1/C

We were docked in Pearl Harbor on December 7, 1941, when the Japanese struck their surprisingly bold and deadly blow. It came at 7:55 AM on that infamous morning, bringing death and destruction to battleship row. At that precise moment, I was on the third deck below standing at my locker, wrapping a bottle of perfume I had bought for my mother. Suddenly, the bugle alarm sounded and a boatswain's voice screamed menacingly through the ships loud speaker systems, "All hands, — man your battle stations!"

I thought, how peculiar it was to have a general quarters drill in port? We never had drills in port, we only had them at sea? However being well trained, I quickly dashed to my battle station on the main deck. Men were scrambling in all directions. The boatswain repeatedly sounded the ominous call, "All hands man your battle stations! This is no drill!"

Breakfast was being served below at the time. I scrambled to my battle station through passage ways, compartments and the debris of overturned mess tables. Breakfast has spilled everywhere!

Climbing the last ladder to my battle station on the boat deck, (A 5 "25 caliber Anti-Aircraft battery), I heard the resounding sound of guns pounding from our ships on battleship row. Low flying Japanese torpedo planes and dive bombers were dropping bombs and torpedoes everywhere! (We recognized immediately that they were Japanese, because of the large red ball insignia on their fuselage and wings.

Suddenly, all hell broke loose! I saw the battleship *West Virginia* burning uncontrollably. She was listing severely, having been hit hard by several Japanese torpedoes. She quickly settled to the bottom, where she was anchored. The same destruction happened to the nearby battleship USS *Tennessee*, docked just astern of us.

The Battleship USS *Oklahoma*, tied to the port beam of the Battleship *Maryland*, had caught five torpedoes in rapid succession. I watched the heavy lines snap like thread, as she rolled over amid heavy smoke and debris!

In the next moment, the powder magazines of the USS *Arizona* exploded furiously, sending 1,103 Marines and Sailors to a watery grave. The strong force of concussion whipped across our knees, while we still held live ammunition in our hands, firing shells as fast as we could load them!

The vulnerable *Oklahoma* had taken one torpedo hit after another. The fact that the USS *Oklahoma* was tied to our seaward side, saved the Battleship USS *Maryland*, from similar destruction!

A 500 pound fragmentation bomb exploded on the *Maryland* forecastle forward. It killed two crewmen and blew a gaping hole about 12 by 20 feet in diameter into our topside deck. Another crushing bomb caused widespread structural damage and flooding to our port bow and torpedo air-compressor rooms. Both compressors were put out of commission.

My job, was to load live ammunition into the number 5 gun fuse pots, and to shoot incoming Japanese dive bombers which flew through the dark smoke filled sky. Bombing was followed by enemy machine gun strafing. Only moments earlier, it had been a very beautiful Sunday morning!

We had to move quickly. The harbor was rapidly filling with acrid, black smoke from torpedoed American naval ships. It made it very difficult to sight incoming enemy aircraft. At the beginning we didn't have live ammunition topside. However, it finally arrived from ammunition rooms below. Shells rolled onto the deck, where they were quickly placed in "ready boxes". As second loader, I passed hundreds of live shells.

Scanning the smoke darkened harbor, I spotted a group of Japanese fighter planes coning in extremely low over Ford Island. They pounded hangars and blew up everything in their deadly paths. All of our aircraft still on the ground exploded before my eyes. There must have been thirty of them erupting into giant balls of fire! Enemy fighters relentlessly strafed everything in sight, as they neared the Battleship *Maryland*. If I had been standing, it seemed I would have been ripped in half! The splinter shield on our gun emplacement was the only thing topside which offered us protection.

Indiana Johnson, a full blooded Cherokee, was the first loader on our 5 inch twenty 5"-.25 caliber anti aircraft battery. He was mad as a hornet! He demanded more and more ammunition. The other second loader and I barely kept up with his orders. The gun breech was red hot, as salvo after salvo fired in rage at the Japanese.

Until that morning, Indian Johnson had been a very quiet and reserved person. He was so excited with all of the shooting action, he ripped off his grimy clothes down to his shorts, smeared gun grease on his face, (His markings for the "King of Warriors" on battleship row), and did a war dance on the deck, the likes of which I shall never forget!

The Battleship USS *California* lay burning and listed heavily. A few minutes later the battleship *Nevada* sailed past us, desperately trying to get out to sea ... She never made it! The Japanese pounded her relentlessly. After sustaining extensive damage from bombs and torpedoes in her side, the *Nevada* beached herself on the Ford Island side of the harbor. Her skipper was very wise to beach his ship. It could have sank in the channel, thereby blocking it so no other ship could either enter nor leave Pearl Harbor!

I had soon began to come to the realization that we were in the middle of the Battle of Pearl Harbor! My hands and especially my fingers, were bleeding from passing ammunition. I felt no pain,—only anger! I fought on with compassion and determination to preserve our American heritage, which had suddenly taken on a new, more beautiful and important meaning!

The Harbor was engulfed in flames that licked at thick black oil, which rolled menacingly throughout battleship row. Man men attempting to swim to safety were either burned to death, or drowned in the choking, clinging oil, which covered the waters surface. It seemed as though the entire United States Navy had been destroyed. I watched as our tracers hit home on at least three Japanese planes. When exploding, they appeared as torches igniting in the darkened sky. Enemy aircraft crumbled, falling in flames

like hot Meteors. Though it seemed a lifetime, the battle only lasted one hour and fifty minutes!

I lived at my battle station, without going below decks for three days after the Pearl harbor attack. We feared the Japanese might return, in an attempt to administer a coup de grace? The wooden deck was my bed. Our toilet was a five gallon can. My pillow was a navy cap folded into a small bundle. Sandwiches and coffee from the ships galley were brought to our gun positions topside. (We devoured anything and everything we could find). Men were streaked with dirt, oil, blood, and sweat.

I had been temporarily deafened from anti- aircraft blasts which had continuously surrounded us.

Later, when the ships doctor examined my ears, it seemed he must have removed a half cup of gun powder from each ear! He exclaimed that he had "Never seen anything like that before in his entire career!"

Trapped In a Watery Coffin of Hell!
By Charles Forselles, SC 1/C

I kept thinking about the capsized Battleship USS *Oklahoma*, which had berthed along side of us. How devastatingly helpless she looked. She appeared as a huge whale, which had gone belly up. I knew one of her crewmen from basic training at San Diego. I was anxious to learn what had happened to him aboard the *Oklahoma* when she capsized? Thirty two living men were still trapped deep within her bowels, desperately trying to stay alive! * (The *Oklahoma* lost 415 officers and men out of her 1, 354 man crew, during the attack)

The Battleship *Oklahoma*, never had a chance to fight during the attack. She sank within 15 minutes after the first direct torpedo and bomb hits. Her crew were heavily strafed by Japanese aircraft as they desperately scrambled to climb over the rolling hull. The rolling stopped as her mastheads dug into the harbor's murky bottom. Rescue efforts by military and civilian workers began amid blazing oil fires which surrounded the area.

Surviving *Oklahoma* crewmen caught below decks, were trapped for hours inside the overturned battleship. More than 400 shipmates had drowned, and many were trapped, imprisoned in an upside down world. They dove and swam through compartments being flooded by rising polluted sea water, desperately trying to find trapped air to breath and a hope for freedom from their depths of containment!

The story you are about to read, was related to me by my friend, who was one of the few who survived a terrifying 34 hours in a seemingly hopeless, watery grave! ...

My friend told me he scrambled below decks to his battle station. He grabbed the nearest stanchion as the ship shook from the five torpedo hits amidships. He had to climb two decks down, to the handling room loading station, which served the huge 14 inch guns of the main battery.

The rushing force of oily putrid sea water bearing dead body, after dead body, almost swept him away. He was cut with flying metal from another torpedo hit. Nevertheless, he reached his battle station. He and other crewmen secured the watertight hatch which cut off the rushing flow of fouled, oily salt water.

The *Oklahoma* began to list badly from the five direct torpedo hits. The entrapped men hung on to the angle irons running parallel to the ship's bulkhead, as she listed heavily. Some were unable to accept the fact that they were trapped underwater! Temporary insanity swept over them, (Which medical science later attributed to battle fatigue), as they clawed at the hatches to free themselves from certain death by drowning! Seemingly, deep inside the overturned *Oklahoma*, surrounded by rapidly rising water, there was no escape! Auxiliary lights were dimming!

Men trapped inside various compartments could hear loudspeakers screaming "Abandon Ship! Abandon Ship!" Suddenly, 1400 pound target projectiles fastened to the bulkheads broke loose, crushing who men before the terrified eyes of their companions. Six men in the compartment above them drowned as the stricken *Oklahoma* lurched!

* (*Japanese torpedoes were especially effective at Pearl Harbor. There were no torpedo nets spread for the protection of battleships at Pearl Harbor. Each battleship was a stationary target which could hardly be missed by forty torpedo planes flying 50 to 100 feet above the water*).

As the *Oklahoma* was capsizing in the harbor, sea water continued to rise inside the compartment holding my friend and four other survivors. Their escape plan was to take deep breaths, fill their lungs with air, dive into the darkness of the oily water, and attempt to swim through a hatch, into an adjoining compartment. There, they would rise to hopefully gulp another lung full of captured air, dive again, and so on, until they found a way out! The plan was a desperate one, without choice! (Two of five

The capsized Oklahoma BB-47 and the USS Maryland BB-46 after the attack on December 7, 1941. Crew on the updturned hull of the Oklahoma burn holes through the hull to permit rescue of men trapped inside. One of the Oklahoma launches is in the foreground. The USS Maryland is in the background. (Courtesy of Walter J. Mycka)

young men drowned in the process. They had lived their lives. Their day had come as they sank into their watery graves).

The surviving three men dove again, maneuvering their way into another compartment. There, they found eleven more crewmen caught in the same predicament. Three of these men had decided they would attempt to swim to the overhead of the main deck, find a hatch, cross it some thirty feet under the surface, then scale the side of the ship. (Later we found that only one of them miraculously accomplished this feat!)

The remaining eleven men finally reached the last compartment forward. It was as far as they could go. The exhausted crewmen slept standing erect, in water up to their shoulders. (Air pressure held the flooding at that level temporarily).

Hours had passed since the first attack. Treacherous seawater continued to rise slowly again in their darkness. Time seemed to stand still. Emotional and physical strain became unbearable!

Finally, at last the trapped men sealed in their supposed tomb, heard the sound of drilling! Some were impressed that it might be the enemy, trying to take them prisoners? Two more crewmen trapped in adjoining magazine compartments were screaming for help! "How could they reach them", they wondered? Suddenly, the screaming stopped...Their compartment filled with water, to end their heroic effort to live...

The other eleven trapped men could feel the water rising around their own necks. Heads pressed against the steel surface above them, they could still hear the steady sound of drilling. One man dove into the depths of the compartment and found a wrench. He desperately used it to signal that they were alive! Would anyone hear their SOS message? The situation seemed hopeless, as they made feeble half hearted attempts to free themselves. The stale supply of air had almost dissipated. The men were lacking physical strength to endure.....

A launch crew made a final cruise around the capsized Oklahoma's hull, looking, —listening for survivors trapped within, when weak tapping sounds were heard through the hull now barely visible above the water level of the harbor! Cutting through the many layers of steel, was an enormous and tedious job.

Extreme caution was required to avoid hitting ammunition or oil storage compartments. Acetylene torches were very dangerous to use! Rescuers were forced to use air hammers, making progress slow and difficult.

Inside, the drilling sounded louder and louder to the entombed men. After what seemed like an eternity, a drill finally penetrated through the thick hull! Immediately the remaining air escaped, as the dark harbor water rose rapidly to flood their compartment! It meant swimming under water to another compartment, or drown! One of eleven men dove under the water, managing to open another hatch. The survivors hurriedly squeezed into a less water filled compartment, securing the hatch behind them. They realized however they had lost the wrench used to tap their S.O.S. distress call! "How much longer can we last," they wondered?

They finally heard noises unexpectedly from the other side of the ship! They banked their fists furiously against the steel walls, shouting and screaming desperately for help! Finally the trapped crewmen were pulled from their watery grave one by one, after a heavy lid opening was made by rescue parties.

After facing the tensions of certain death for 27 hours, in what seemed a hopeless situation, they were free at last! Twenty one other survivors were also rescued from the hull of the overturned battleship. The first group of survivors were released at 0800 (AM) on December 8, 1941. The last were rescued at 0230 (AM) on December 9, 1941. Basically, all were in fair condition, except for a lack of sleep, food, sufficient oxygen and exhaustion.

The trapped survivors were completely naked. It became impossible to wear wet heavy clothes in water filled compartments with little air and no ventilation.

A gut -wrenching sight greeted the survivors. The USS Arizona was a twisted ruin, smoldering aft of the Oklahoma, Maryland, Tennessee and the West Virginia. The Arizona burned for two days in the harbor, before yard tugs were able to extinguish the raging flames. Fires illuminated the harbor which held the shattered remnant of our proud fleet.

From a nearby ship, a lone bugler played taps. Tears filled my eyes. I lowered my head in prayer for lost comrades, as pensive notes echoed across the black smoke filled harbor. We knew then we faced a long hard war.......

The Congressional Medal of Honor
For Father, Lt. J.G. Aloysius H. Schmitt
Submitted by Charles G. Forselles

Of the twenty two officers attached to the Battleship USS *Oklahoma* on Dec. 7th, 1941, one was a heroic Chaplain, Father Lt. J.G., Aloysius H. Schmitt. He was posthumously awarded our nation's highest honor. He unselfishly sacrificed his own life, to save the lives of other shipmates trapped in a water filling compartment of the USS *Oklahoma*, as the ship settled to a watery grave at the bottom of Pearl Harbor.

Chaplin Schmitt was stationed with the sick Bay Medical Staff, giving of himself unselfishly to the comfort of others. As the torpedo stricken vessel increased it's degree of list, word was passed to abandon ship. Men scrambled desperately towards the only route of escape, — one single open porthole. As Chaplain Schmitt's time came to squeeze through the narrow opening, the breviary he carried in his back pocket prevented his passage to escape. As he pulled himself back into the water filling compartment, he felt convinced that his duty was to help others out first! One crewman after another clawed past in a frantic attempt to escape the watery gave which awaited them. The *Oklahoma* had passed horizontal mark and now settled on the bottom of the harbor. Stale putrid air filled the last space in the darkened compartment. The last surviving crewman to leave said that when he looked back at Father Schmitt, he appeared to be enveloped in a euphoric feeling of great happiness and well being.

It was said by the Medical Staff, that Father Schmitt helped save many lives, at the sacrifice of his own. "Greater love hath no man, than this, who would lay down his own life for his friends — Well done, thou good and faithful servant!"

*The refloating operations of he USS *Oklahoma* was difficult for navy salvage crews, as was the beggarly job of removing human bodies in various compartments. Two or three feet of water were left in each compartment, so bodies could be floated into canvas bags. The bags were then tightly tied and transported to the Naval Hospital for proper identifications and burial. The total dead reached as many as 400 to 500 men.

* A total of 5000 dives were made, with about 20,000 hazardous hours under water, by men who put their lives on the line, in search of imprisoned survivors in sunken warships and salvage efforts.

The Memoirs of Ed Swanson, CBM

Soon after morning chow, Frank (my bow hook), and I were leaning against the hammock netting, engaging in small talk. Lapsing into silence, we wondered to ourselves what this beautiful new day would bring. Cloud formations began to disperse, as their attempt to hold back the dawn failed ... Rays of morning sun filtered softly through the hatchway and down the ladder, to form golden shafts of light ... The splendor of a morning that was.....

Their colors deepened, as swirling dust particles bathed in it's glow, chasing shadows across the deck and up the lockers of the First Division compartment. It was an uplifting experience, which made our spirits soar. We turned to look out the open portholes, towards nearby Ford Island. The effect was tranquilizing. Slanted amber rays of the sun brushed the palm trees and lush green foliage with brilliant hues which transformed the view into an almost paradisiacal scene.

Frank faced me with an earnest appeal in his voice. The essence of our conversation remains clear in my mind..... "Ed, why can't we get permission to have our motor whale boat hooked up, (hoisted to the boat deck), since we're only on stand by since today is Sunday? Perhaps we'll be able to go ashore when liberty begins, around noon?"

Having just witnessed God's nature in it's finest apparel and not trying to do something uplifting, would be tantamount to holding our spirits in contempt! We wondered if Frank's idea would pass approval, as we headed aft on the port side. On the quarter deck, the Officer of the day was not standing by the gangway which extended over the Battleship *Oklahoma*.

As we crossed over to the starboard side of the *Maryland*, we spotted the Officer, but noticed a fuel tank on Ford Island engulfed in flames? Moments later, the Public Address System bellowed "Away fire and rescue party!" Then immediately afterwards, it was "All hands — Man your battle stations!"

The unmistakable sound of an aircraft engine caught everyone's attention, as it roared by.... We had a ringside view of a Japanese "Kate", (I.D. code name) as it roared by. We could plainly see the pilot, wearing a white scarf and a dark moustache as he peered down at us! The flaming red "Meatballs" on wings and fuselage brought everything into proper focus. I suddenly came to the realization that our two countries were now at war!

The enemy aircraft began to surge with a visible bouncing motion, clawing for altitude, as it skimmed over the USS *Maryland*, having launched it's torpedo into the Battleship USS *Oklahoma*. The action occurred within a matter of seconds. The visual picture would be indelibly etched into my memory for these almost five decades that have passed...

On the double. I headed towards my battle station, (The upper handling room of our huge 16 inch guns (Turret #1). My heart pounded with excitement, as there came a flashback of the evening before, as I had stepped off the motor launch onto the boat landing. A newspaper with banner headlines in bold faced letters seemed to shout for attention, as it proclaimed: "F.D.R. SAYS JAPAN LIES!"

A Bittersweet Christmas
By Ed Swanson, CBM.

The seas were running heavy with strong winds and swells, which forced the Battleship USS *Maryland*, to tolerate it's fury. The weather was a picture of dreariness. Being at sea seemed so out of place. Today was Christmas! Our thoughts were of the up-coming feast, together with memories of past Christmases as home with our loved ones.

What a welcome sight it was, to enter the straights of Juan De Fuca, leading into Puget Sound. These warm and cheerful reflections obviously helped to roll back the dismal days at sea.

The sad memories of three Sundays ago persisted to linger in the corners of my mind. Several of our shipmates would not be with us to enjoy fellowship at the Yuletide and Hanukkah Season. However, fate had decreed that the Battleship *Oklahoma* moored along our port side, would shield the *Maryland* from enormous casualties ... and we were grateful.

The Memoirs of Rudy Keihne, GM1/C
Served Sept. 1938 to Oct. 1942

I joined the United States Navy in the town of Fredericksburg, located in the hill country of Texas, in June of 1938. (Fredericksburg was also the birthplace of Admiral Nimitz) After completing boot camp at the training station, in San Diego, California, I was assigned to the Battleship USS *Maryland*, BB-46., which was at that time based in Long Beach. We had a limited choice as to where we elected to serve. I requested duty aboard the USS *Maryland*, because a couple of my friends from home were serving aboard this ship at the time. Fredericksburg was well represented aboard, with as many as seven crewmen form my home town.

I was attached to the Fifth Division, and assigned to a five inch broadside gun battery unit. The guns were located in individual compartments called "casements". These casements were my home for years.

Shortly after coming aboard ship, the *Maryland* weighed anchor and headed out to sea for night gunnery practice. I was about to have my first experience in what life was like to be stationed on a "floating" gun platform! The Battleship *Maryland*'s main function and purpose of being, was her tremendous fire power. I must admit, I was at that time a bit apprehensive of what I had gotten myself into?

I had been assigned as a "pointer" on gun number three, while John Land, a home town friend, was the "trainer". We were a good team. We had engaged in short range firing practice, because of heavy seas. Only two guns aboard the ship earned the much sought after "E's" for efficiency and performance. Ours was one of them. This award involved not only prestige, but extra pay!

I had only about six more months to do on my four year hitch, when we were attacked at Pearl Harbor, but the plans and hopes of many were altered on that morning of December 7, 1941... I wakened to reveille, stowed my cot in the hammock netting, and enjoyed a nice breakfast. I had bought a Sunday paper, and was headed towards the forecastle, near our big sixteen inch gun turret #1, to read it. While sitting in it's shade, I heard an explosion, and saw a fire on nearby Ford Island? I instinctively walked toward my battle quarters located in the casements. Then I heard other explosions? As I entered the door to the casement on the starboard side, an aircraft zoomed over the *Maryland* at extremely low altitude. I caught a glimpse of the rising sun emblem as it passed. It had apparently launched a torpedo towards the doomed USS *Oklahoma*, which was secured to seaward side of the Battleship *Maryland* ... The infamous attack at Pearl Harbor was well underway!

Though I do not recall hearing General Quarters being sounded, I immediately dashed to my general quarters station at the port side battery. Shortly afterwards, the Battleship *Oklahoma* snapped her big ten inch mooring hawsers, which secured her to the *Maryland*. After about five successive Japanese torpedoes in her side, I watched the *Oklahoma* heave to, roll over and slowly sink, before our horrified eyes! Being on our seaward side taking the brunt of the attack, she absorbed the deadly enemy torpedoes, protecting the *Maryland* from a similar fate!

We were unable to fire our broadside guns. Had we done so, we might have unwittingly bombarded our own installations across the harbor. I never unlocked the compartment which contained the firing locks to the broadside guns of the port side, even though there was pressure on me to do so.

I reported to my alternate battle station on the 5 inch 25 caliber anti-aircraft battery located on the boat deck. I helped there until all of the ammunition from the ready boxes had been expended. While we waited for ammunition to be sent up from below, a number of us took cover in the tailor shop. There, we used cotton from the steam press to stuff in our ears, in order to abate the concussion and noise. Our five inch guns blasted away at Japanese aircraft flying low to the water as they opened up their machine guns on us.

Ammunition finally began to flow up the ammunition hoists below. Again, we were able to pass ammo, as we fired at high flying enemy bombers. I glanced at the capsized hull of the *Oklahoma*. I felt thankful that I didn't have a battle station in the powder magazine, three decks below...

Finally the attack ceased — However, we still expected there might be more to come. That December 7th evening, rumors circulated that Japanese battleships were at the harbor entrance, and Japanese troops were ready to land? We continued to man our guns. That night, we had mistakenly opened fire on some B-17's landing at Hickham field. Fortunately, no serious damage was done.

Bombardments from Japanese warships had never taken place, nor did foreign troops ever land on our shores. Ship routine changed. Gun watches became a part of life. Brass was not shined, but painted over, to discourage reflections. The ship was kept clean, but not for close inspection.

The *Maryland* had sustained a bomb hit on or near the forecastle. Her bow rested on the bottom. As I remember, this was the only major structural damage received. However, five of our crewmen were killed. Among those who lost their lives, was an outstanding officer from the fifth division, Ensign Crow, from Goldwaite, Texas. A number of Petty Officers with high proficiency ratings, were transferred a short time after the attack. Many of these fine sailors, whom I knew very well, lost their lives on cruises in the Java Sea naval battles of 1942.

I saw no panic before nor during the attack. We went into action and fought with valor that day. I am proud to have been a part of such a gallant crew.

Unidentified aircraft were contacted by radar well before the attack started. Also, a foreign submarine had been sunk at the harbor entrance almost an hour before the attack.

On Christmas day, 1941, the Battleship *Maryland*, BB-46, got underway in heavy seas, headed for the Bremerton, Washington navy yard, for repairs and service. The *Maryland* had extensive renovation work done. We had improved radar installed, and our anti aircraft gun batteries were modified as well. Twenty millimeter anti aircraft guns replaced the almost worthless 1.1 inch pom-pom quads.

In this short time, our navy learned a lot from the Pearl Harbor experience, concerning anti-aircraft warfare.

The Memoirs of Francis J. Walch, YNC. USN Retired
Served aboard Nov. 1939 to July, 1942

On that Sunday morning of December 7th, 1941, I was taking a shower in the engineer's washroom, getting ready to go to Catholic Mass aboard the USS *Oklahoma*, when the Japanese struck. General Quarters sounded and the word was passed, "All hands man your battle stations! This is no sh-t!" My battle station was Central Repair, telephone talker. Boatswains mate Mackay detailed me to a repair party to take down the awnings on the forecastle. As we were doing this, we witnessed the destroyers USS Shaw and USS Downs blow up in drydock. It was the same scene that was captured on film.

Later, when our forecastle was hit by a bomb, I was amidships on the main deck. Although water tight integrity had been set, the concussion of

Captured Japanese photograph taken during the attack on Pearl Harbor December 7, 1941. Observe enemy plane above battleship row after launching first torpedo hitting Oklahoma; Arizona, Utah, West Virginia still afloat; also, Oklahoma before she capsized. (Courtesy of Walter J. Mycka)

the explosion caused a rush of air in the compartment, ripping off my hat, and tearing the shirt off of one of my shipmates! The *Maryland* was at general quarters. The bomb hit did not cause any personnel casualties. However, it devastated the forward crew's head and did some damage to sick bay. It did not break the anchor chains, but shrapnel took small chunks out of some of the huge links.

Later that day, Lieutenant Taylor, the Personnel Officer, pulled me from the repair party to be his messenger and aide. We roved the ship to observe damage, damage repair, fire fighting and rescue efforts, then reported to the Executive Officer on a continuing Basis.

Oil from the damaged ships in the harbor caught fire and threatened the *Maryland*. Fire hoses kept the flames away from the stern. Billowing black smoke from the Battleships *West Virginia*, *Tennessee* and *Arizona*, filled the sky, completely obliterating the sun. It seemed almost like night topside.

Rescue Parties
By Francis J. Walch, YNC, Retired.

Survivors from other ships were being pulled on board the Battleship *Maryland*, in oil soaked clothing. They were ministered to and issued clothing available form small stores. While on my tours with Lieutenant Taylor, I saw rescue parties in boats, groping for bodies that could not come to the surface, because of the thick layer of oil on the water.

I observed other rescue efforts to the exposed hull of the USS *Oklahoma* by the "R" Division personnel. Drills, torches, air hammers, etc. were being used in attempts to rescue trapped victims. They worked around the clock. Sandwiches and coffee were sent to them. One of the last survivors to be rescued came out of the small exit in the hull, carrying a basketball. He said he would have "cracked", if he didn't have that

basketball to dribble in the dark upside down compartment while he waited hopefully for rescue.

The Battleship *Maryland* after temporary repairs, was ordered to depart to Bremerton, Washington, for further repairs and service. It was Christmas, and we were underway. We arrived in time for New Years eve. One fourth of our crew was allowed liberty until midnight. We were not allowed, however to leave the vicinity of the shipyard. Most of us wound up in a bar near the gate, which was packed with sailors. A small radio in the back of the bar was playing and could barely be heard. However, when Bob Hope's program opened with "General Quarters", all hands made a beeline for the exits and their ships!

The Battleship *Maryland*, soon rejoined the fleet in February. I recall the cruise off of Alaska, which cost the loss of all of our seaplanes, floundering in a blinding fog. I remember the continuous eerie sounds of our ships fog horn, and of bells clanging their warning to other vessels in the area. Our lookout posted on the bow, couldn't see even a foot in front of themselves.....

The Memoirs of Harold N. Kinsey, GM2/C
Served April 1936 -March 1942

Just after breakfast on Sunday, Dec. 7th, 1941, I was sitting top side enjoying the beautiful fresh morning air. I was looking towards Ford Island, when a low flying plane roared by. As it tipped it's wing, I recognized the big round red insignia. Startled, I just froze in my tracks for a moment, as it hurled on it's course towards Ford Island to drop it's deadly bombs. A second Japanese plane winged by, as one of the U. S. S. *Maryland* machine guns fired what might have been the first retaliation against the Japanese at battleship row.

Between shooting at enemy aircraft and while waiting for more ammunition, I watched the Battleship *Arizona* explode furiously in one tremendous burst, as her powder magazines blew. It's superstructure and debris flew skyward in a cloud of flame and black smoke. The explosion caused a tidal wave which swept through the harbor, causing every vessel in battleship row to rise abruptly three feet in the water, then rock back to a settling position.

We were machine gunned by enemy aircraft, which wiped out some of our personnel. Then a bomb smashed through our bow, as black smoke from the *Arizona* and other sinking battleships enveloped us in it's darkness. The Japanese enemy aircraft even had a difficult time finding us during the remainder of the attack. It was a day in which every Pearl Harbor survivor will never forget!

The Memoirs of Floyd R. Welch, EM I/C
Served March 1940 — March 1996

I was assigned to the "E" (electrical) Division. My maintenance duties took place in the lighting and power shop, sixteen inch Gun Turret One, Gun Turret Two, electrician, and IC Shop, where I was in charge of the gyro compass.

During one of our fleet exercises off Hawaii, one of the interesting experiments the USS *Maryland* conducted, was towing another battleship. However, it proved unsuccessful, as the cable would snap in ocean swells.

The attack on the early morning of December 7, 1941 would be a day that will live through history. My General Quarters station was well below the water line. We could hear explosions very clearly. Soon word came that we were under attack from Japanese forces.

After what seemed like many hours, as an electrician's mate, I was called topside, to rig light and power circuits for rescue work on the already capsized Battleship *Oklahoma*. It had been securely tied along side of us only moments before. She had already rolled almost completely over, trapping many crewmen inside.

I could hardly believe my eyes when I first came topside, even though word had been passed down to us as to what was going on. Suddenly, enemy aircraft approached, and I ran under the barbette of 16" Gun Turret #1 for protection.

The Battleship *Oklahoma* rolled over, pressing the USS *Maryland* tightly against the concrete quays that she was tied to. After the attack was over, we had to blast the quays away. This was done to release the USS *Maryland* from her tightly wedged position. She then moved out to the Pearl Harbor shipyard for temporary repairs on her bomb damaged bow and forecastle.

After final repairs and improvements were made to the *Maryland* in Bremerton, Washington, we sailed back to Pearl Harbor, then on to Viti Levu, in the Fiji Islands, November 2, 1942. Our Presence there prevented Japanese invasion of these outpost Islands. We spent a few months in the harbor with torpedo nets surrounding us. The crew were allowed to go ashore for recreation in groups.

There, we enjoyed horse back riding and diving for "cat eye" shells in the clear lagoons. We later converted them into various forms of jewelry. While in this port, the local natives performed unique ceremonies and entertainment on our quarter deck. It was a most memorable port. The native Fijians were well over six feet tall and very muscular in contrast to other native Indian tribes in the area, who were quite small in stature.

The Memoirs of Bob Hansen, GM 2/C
Served July 1941-March 1944

On November 27, 1941, while on maneuvers in the Pearl Harbor area, shipmate Bob Manahan and I spotted a periscope. We immediately reported the incident to the bridge. We were questioned extensively by several of the officers. I never heard any further about the incident, until the 15th annual *Maryland* Veterans Association Reunion in Denver, Colorado, in 1989. There, I ran across a copy of the following original memorandum sent to all officers:

"Subject: *Emergency situation due to present International conditions in war time.*

At 1545 on Thursday November 27, 1941, a report was received by the officer of the deck from the lookouts in the Maintop, that a Submarine periscope was sighted, bearing 145" relative distance 3,000 yards. This report, less the distance was immediately reported to me in the Captain's

Emergency Cabin with the added information that it was not confirmed by the bridge. I enquired and was informed that the estimated distance was 3,000 yards".

The above report was confirmation of the sighting we had reported. *It was later reported that a submarine had been sunk at the mouth of the Pearl harbor channel!*

The Memoirs of Stirling M. Oldberg, RM 3/C
Served aboard, March 7, 1941 - April 10, 1942

I remember coming from an early breakfast to my work station in Radio Two, where I stood watches on the ships radio transmitters and assisted in keeping the radio equipment in good repair. I was just about to leave for liberty ashore when all of a sudden, I heard the rattle of a machine gun firing. It came from one of our deck levels which overlooked the Battleship *Oklahoma*, which was moored to the Battleship *Maryland* on the harbor side. I thought to myself, "boy, some guy is going to get it!" Then suddenly, I saw a plane burst into flaming smoke! As it flew over us, I saw the orange emblem on it's side, and thought "Hmm, the Army is going to be mad about that! *I didn't realize that the Battleship Maryland had just shot down the first enemy plane in World War II!*

As General Quarters sounded, I headed for my battle station. Then as a Japanese torpedo exploded into the Battleship *Oklahoma*'s side, the *Maryland* rolled very hard. The next sound I heard, was like a million dishpans being dumped on the deck! I was a bomb hit on our bow!

I reported to the main radio room and was ordered to bring the emergency radio to the bridge. It was there in a matter of minutes. I was advised to set it up on a special frequency, and *listen* only. I set it up on the bridge, outside of the navigation area. As I did so, I stood up to see what was going on? A most frightful scene took place before my eyes! The harbor waters were covered with burning oil! Men were swimming away from the fire, trying to get back aboard the ship, from which they had been blown from, when suddenly a tremendous explosion occurred as the Battleship *Arizona*'s magazines exploded thunderously into flames! Heavy black smoke clouds boiled furiously into the darkened skies.

The Battleship *West Virginia* was burning fiercely from torpedo and bomb hits. The Battleship *Tennessee* also settled into the muddy bottom in flames, having taken several torpedoes, and suffered heavy damage.

As I turned to look across the harbor, the battleship *Oklahoma* lay nearly on her side, while flames licked at the thick oil covered water around us. I was then ordered to get to the quarter deck, to help oil covered survivors, trying to come aboard. As I climbed down a ladder, I saw the Battleship *Nevada* get underway, as she headed for the open sea. There were cheers as she sailed by with her colors streaming out! The Japanese dive bombers and torpedo planes concentrated on sinking her, preferably at the mouth of the harbor, hoping to block all shipping in or out! As the *Nevada* began to settle taking on more and more water, she purposely ran herself aground away from the harbor entrance from the sea.

Haunting Rescues
By Stirling M. Oldberg, RM 3/C

I arrived at the quarter deck, where a Jacob's ladder had been put over the side to help survivors climb aboard to safety. I reached down to help one man whose uniform had been burned to his skin. I took his hand and assisted him aboard.

He was badly burned. He screamed in pain so deeply from his throat as I laid him on the deck, it still haunts me to this day. A corpsman came over to give him a shot of morphine for the pain, but there was not a spot on his body which wasn't burned. The drug could not be administered .... The corpsman called the doctor over, who tried to give the shot to him in the neck as I held him in my arms, but it was too late. They said, "He's gone... We can't help him any more. Go see what you can do with the others trying to get aboard.

I saw Rear Admiral W.S. Anderson in his white uniform help the gunners to load a British "Pom Pom." (I could tell he was wishing he could fire it.) We all admired Admiral W.S. Anderson. He was a real navy man, through and through.

By this time, our decks were covered with the injured, and sick bay was filled with people who needed to be helped. Most of those on deck were either dead, or beyond any help. High level bombers began to drop finned bombs on the ships in battleship row, and other targets. The Battleship *Oklahoma* now had completely capsized.

When the attack was over, Mr. Proctor took four other radio men and myself in a launch to see if we could help out the battleship *Nevada*. When we arrived, it was a terrible sight. We went to the Radio men's living quarters. It was vacant. A ladder nearby led to "Radio One" where most of the radio men usually were. It was flooded to the ceiling. I understood then, what must have happened to the radio men.....

Realizing that there was nothing we could do on the *Nevada*, we decided to return to the *Maryland*. On the way, we pulled up some bodies which were floating on the water and helped some who were still alive, to come aboard.

As we pulled up to the *Maryland*, the Officer of The Day told us to take the dead to the Aiea landing, where there was a morgue. (The morgue was formerly the fleet recreation center).

As we returned again to them, we had passed many ships which were struggling to stay afloat. As we passed battleship row, the first ship we saw was the *Arizona*. The top of her superstructure was bent forward as if she had her head bowed. The rest of her was underwater, with only a portion of her remaining above, which was still smoldering. Going down the line, we passed the *West Virginia*, also a sad sight, still fighting fires and spraying water on the harbor to keep burning oil away. As we came abreast of the *Maryland*, we could see men still working on the bottom of the *Oklahoma*, hammering and getting answering taps from within. Soon they were cutting escape holes for the trapped men inside.

For the rest of the day, work on the *Oklahoma* went tirelessly on. Many were rescued. Many more trapped inside, died a watery death.

The Battleship *Maryland* escaped with the least damage of all the battleships, having caught a couple of bombs forward and in the bow. One man was trapped inside the compartment which housed a large air compressor. He remained there, until we returned to Bremerton, Washington for repairs.

I came aboard the *Maryland* March 7, 1941 and was aboard until transferred to the USS Massachusetts, April 10, 1942.

The year I was lucky enough to spend on the Battleship *Maryland*, BB-46 was excellent training for me. The crew formed for the New Battleship Massachusetts, was composed of many experienced sailors from the old Pacific Fleet. I was really a pleasure to serve with these men. One other man and I from the Battleship *Maryland* remained together with the radio gang. We both knew that we had gained much from those great old timers who taught us how to be men, and how to conduct ourselves like men when things got tough!

The Memoirs of Newl G. Culver, BM 1/C

Served January 19, 1939 —January 1945

My battle station was in the "crow's nest" high above the ship in the maintop cage mast. I was a look out and observer, who reported anything of importance to the bridge.

As I ran up to the main deck and had my first glimpse of the action which was taking place. I saw Japanese planes flying all over! There were lots of explosions and gunfire. I took a step backward for a running start to my battle station. Strangely enough, I cannot recall to this day one step from all of those ladders going up the that mast? What happened between that time and the time I got to my battle station high up in the "crows nest" remains a mystery?

My shipmate and I got our binoculars and phones on, then immediately tried to report. It was difficult, because the enemy aircraft were flying by so low and fast, we didn't have time to observe them properly!

I can't remember the destruction of the USS *Arizona*, as her powder magazines blew up in all of the simultaneous confusion. It was just another "Woof" among the flames and clouds of black smoke which filled the sky.

The Japanese aircraft were flying at very high speeds, lower than our mainmast!

We had an excellent view of the surrounding action, but were tense and apprehensive, wondering what would happen next? To me it seemed like the end of the world? Everything was on fire — ships, land installations, — even the water surrounding us was filled with flames.

My lookout shipmate standing beside me was hit. He fell to the deck. I dragged him aside and called for a medic. Shortly after, I observed him climbing up the series of ladders to the maintop, with a pack on his back. He looked at my buddy laying on the deck, then began chewing me out, because my friend was dead! I shouted "He's not dead!" The medic replied, "Well, his is now", then down the ladder he went!

Later, the body of my companion was removed, but that is another thing which has been blocked from my mind. They must have used ropes to lower him down from our precarious perch high above. Evidently, my shipmate got hit by flying metal again, as he laid there a wounded and unconscious man.

I looked down at our decks below. My shipmates appeared as ants scurrying around with fire hoses, which pushed the burning oil away from the *Maryland*. Flames were leaping over the side of our ship.

As each wave of enemy aircraft flew by, they would drop their fire hoses and run for cover. Then a quickly as danger had passed, they picked

Oklahoma capsized. Left to right, USS Maryland, Oklahoma, and Tennessee. Heavy smoke eminating from USS Arizona. (Courtesy of Walter J. Mycka)

December 7, 1941 moored inboard of the Oklahoma. The Maryland, damaged slightly, was one of the first ships to rejoin the fleet after the Japanese attack. (Courtesy of Walter J. Mycka)

Two man Japanese submarine above, was captured during the attack on Pearl Harbor, and remains on display there. (U.S. Navy photo)

their hoses up again to fight the fire, until the next wave of enemy planes flew over. It seemed rather comical in a way, as they scurried for shelter,.. but it certainly wasn't at the time!

I remained at my battle station in the mainmast for a couple of days and nights. Then we observed something that really got to us —bodies were floating to the top of the water from small craft which had been strafed in the bay .... Many good men were killed that day.

The smoke was so thick, I couldn't observe anything around us. I thought I had it made, until an unidentified plane flew by! I heard it, —even felt the tail wind from it, yet I couldn't see it! To me, it seemed that it was flying lower that I was in the mainmast! I felt frightened that they would crash right into my battle station.

Memoirs of Orin W. Wright, PFC
U.S.M.C. Marine Detachment, USS *Maryland,* BB-46.
Served aboard Dec. 1940 —Nov. 1942

I arrived aboard the USS *Maryland* on December 6, 1940. We then spent some time at sea on maneuvers in the Hawaiian waters of the Pacific. On December 5, 1941, as we were coming into Pearl Harbor, our lookouts reported the sighting of a submarine believed to be of foreign origin. After Saturday inspection, the Officer of The Day advised all liberty parties going ashore to say nothing about the submarine sighting......

Surprise Attack!
By Orin W. Wright, PFC, USMC

On Sunday morning, Dec. 7, 1941, I was in the Marine Color Guard, waiting for the bugler to sound colors. As we were in process of the ceremony, we observed what we thought was a mock air raid, and what appeared to be smoke bombs at the Catalina base on Ford Island?

Suddenly an unfamiliar aircraft screamed over the *Maryland* at about mast height! That's when we spotted the big "meat ball" on it's side. We immediately headed for out battle stations. General Quarters was sounded shortly afterwards.

The situation became very confused. I remember being in the Casemate, trying to get our anti-aircraft ammunition sent up from the magazine below, for our 5.51 inch gun mount. It didn't arrive? After the initial attack, I passed ammunition to our port side 1.1 inch machine gun, located near the bridge. A gunner's mate took up a position under the gun, attempting to clear the jams, — but finally gave up.   .

I then took up a new position on the quarter deck, along with the chaplain, and many others, passing 5.25 calibre ammunition to our anti aircraft batteries. The ship's doctor was scrambling all over the *Maryland*, wearing only his "T" shirt and a pair of shorts!

Terror In flaming Waters
By Orin W. Wright, PFC, USMC

We Marines, along with many other crewmembers had no battle stations, because of the ammunition foul up. We simply filled in wherever we were needed. For some time, a regular shipmate manned a fire hose on the fantail, to keep the flames from the Battleships *Tennessee* and *West Virginia* from spreading to the *Maryland*.

I witnessed the roaring explosions as the destroyers Casin and Downs exploded into flaming rubble, as they sat trapped in naval dry docks. I can't even remember the *Arizona* blowing up, with all of the other activities taking place simultaneously.

On the Evening of December 7, 1941, we were on constant alert at our gun stations. As some of our aircraft flew up the channel. They were challenged, but gave no indication who they were? As they flew over us, we cut loose with everything we had! They luckily escaped any serious damage. One of the "friendly" pilots said later, "Every inch of the air around us had a bullet in it!"

Seafaring Marines

The United States Seafaring Marines were quite well respected aboard the USS *Maryland*, BB-46. They were always impeccably dressed and a revered lot. They were always prepared for any land assignment which might be required and had a multitude of assignments, such as guarding officers quarters, brig guard duty, manning battle stations aboard ship and were prepared to go on land assignments at any moment in time!

These men were our shipmates, who served in a very specialized service, and were well respected among the Officers and crew. They were truly "Marines" in every sense of the word, trained to perform their duties at sea as well as any seaman. They were prepared at all times to do combat one on one with enemy troops on land as well. They were indeed special, and conducted themselves as a well disciplined team force which provided the USS *Maryland*, with a great deal of diversified action capability.

Many of our sea going marines who served aboard the USS *Maryland* not only distinguished themselves in action aboard the USS *Maryland*, but went on to fight America's enemies on land, in other wartime experiences and assignments. We proudly salute them!

The Battleship *Maryland* Strikes Back!

After the shattering surprise attack at Pearl Harbor, the people of America rallied with unprecedented determination to strike back at their antagonists. No individual sacrifice was too great. Out of the devastation which virtually destroyed our naval strength emerged the sleeping giant — a nation bent on retaliation and revenge!

Never before in the annals of history, had a nation been more solidified in purpose and determination to beat back the oppression of freedom. — The Japanese War Lords had unwittingly opened a pandora's box which would ultimately lead to their resounding defeat!

Our first major offensive was taken at Guadalcanal in the Solomon Islands, which provided bases from which to keep the Japanese at bay. It halted their unprecedented advances against the South Pacific Island and Nations. It bought us time to prepare an effective strategy and to protect our supply lines to Australia and other pacific fighting fronts.

On the twelfth of November, 1943, a large task force began to assemble at Havannah Harbor, Efate Island. The USS *Maryland*, flagship of our first offensive operation against the Japanese, got underway.

It would be one of the bloodiest operations to date, against one of the most fortified and defensively prepared Japanese strongholds in the Pacific.

Aboard the *Maryland*, were the key players in the drama of this operation: Rear Admiral Harry W. Hill, Major General "Howling Mad" Julian Smith, Commander, the 2nd Marine Division, and Colonel Carlson, of "Carlson's Raiders."

In the early morning of November 20, 1943, as the invasion force came within sight of their objective, (Betio Island in the Tarawa Atoll), a shore battery on the southwest point of the Island, began to fire on the *Maryland*. Almost immediately, she commenced return fire, with five well placed salvos, which quickly silenced the enemy position forever! Following this action, other support ships began to move into their assigned positions.

The Battleship *Maryland* gallantly moved in very close to the Island, to deliberately draw enemy fire, thus revealing their many well camouflaged positions for elimination, as heavy bombardment began to soften up the beaches.

The orders of the day read: AT O620, COMMENCE SCHEDULED BOMBARDMENT ...." GIVE THE BASTARDS HELL!"

Main and secondary batteries hammered away at gun emplacements, control posts, pillboxes and many other vital installations.

As the first wave of Marines landed on the beach at 0900 (AM), after almost three hours of bombardment by American naval forces, they penetrated a far as the airstrip. The second and third waves of fighting marines met heavy opposition and suffered heavy casualties. Many marines were killed in a vicious enemy cross fire, by well placed enemy machine guns which covered the beachheads. The *Maryland*'s gun batteries efficiently wiped out several of these harassing positions, perhaps averting larger numbers of marine casualties.

As the Flagship *Maryland* stood by for call fire, it's spotter planes observed the general progress of the assault. They radioed first hand reports on conditions and movements.

Lt. Commander. R.A. Peterson, one of the *Maryland*'s pilots, was awarded the Silver Star for heroic and gallant service while on his mission.

The pilot of our second plane, Lt. (jg) F.C. Whaley, attacked machine gun nests and various other types of positions with hand grenades and machine guns. For this unusual and daring action, the enemy retaliated by puncturing the plane with machine gun fire, seriously wounding radioman, Bob Houle.

As the flagship *Maryland* stood by for call fire, it's spotter planes observed the general progress of the assault, then radioed first hand reports on conditions and movements of the Japanese troops.

Lt. Commander. R. A. Mc Pherson, another one of the *Maryland*'s pilots, was also awarded the Silver Star for heroic and gallant service, while on his mission.

That evening, bitter fighting raged on the Island, as the Japanese defenders tried in vain to counter attack. They began to stealthily infiltrate our lines across the intervening waters. From the decks of the Battleship *Maryland*, it's crew watched occasional flashes of flame throwers and artillery which subdued the aggressive fighting of the Japanese defenders.

After three days of intensive call fire, the Battleship *Maryland* moved to the Island of Apamama, to support a landing of U.S. Marines there. The Island's only resistance was a group of 30 Japanese, most of whom formerly committed Hari-Kari.

There were two surviving Japanese prisoners taken on the Island, who were promptly cast into the USS *Maryland*'s brig. One was a Japanese Marine, the other a Korean laborer. The prisoners were promptly stripped naked, except for their sandals, then were issued oversized regulation underwear, several sizes too large. They were forced to hold them up when moving from the brig to the washroom and head. Six days later, the Island group was declared secured.

The Memoirs of Charles Peay, GM 1/C

Tarawa, November 20, 1943. I was assigned to the 20 millimeter anti aircraft guns up forward on the forecastle. We had encountered no enemy aircraft of consequence, therefore we were assigned to the 16 inch gun powder magazines. We handled 45 lb. black powder bags, which were encased two bags to each metal container. As soon as the metal containers were opened, fumes of ether, (used to preserve the effectiveness of the powder) , escaped into the magazine compartment. During the bombardments of enemy positions, the compartment filled with ether fumes. Over half of the magazine crew passed out! The decks were wet with perspiration, during lengthy bombardments.

We had voice communication only, and wondered what was happening topside? We could hear noisy movements of the ships maneuvers, as our 16 inch buns relentlessly pounded enemy installations on the Islands. In our enclosed powder magazine compartment we also sensed the movements of the *Maryland* as it moved about. It was a spooky experience to be several decks below the water line, not knowing what was transpiring above.

Japanese Admiral Keijo Shibasaki told his people who were dug in on the Island fortress of Tarawa, that it couldn't be taken in a hundred years? (Our engagement to subdue their stronghold took less that three weeks!)

The Memoirs of William H. Chase
Ship's Photographer Mate, First Class, served Aboard Jan. 1943 to Mar. 1945

I was transferred aboard the Battleship *Maryland* in a motor whaleboat at the harbor of Efate, New Hebrides, in the early spring of 1943 from a jeep aircraft carrier, the USS Sangamon. We had just come into the Pacific after participating in the invasion of North Africa. The Sangamon had received orders to return to the West Coast. The flag officer on the Battleship *Maryland*, Admiral Hill, needed a Photographer? The photography lab aboard the *Maryland* in the Aviation Section, two decks down was very small. The Lab dark room was about 4 ft x 12 ft long, consisting of a 5 x 7 enlarger, contact printer and misc. trays, etc. It was cool in there, because

The Maryland's OS2U Spotter Plane above, piloted by F.C. Whaley, with unusual daring action, boldly attacked machine gun nests and various other enemy positions, armed only with hand grenades and machine guns. Bob Houle, Radioman, was wounded in this action, by the Japanese defenders. Note holes in fuselage, wing, and pontoon. (Photo by ship's photographer 1/C, William H. Chase)

there was an air circulation duct going through it with a small inspection plate. By removing a few screws and sliding the plate to one side, it would allow cool fresh air to flow in. (I slept there most of the time)

The Private Beer Bust
By William H. Chase, Ship's Photographer 1/C

I remember how that duct almost got me into trouble! In one of the operations a Japanese plane had attacked us and dropped a bomb off of our stern. It sent a large gush of water shooting into the air. The USS Battleship *Tennessee*, which sailed with us at the time, had photographed the action. Upon returning to our rendezvous point, I went aboard the *Tennessee* to swap some photography supplies. I knew the photographer, and he loaned me a negative. I made up quite a few prints, which were in much demand for our officers and men. I'm sure many have them to this day. I recall coming off watch one morning, after standing the 4 to 8 watch on the bridge, manning the E.O. I. (Engine Order Indicator). Coming down the ladder, I came face to face with a Chief Radioman. He wanted one of these photos? I hesitated for a while, until he said he would give me a six pack of beer and a $5.00 bill! The money didn't mean much to me, but the beer sounded pretty good! That night he brought the beer down to me. I don't recall who else was with me at the time, but we went into the photo compartment and drank that delicious beer! We didn't want to get caught with any beer, so we opened the air duct, where we placed the empty cans. What we didn't realize, was that the fumes from the beer would travel throughout the ship!

It wasn't long, before the Master at Arms and his "henchmen", came looking for the culprits who were drinking beer? They pounded on my door! I was friends with one of them, but they did not find the cans, for we had screwed the cover back on the air duct! I'm sure they suspected, but they went away ... Whew! (This happened somewhere off the coast of New Guinea).

Downed In The Pacific
By William H. Chase, Ship's Photographer

Around three days out from bremerton, Washington, I was flying scout observation ion one of our OS2U's, with Pilot Lt. French. Upon returning to the ship, we found thy were having a problem with the crane on the fan tail?

The first OS2U, finally landed in the smooth wake of the *Maryland* and was hauled aboard. By this time, we were running low on fuel and were given approval to come in. We landed in the wake and were caught by the sea sled to hold us steady. I had just hooked the cable to the center of gravity of our aircraft as they began to hoist us up to the deck. Suddenly our cable broke free! Our aircraft splashed nose down into the foaming wake. We were being dragged by the ship!

The next thing I knew, I was sinking in deep water. All I could think of was that the ships pounding screws pounding below could suck us into them, to viciously cut us to bits! God, I didn't want to die like that!

In a few moments, I surfaced onto the rolling sea, gasping for fresh air. One minute I could see nothing, in the huge rolling swells, then the next, I would be on a crest. I could see our ship fading off into the distance. I thought of my lovely wife and what a short marriage we had? I couldn't see Lt. French. I groped desperately, trying to get my may west life preserver to open. I had trouble pulling the cords, but finally got one side to work. Then it finally puffed out, lifting me higher upon the water. My gunners belt was still strapped around my waist. The next frightening thought was being attacked by sharks! With a sense of urgency, I quickly released the shark repellant which was attached to my May West.

There I was, — floating around in the great expanse of the Pacific! .... I had bad thoughts that day, for the ship to just sail off and leaving us.....

Finally, I came to a crest in the rolling swells and saw a destroyer heading in my direction! They spotted me first, lowered a lifeboat and picked me up. They finally located Lt. French, and picked him up as well. He was quite ill from having swallowed a lot of sea water. The Officers and crew really treated us great.

This same destroyer had sunk our plane by gunfire. After our rescue we proceeded on into Pearl Harbor. I can remember waiting at the quay for the *Maryland* to come in. I had no shoes and wore a Chief's hat with no emblem, which was given to me on the destroyer. I can't remember her name, but I shall never forget the kindness and royal treatment by her crew. I believe the *Maryland* had proceeded on for more sea maneuvers. It was a few days before I saw her sailing proudly into Pearl harbor..

Photographing The Taking of Tarawa
By William H. Chase, Ship's Photographer, First Class

Our submarines had taken panoramic views of the Tarawa Atoll and it's Islands... I was given the job of copying the photographs, so each squad of Marines going ashore the next day, would have a view of their designated landing area. I believe it was the second day of the operation that some of the Flag's Staff, along with Admiral Hill, were to go ashore.

I was sent for, then told to get ready with my camera and plenty of film. I was assigned to photograph the operation ashore at Tarawa.

After boarding the LCM, they handed down guns and ammunition ... but none for me? I thought at least they could have given me a 45 calibre pistol? Upon going ashore we made contact with the command post. There, I was assigned two Marine body guards and was told to photograph Japanese installations, construction of the pill boxes and tank traps.

I shall never forget this assignment. We had not taken the island yet and nothing had been done with the dead from either side. The hot tropical sun had beat down upon the corpses, which were swollen and distorted. They were strewn all over the place, lying where they had been killed.

I had started to climb on top of a pill box. As I reached for a hand hold, a body came tumbling down at me. When I got to the top, I began taking photos of the front lines. Suddenly, I was knocked down to the ground by one of my Marine body guards! "You damned fool", he screamed, "You're a perfect target up there!" ...Well, It sure didn't take me long to get down from that spot!

As we continued on, one of my Marine body guards calmly lifted his rifle, took quick aim and shot a sniper less than two hundred feet away from me! They took me over to his body which was covered with blood. One of my body guards kicked him over on his back. They were always cautious, taking no chances. One of them asked me if I had any souvenirs yet? I said no. He reached down with his bowie knife and cut the Japanese Marine's ammunition belt in half, and pulled it out from his limp form. The belt contained a bullet case. "Here" he said, as he tossed it to me. It was still covered with blood, as I shoved it in my shirt. I had that bullet case for a long time, as a grisly memento of the horror of war.

The stench of rotting flesh filled our lungs as we continued our photographic assignment. It was so bad, that even as we flew over the Island to photograph the chaos of enemy installations, we could still smell that unforgettable stench of death!

The Memoirs of Harry D. Johnson, GM 2/C
Served aboard Jan. 1942 —Dec.1945

This story took place on the morning of November 20, 1943. It was the landing at Tarawa, called "Operation Galvanic".

During anti-aircraft action, below deck you could hear the five inch guns blast away first. Then as enemy aircraft closed it's range, the forty millimeter guns began to join in. The when the 20 millimeter guns opened up, there was a bit more reason to be concerned. The whole ship would began to rattle! You knew then, that the enemy was close enough to slam home, when they couldn't drive a pin up your butt with a sledge hammer!

Destruction of a Tarawa fortress and Japanese aircraft. (Photo by ship's photographer 1/C, William H. Chase)

The Memoirs of F.R. Welch, EM 1/C
Served aboard March 1940 to March 1946

Tarawa was the first of many battles we engaged in that consisted of destroying shore installations and softening up the beaches for our Marine landings. We were always there a week or more prior to the actual landing of troops. We then stood by for call fire, to protect their flanks and destroy any target which we could reach with our heavy sixteen inch guns. (Our guns had an effective range of about 26 miles distance).

In the taking of Tarawa Atoll, in the Gilbert Islands, we witnessed wave after wave of our landing craft go aground on razor sharp corral reefs, a few hundred yards from shore. Our fighting marines bravely leaped into the water, forging onward towards the enemy. Many were easy targets, and were slaughtered in withering enemy fire, as they approached the beaches. Nothing could be done to help them. After what seemed an eternity, we managed to silence the skillfully hidden enemy guns ashore. By then, an enormous number of our men were floating dead in the water. This carnage imprinted itself on my mind more than anything I had witnessed during the remainder of the entire war.

A Sign Board Placed On The Sands of Tarawa Reads:

JAPANESE EIGHT INCH BATTERY
THESE EIGHT-INCH GUNS OPENED THE BATTLE OF TARAWA, FIRING TO THE SOUTH WEST. THE BATTERIES THEN TURNED TO OPEN FIRE ON THE TRANSPORTS JUST NORTH OF THE ENTRANCE TO THE LAGOON. THESE GUNS WERE THEN TAKEN UNDER FIRE BY THE USS *MARYLAND*, WHICH SILENCED THEM.

AFTER TWO SALVOS. THE *MARYLAND* THEN MOVED IN TO APPROXIMATELY 2,300 YARDS AND ENFILADED GREEN BEACH 1 AND 2 DOWN TO THE OTHER BATTERY ON THE NORTHWEST POINT FOR A PERIOD OF THREE HOURS.

ON "D" PLUS ONE DAY, THE CRUISER USS *SANTA FE* METHODICALLY RIPPED THE SAME AREA TO PIECES FROM AN AVERAGE RANGE OF 3,000 YARDS, USING SLOW FIRE AND WORKING FROM THE NORTH TO SOUTH POINT, FOR A PERIOD OF TWO HOURS.

THE JAPANESE EIGHT INCH GUNS WERE OF BRITISH MANUFACTURE AND WERE POSSIBLY MOVED TO THIS SIGHT FROM SINGAPORE.

Kwajalein Atoll, Roi Island—Hub Of The Marshall Island Defense System

Task for 53, was assembling in the Hawaiian Islands for a strike at the well protected Marshal Islands group, in the Kwajalein Atoll. The selected major targets were Kwajalein Island itself and the Island of Roi.

The Battleship *Maryland*, as flagship for the Northern force, with it's supporting warships, the Cruisers *Santa Fe*, *Biloxi*, and *Indianapolis*, began firing in the early hours of morning, January 31, 1944, at Roi Island, which contained a major airfield, a seaplane anchorage and enemy submarine facilities. Our predetermined targets consisted of Pillboxes, gun emplacements and storage areas. The pillboxes were made of steel and concrete, covered over with many feet of sand and coconut logs.

Strong defenses were secretly installed, when the Japanese took over the mandate from the League of Nations in 1920. They were low, narrow, coral formations, studded with islands which enclosed lagoons.

In this dramatic photo, U.S. Marines inspect a gallantly defended Japanese bunker, a portion of their well camouflaged defensive systems. The Japanese were tenacious fighters. Several bodies strewn about, graphically illustrates the effect of naval bombardment and the senseless waste of human life in times of war. (Photo by ship's photographer 1/C, William H. Chase)

It was Roi Island that the *Maryland* witnessed it's first devastating air raid, since Pearl Harbor, which was directed at the supplies on the recently captured Island. Our land-based aircraft in the Gilberts continued their attacks on the Marshal Islands to support our invasion forces.

The enemy was expected to react more strongly to this operation than they did in the Gilbert Islands, particularly with submarines and air attacks. In a Memorandum for all hands, dated January 24, 1944, it was stated:

"Whether his ships will come out and fight, will depend upon the success he achieves with his air raid and submarines.. We must be alert to combat submarine and air menace and be prepared to take on any enemy vessels which may attempt to interfere with our operation. While it does not seem likely that the Japanese Fleet will come to fight, except under the most favorable circumstances, if it does, the war will be over for all practical purposes when the two fleets clash. Let us be fully ready to play our part.
H.J. Ray, Captain, U.S. N. Commanding.

The Memoirs of William Chase
Ship's Photographer Mate First Class

I remember the bombing of Kwajalein Island. The *Maryland* with other ships were on one side of the Island firing, while the *Tennessee* and other ships were on the other side firing at targets there. I remember those strange sounds going by us ... Whomp - Whomp, several times? I was on the open bridge photographing the action when I heard a radio transmission telling the *Tennessee* to cease firing, as her armor piercing shells were actually ricocheting off the Island and going all around us! Luckily, we were not hit by one of our own ship's shells!

The Memoirs of Charles Richard Peay, GM 1/C

Kwajalein was a very impressive and scary operation. The Battleship *Maryland* bombarded Roi Atoll from 2000 yards. Admiral Connolly ordered her in close.

The Navigator told the Captain of mine fields, and warned we shouldn't go any closer? The Captain said, "Take her in!" We went in to 1,000 yards. Small arms fire began ricochetting off our bulkheads and superstructure of the ship! The *Maryland* retaliated with very accurate and effective firepower, which destroyed the Japanese poll boxes, large guns and their organized defense. About February 14, 1944, we departed for Pearl Harbor and Bremerton Washington for overhaul and repairs.

The Memoirs of Fred R. Vreeken FCR 3/C
Served Dec, 1943 —1946

When the Japanese surrendered at the end of the war, I was transferred to Roi Island, in the Marshals Group. The voyage was one of mixed feelings. Many of the crew we knew so well were transferred. The scuttlebutt was that all but a skeleton crew would be transferred at Pearl Harbor. The Battleship *Maryland* would then be assigned to "Magic Carpet" duty, to transport our armed forces from the Pacific, home. I had become very attached to the old "Mary Maru." (A nickname given by the crew at large) We had been through so much together. It would be like leaving an old and dear friend. I began to prepare for the eventuality of being transferred. I knew inside that there would always be a soft spot in my heart for the old girl!

Post War Duty On Roi Island
By Fred R. Vreeken, FC 3/C

At Pearl Harbor, I received my orders to proceed to a waiting station in Honolulu, for a new assignment to Roi Island In the Marshals. It was one of the Islands in which the *Maryland*'s big 16 inch guns had wreaked havoc, destroying bunkers and other installations. It would be very interesting to see first hand, the damages which The Battleship *Maryland* inflicted upon this Island!

As I walked down the gangplank for the last time, my heart filled with a strange empty feeling. I looked back at her majestic masthead and awesome sixteen inch guns. A lump filled my throat and I felt proud, because I knew I would always be a living part of her historic past! I strode away contented for having served aboard this wonderful old Lady of the sea. I knew in my heart that she would always be an important part of my life and she was, for more than a half century ago!

My new assignment, had taken me on a journey to the Marshal Islands

Unexploded projectile—Kwajalein, Marshall Islands. U.S. Marines inspect an unexploded 16 inch in diameter shell fired from one of our participating battleships. Comparing the size of the business end of the projectile against the size of the U.S. Marines will provide the layman with an idea of the awesome firepower of a battleship. (Photo by ship's photographer 1/C, William H. Chase)

on a troop transport. The bunks were stacked so close together, a man did not have room to roll over on his side! The holds were cramped and poorly ventilated. I selected a top bunk. They were stacked eight high! It appeared to have a bit more space. Directly above, was a sheet metal air conditioning conduit — but no vent? The stifling heat was unbearable? However a few punches into the conduit with a borrowed bayonet, made life a lot more comfortable!

Finally, we arrived at our destination. The Island itself was as flat as a table top. What was once a lush paradise, studded with palm trees, now had only one palm remaining in tact — and it only had three mangy fronds sadly drooping from it! The USS *Maryland* certainly "Wiped the table clean," when the Island was taken!

A row of quonset huts housed the crews which were helping to dispose of American "war surplus". There were American jeeps, armored cars, fighter aircraft, boxes of brand new luger pistols, tons and tons of bombs, ammunition and surplus supplies of other sorts. All of these materials were considered war surplus. My job, was to operate a huge northwest crane, loading all of these and other "war surplus materials", onto barges. They were then taken ten miles out to sea, and given the deep six! It was difficult to comprehend such waste?

If one of us were caught with as much as a clock from a fighter aircraft cockpit, it would be a Court Marshall offense! For some unknown reason (if you can call it reason), the wheels of aircraft were the only items saved? There were huge stacks of them on this barren flat Island, which it seemed one good big wave, could wash away, Island and all!

We were allowed to take souvenirs that were recaptured from Wake Island, then stored here. Among them were both Japanese and American bayonets. I took one of each, and I wondered what stories they could tell, as I examined them from time to time, through the more than half century that has passed.

The water surrounding Roi Island was crystal clear. Fish of all varieties were abundant. The shores were littered with strange cone-like shells containing crab like creatures, which shot out of them like a cannon when the shell was heated with a match!

Fishing was another pastime. Fish were very plentiful, however fishing gear was not? However, American ingenuity made the best use of the materials at hand. We simply tossed a hand grenade amidst the unwary schools which were always there. A large portion of them would simply float to the surface — fish for the taking!

During my tenure on Roi Island, Danny Kaye, singer and actor, with his troupe, put on a great show for the men. Having a chance to talk to Danny at some length was an interesting and memorable event.

The uniform of the day, was high top shoes, marine green poplin shirts, (never buttoned, but tied in a square knot by it's tails), and marine

Heading Home For a Break....

large gun installations, crediting the Battleship *Maryland* with the destruction inflicted.

Bunkers, destroyed by the *Maryland*, but still standing, were solidly constructed. Walls were from four to six feet thick. They were constructed of rock, corral and steel reinforced concrete. They were interesting to explore. One could only imagine the commotion and struggles to the death which had taken place there, as American and Japanese Marines locked themselves in mortal combat? I wondered of their thoughts as they struggled to keep alive? It was as if I could hear the ghostly cries and last moment gasps for a breath of life...and I was glad to have been a sailor, relatively safe from the horror of hand to hand combat.

The Memoirs of Charles R.Peay, GM. 1/C

Kwajalein was a very impressive and scary operation. The *Maryland* bombarded Roi Atoll from 2000 yards. Admiral Connolly ordered her in close. The Navigator warned the Captain of mine fields and that it would be dangerous to go in any closer? The Captain replied, "Take her in!" We slowly drew closer to the Island — 1,000 yards! Small arms fire ricochetted off of bulkheads and superstructure of the ship. The *Maryland*'s bombardments were very accurate and effective. She destroyed large guns, pill boxes and disrupted all organized defense systems.

Saipan.. A Strategic Stronghold!

Just as the Yanks began to storm the beaches of Normandy, in the great invasion of Europe, a huge amphibious force with a covering fleet of battleships, cruisers and destroyers streamed ominously towards one of Japan's most important strongholds — Saipan.

This operation in the Marianas Islands, would become one of the most

Roi Island bunker destroyed by USS Maryland. (Sketched by Fred R. Vreeken while stationed on the Island)

trousers cut off just below the pocket line. Our skin soon turned native brown and our hair bleached blonde, as we waited to be called home under the point system.

I witnessed first hand, the devastation wreaked upon the Island by the *Maryland* and the cruisers which supported the task force. There were many huge mounds of earth running about 100 feet in length, each with carved wooden signs marking "400 Japanese dead, 600 Japanese dead, etc." Over forty years later, relatives of the dead Japanese defenders were able to come to Roi Island, to claim their remains. A portion of this event appeared in the American newspapers.

There were also bronze signs embedded in concrete, posted at several important campaigns of the Pacific. Once Saipan was taken, it would provide an extremely valuable air base from which Japan itself could be attacked by American long range bombers. From Saipan, the infallible B-29 could fly all the way to Japan and back without refueling.

En route, the crew of the USS *Maryland* listened to Japanese radio broadcasts for amusements sake. The suave propaganda voice of "Tokyo Rose" blandly announced that the garrison and defensive air groups of Saipan were "eagerly waiting", the arrival of American forces.

The big sixteen inch guns of the Battleship *Maryland* would soon be pounding relentlessly at the enemy installations and specified targets, and to soften up the beachheads for our invasion forces three days before "D" day!

On June 14, the firing commenced. Two coastal defense guns on a small Island nearby were quickly silenced in a brief duel. There appeared to be little opposition. Our OS2U spotter aircraft took off from the launch ramps of the *Maryland*, to direct and report the accurateness of her powerful heavy guns. We fired at and destroyed coastal defense guns, anti-aircraft guns, blockhouses, heavily constructed buildings, and other selected targets in the town of Garapan.

Gunfire from American ships leveled the town of,Tanapag, which had been thick with troublesome snipers.

The invasion which took place three days later on June 17th was very successful, as our Marines and armed forces swept through Japanese strongholds. The enemy resisted stubbornly, as they were purged from their caves and fortifications.

On June 22nd the battle had progressed well enough that it was presumed that the enemy presented no threat to the naval forces offshore. Orders were given by flag ship *Maryland*, to secure the guns and anchor off the southeast coast of Saipan.

The Memoirs of Fred R. Vreeken FC 3/C
Served Dec. 1943 — Jan.1946

Our awesome amphibious force under the protection of our battleships, cruisers and destroyers, steamed ominously out of Pearl Harbor, setting it's course to an unannounced destination in the Pacific.

Speculation among the crew ran rampant. I remember talking to one of our Philippine crew members who seemed to have an uncanny way of knowing where we were going. I suppose working in the officer's quarters gave him a little more insight than the rest of us? When I asked him where he thought we were going, without hesitation he answered, "Saipan!"

"Saipan", I inquired? "Where in the world is Saipan," I thought to myself? I would soon find out that Saipan's neighbor was the Island of Tinian, and Tinian's neighbor was Guam, (Now that was a name I could relate to!) (*All of these were in the Marianas Group of Islands.*)

Our objective was to invade and take command of all three of these Islands. It was from Saipan, that our bombers would eventually depart, to drop the first atomic Bomb! — A decision which without question, saved countless young American lives!

The dedicated Japanese soldiers and marines on Saipan, fought

Torpedo to the bow! Only one thin bulkhead kept the sea from flooding the decks below. Huge timbers placed to support the weakened bulkhead by the Maryland's efficient damage control crew, kept her afloat. (Several decorations were awarded to these men who took great risk upon their lives). Compare size of opening with the workman show encircled. (U.S. Navy photo)

gallantly, without hesitation, to their deaths, to preserve this important foothold in the Pacific. The enemy was well trained and demonstrated an uncommon willingness to sacrifice their very lives for their honor, Emperor and homeland. (Our armed forces were more than happy to accommodate them.) Even so, they exacted substantial casualties to our fighting marines and soldiers.

It was an exhilarating experience to be a part of this vast armada of fighting ships. Our sleek 32,500 ton battleship sliced through the deep blue Japanese controlled waters of the Pacific with determined force.

A surge of pride swelled within my bosom for my American heritage, and the opportunity to defend our country against it's enemies. I pondered about the new changes I would have to face and what it might be like to die in battle? How strange it was that I never feared death? Deep inside, a strong inner feeling of confidence told me that I would survive!

It was at Saipan, that I first observed the awesome destructive abilities of rocket power. Smaller vessels loaded with racks of pencil like missiles angled ominously at the beaches and fortifications, fired these deadly projectiles in extremely rapid succession: "Swoosh! Swoosh! Swoosh! Swoosh! Swoosh! … and a momentary pause as they swiftly sped to their objective …Then along the beachhead, equally rapid explosions commenced from left to right, kicking up huge clouds of earth and debris — "Blam! Blam! Blamb! Blamb! Blamb," reported the echoes, reverberating the awesome impact of destruction through the calm sea air …

A Battle Station Five Decks Below

My first battle station was five decks down, below the water line, in the lower Handling room (powder magazine) of sixteen inch gun turret number four.

As part of a crew of six men, our job was to send powder bags up on a special elevator, to the loading room within the turret. The breech of a sixteen inch gun was so huge, it had to be handled hydraulically. There was a "catwalk" along the breech, which required a crew of two, to operate the controls in order to open and close it!

After each firing, these huge guns would have to be lowered to a horizontal position for reloading. Each huge gun was loaded with a projectile approximately five feet tall, and sixteen inches in diameter, followed by five bags of gun powder. The loading room was very large and open in order to allow for recoil and elevation. Each gun was thus loaded simultaneously, utilizing long cove shaped steel ramps and a hydraulic ramrod.

Pushhhhh - they hissed, as the ramrod jammed the projectile deep into the breach, then swiftly returned to it's starting position. Then came five bags of powder from the elevator onto the steel ramp ... Pshhhhhh! — Into the barrel they were quickly placed as the huge breech closed. Personnel scrambled clear from the loading area to avoid the recoil of the huge guns as they swiftly moved back into firing position. It was indeed the essence of teamwork, requiring split second timing and hours of training and rehearsal.

The complete loading procedure for both guns was accomplished in 60 seconds! As fast as that might seem, it would be an eternity, when under enemy fire. The only consolation? The enemy had the same problem. Battleships of today, are even more efficient, thanks to computers and sophisticated electronics.

Unlike modern vessels of today, the air conditioning aboard the *Maryland* was very poor. It existed only in certain areas such as officer's quarters, and sick bay. During a bombardment, the crew in the lower handling room deep below the waterline poured perspiration continuously, until their skin became wrinkled. The entire deck was wet, — puddled with human sweat! We manned our battle stations garbed only in our regulation shorts! Whenever a lull in the bombardment took place, the small, narrow "one man at a time" hatches at each of the five deck levels were opened. It allowed a feint portion of air to trickle down into our hellish depths below. The five man crew would lay on their backs upon the sweat smothered deck, heads in a circle, to rest and suck up any fragment of air which might find it's way to relieve the discomfort of their private hell.

Between bombardments, we were allowed to go topside for a few precious minutes of fresh air, two men at a time. With great anticipation, a mate and I threw on our clothes. We then began the long climb up steep vertical ladders and narrow hatch openings. The moment we cleared the last hatchway into the open fresh air and blinding sunlight topside, our wrinkled flesh instantly broke out into a terrible rash,—but oh, how good it felt to be in the open air!

It was easy to become addicted to claustrophobia. To this day, I still feel uncomfortable in confined spaces. In the event we were to sink in action, it would be one of the most hopeless areas aboard from which to escape drowning. (These pristine conditions are practically non existent aboard newer modern men of war vessels).

A Duel With Japanese Shore Batteries

It was a clear tropical day. Our gunfire had all but leveled the towns of Garapan and Tanapag. The *Maryland* had drifted close to a small, heavily foliaged peninsula. I had come topside for a welcome break and sat myself down against on of the huge mushroom shaped ventilators, observing the Islands which echoed thunderous sounds of gunshot in the distance.

Suddenly, a huge yellow splash just yards from our quarterdeck leaped from the water. I watched in stunned awe, as I heard the unmistakable shrill whine of another shell passing overhead ...." Whrrrrrr ... Splash! Then another huge spout of colored water burst menacingly, high into the sky! As a rangefinder operator I knew that we had been "bracketed" by our enemy! He now had our exact range! The next shell would have landed right in my lap!

There was no time to run, nor find shelter! Quickly I laid on my stomach and waited to be blown to hell! Our 20 millimeter , 40 millimeter and five inch guns instantly retaliated with a devastating, deadly barrage at the tip of the heavily foliaged peninsula.

A camouflaged Japanese 5 inch gun emplacement lay hidden there. The ship shook with the rapid intensity of it's thunderous firepower. Then ...deadly silence, as the smell of gunpowder filled the air. I looked toward the enemy gun position in the once heavily foliaged peninsula, which dared to take on a battleship! The one lush jungle where the enemy emplacement once existed now looked like a plucked chicken!

I quietly admired the determination and sacrifice made by the Japanese defenders, who had hopelessly forfeited their lives for their country. It was indeed an act of uncommon courage and commitment ......and I was glad to be alive!

A Mass Suicidal Tragedy!

On the Island of Saipan, Japanese civilians, families and farm workers were told by their governing body, of American tortures and atrocities which would befall the people who lived there, should they be captured. Women would be raped, children killed, and homes pillaged, etc.. The native villagers, bound by inborn loyalties and traditions, were filled with fear. Rather than suffer such indignities, they took their young children to the brinks of the highest cliffs, held hands, and leaped into their watery deaths below! Women threw their babies and young children into the waves dashing upon the rocks below, then flung themselves after them. It was one of the greatest incomprehensible tragedies of the war! To American minds, it brought a certain sadness, —yet in a strange way, admiration for such loyalty to tradition.

The bodies of these victims of self destruction floated with a variety of other debris, past the *Maryland* on the outgoing tide. Shipboard marines were required to shoot all bodies and other floating debris which drifted close to the ship, for fear of mines or explosive devices which might be attached to our hull, — a rather sickening but necessary evil.

Modern Day Dog Fights In The Air

There were days when our P-38 fighter aircraft would have dog fights with Japanese Zeros in the skies above us. In the melee, one of our battleships shot down one of our aircraft! The Battleship *Maryland* splashed one Japanese "Judy", type aircraft as it made an attempt to bomb us. The enemy plane crashed into the water off of our fantail.

Tokyo Rose, broadcast regularly of aid that would be coming to the "Brave defenders of Saipan." We kept a wary vigil for Japanese warships, —but they never materialized.

Finally, the fighting on Saipan was reduced to a mop up operation, with isolated pockets of resistance hopelessly holed up in caves. For all intents and purposes, the Island of Saipan was secured. The American fleet anchored off shore, and battle conditions were recalled. At last, we could relax!

Torpedoed!

June 22, 1944 .... It was a heavy, humid evening. The enclosures of steel walls below decks were filled with stale, humid air. Crowded quarters added to the discomfort. Most of us went topside to enjoy the cool of the evening. My favorite spot to relax, was way forward at the point of the bow where the teakwood deck ended. That's where the gaping holes swallowed the huge links of the anchor chains, which slipped down into the depths and held us steadily in place. Here, I could look back at our massive bridge and rising masthead against the blue sky, with a feeling of pride in simply being there. This was my ship! My home! It was a part of my life that would always live vividly in my mind. She was majestic, magnificent, and I knew that one day, if I survived, I would leave a legacy of these historical exploits and experiences to my posterity!

The decks topside were filled with sailors, spread out on blankets, chatting and swapping yarns. I pulled off my shoes and laid on my stomach. The teakwood deck was my bed, a seaman's hat was my pillow. I closed my eyes, and listened to the chatter of the crew, gathered in small groups playing cards, and laughing and jokes. It was pleasant and peaceful.

My good friend, "Snuffy" Smith, wasn't far away. I could recognize his voice with my eyes closed. "Snuffy" was a good fellow. You'd never hear a foul word come from his mouth. Indeed, he was a good natured person. When he was really mad or upset, he would shout, "Gol' dern it!" or "Dad blast it!," But never, ever did I hear him swear! I was very fond of him ... he kind of grew on you. One couldn't help liking ol' "Snuffy"!

I had just begun to drift off into pleasant slumber, when "Snuffy" quietly got up, (his blanket in hand), and without a word, swiftly began to make a hasty departure through the crowded deck.

"Hey Snuffy", a voice called out, "Where are you going?"

"I'm getting' hell out of here!" He hastily exclaimed, shaking his finger vigorously at a distant drone, "That's a Betty!" (Identification code name for a Japanese torpedo bomber). Without so much as turning around, he quickened his pace, as all eyes looked into the direction that Snuffy's finger pointed. The lone twin engine Japanese torpedo bomber had already flown over the bow of the battleship Pennsylvania without a shot fired, skimming low to the water, towards it's pre-selected target, the flagship of the fleet, — USS *Maryland*, BB-46!

All heads turned in disbelief, to look into the fading sun, ...and there it was, almost upon us! The crew began to make a hasty departure aft. The undetected enemy torpedo bomber had already dropped it's deadly torpedoes, as it continued it's collision course towards us, saving the second torpedo for a sure "down the throat" shot!

I lifted my head just in time to see the second torpedo slice into the water! I was on my elbows, as the Japanese torpedo plane screamed by just above our port side deck level! It was so close, it seemed you could almost touch it! I could plainly see the tense faces of the pilots as the flash of a huge red "meat ball" insignia painted on it's wings of death roared past. The heavy drone of turbulent engines faced in it's wake. Had they strafed, they would have easily killed a hundred or more men who were sprawled on the deck!

"Ker-Boom", Thundered the jarring impact of the torpedo directly under where I laid. The tremendous impact of the torpedo threw my body into the air. I fell back to the deck on my knees. A few feet away from me a steel hatch to the boatswains locker had blown into the sky like a tin can with a fire cracker under it! A huge splash of sea water and aviation gasoline shot ominously upwards into the sky.

The torpedo had struck our bow from the port side, ripping a huge , gapping hole below. Emergency klaxons sounded that steady, familiar, "PING! PING! PING!," as bugles sang out an urgent call to battle stations! I found myself running barefoot towards my station on the quarter deck. As I looked back, at the huge splash it was now still gracefully descending onto her wounded deck and back into the sea. Aviation gasoline vapor spread rapidly into nearby compartments, greatly increasing the danger of another explosion.

Sound powered telephones throughout the ship ran rampant with rumors concerning our damage. Soon it became apparent that there remained only one weakened bulkhead between us and the Pacific Ocean! Huge timbers were placed into position to support the remaining bulkhead as we weighed anchor and moved slowly out of the area with a destroyer escort, bound for the Island of Eniwetok for temporary repairs.

Upon arrival, divers were sent down to inspect the damage.....

"Well," called one of the damage control party, "How does she look? What's the damage to the bow?"

"What bow" came the response? There ain't any bow!"

The Battleship USS *Maryland* again immediately put out to sea, headed for Pearl Harbor for major repairs. She limped at a very slow speed to avoid the collapse of the one steel bulkhead between us and total disaster. Even at relatively slow speeds, the great force of the sea pressing against the torn jagged steel plates began to peal and tear dangerously backwards. They banged noisily against our wounded hull Speed had to be reduced even more, to prevent further damage. Destroyer escorts kept a wary watch for enemy submarines bent on administering a "coup de grace".

Each time we plowed through huge ocean swells, air was captured in the gaping hole. Then as her bow plunged downwards, both water and spray screamed menacingly up through the narrow hatch opening, it sounded like the ominous shrill of a wailing banshee foretelling death! I shall never forget that weird and terrible sound which could have brought fear even into the heart of Edgar Allen Poe. She was not unlike a wounded whale, screaming in pain....

The Ghost Battleship!

On July 10, we entered Peal Harbor for urgent repairs, as Tokyo Rose and the Japanese press boldly reported that The Battleship USS *Maryland*, BB-46, had been sunk! American newspapers reported, *"Ghost Battleship Plagues Japanese Fleet!"* Later, many of her crew would affectionately call her, *"The Mary Maru"* in bland defiance to her enemies.

During our period of repair, there were liberty parties into Honolulu, and a short respite at a recreation camp. Bob Hope, Jerry Colona and their troupe visited the *Maryland* while she was in drydock.

We were also honored with a personal visit from President Franklin D. Roosevelt and his entourage, who had inspected the damage while we were in drydock. It was exciting to see the President, as we proudly "manned the rail" in his honor.

Sometime later when we were somewhere in the middle of the Pacific, headed for further engagements with the enemy, we received word that the President had passed away. Our ships bell rang in slow cadence, as bugles sadly sounded taps in final salute to our Nation's leader, followed by a period of absolute silence. He was the man of his time, honored and respected by all, as our commander in Chief. It was an unforgettable moment.

Getting Ready To Fight Again!

Construction of the bottom half of our bow was started even before our arrival at Pearl Harbor. The relatively undamaged top portion of the bow was sliced off like a piece of cheese, then placed on huge wooden blocks in the drydock. The bottom half of the bow which remained was neatly

Buried at sea: R.N. Woolridge, Seaman 1/c; F.R. Bone, Seaman 1/c—killed in action June 22, 1944 at Saipan. Chaplain C.M. Sitler officiated at the ceremonies. (Courtesy of Fred R. Vreeken)

USS Maryland BB-46, starboard side view of damage from Saipan torpedo. Note ship repairmen standing at left near water line level. Anchor chain has been removed, and level steel supports welded to top of bow. Top of bow will be detached, and placed on blocks, while the bottom half will be cut out, completely rebuilt, and set in place. (U.S. Navy photo)

severed from the rest of her body. A new bottom half, was brought to the site, already completed. Two very huge cranes on railings lowered it carefully into place, where it was welded solidly together. When this step was completed, the repaired original top half was lifted carefully into place. It was amazingly clever work to behold!

The fighting "Mary *Maru*" and her crew were soon ready to face their enemies once again!

Memoirs of Charles Forselles, SC I/C

I'll always remember when the Japanese torpedo bomber dropped her two torpedoes, one of which crashed viciously into our bow. The blast sent fifty thousand gallons on aviation gas from the storage tanks in our bow soaring upwards into the sky. The Sea, some compartments and decks were filled with dangerous fumes. The possibility of another catastrophic explosion was entirely likely. Incredibly, no explosion occurred? If only one man had been smoking, the USS *Maryland* would have gone up in flames, carrying with it many lives.

When the torpedo struck, I was standing on the starboard bow. The blast hurled me 10 meters into the air! I landed with my back to the deck, and felt fortunate to have not been seriously injured.

The following report by Associated press, was printed in newspapers across the nation:

"Ghost of Saipan With Big Guns Hits Leyte Japs"

WASHINGTON, Oct. 30, 1944 (AP) — That battleship the Japanese claimed to have sunk at Saipan, rose up to plague the enemy in the battle of the Philippines.

The Navy disclosed today that the USS *Maryland*, torpedoed off the Marianas, was repaired in less than seven weeks and took part in the rout of the Japanese fleet last week. It was the *Maryland*, the Navy said, which the Japanese claimed as sunk. The speed of it's repair was described as typical of the work at Pearl Harbor, where repairs have been made to more than 50 vessels of all sizes and types since the war started.

Describing the attack on the *Maryland*, the Navy told how a torpedo

from a plane smashed into the battlewagon on the port bow, releasing the vessels aviation gasoline.

Why the gasoline didn't flare into a blazing inferno will forever remain a mystery," the Navy's version read.

Under escort, the Battleship *Maryland* limped to an advanced base and after temporary repairs sailed to Pearl Harbor.

The *Maryland* was straddled with two 500 pound bombs when the Japanese struck at Pearl Harbor Dec. 7, 1941, but remained afloat..

The Memoirs of Lawrence E. Dibb, CM 1/C
Served aboard 1942-1945

The Man Who Caught a Fish At Saipan

One evening while at anchor off of the Island of Saipan, "Old Horse" (Harrison D. Mathews, SF 2/C), and a bunch of the other guys from the "R" Division, were relaxing up on the forecastle, cooling off. "Old Horse", was laying on his back, port side, forward, with his shoes off. He had a fishing line tied to his big toe, which hung over the lifeline at about the break of the knee, and into the water below. Just about the time his fishing line started jigging, a plane suddenly screamed by low to the water. We all agreed it wasn't ours, as it's torpedo smashed into the bow below us!

We all scrambled for our battle stations, including "Old Horse!" I don't think he stopped to untie that fish line? ... So if anyone got "hooked" at Saipan, you'll know now where it came from?

Repair Division Citations

A number of our gang received Citations for making emergency repairs to the ship, which may have prevented the *Maryland* from sinking. We made a slow and precarious journey to the Island of Eniwetok, where divers inspected the damage to our bow. Then we limped at a very slow speed with a destroyer escort, to Pearl Harbor for repairs. The Citations read as follows:

UNITED STATES PACIFIC FLEET
Flagship of The Commander-in-Chief

The Commander in Chief, United States Pacific Fleet,
takes great pleasure in commending

LAWRENCE EUGENE DIBB
Carpenters Mate 1/C

For service as set forth in the following CITATION:

"For meritorious achievement while serving in the repair force on board a United States Warship engaged in operations against the enemy in the Pacific. By his outstanding performance and skill in shoring decks and bulkheads in the battle damaged area following a hit on this vessel, he contributed materially to the reduction of damage and the safe return of his ship to a navy yard. His actions were at all times in keeping with the highest traditions of the naval service."

C.W. NIMITZ, (Signature)
Admiral, U.S. Navy.

*Commendation Ribbons Authorized.
• Nineteen Commendations were authorized similar to the above.
and A Bronze Star Medal was with Combat Distinguishing Device was awarded to Lieutenant Commander Oscar Ezra Poole, USNR
(*Ironically, several of these shipmates were killed or wounded in the Leyte Gulf Campaign.)

Memoirs of James W. Howel, QM. 1/C
Served Dec. 1943-Jan 1945 • Deceased Mar. 23, 1989

I was a Quartermaster In the "N" Division. Assistance with navigational matters was my primary duty. I was also frequently assigned the duty as a helmsman. It was my good fortune to land a spot in a quartermaster training school, before being assigned to the *Maryland*, along with two of my classmates. The Battleship *Maryland* was simply awesome to this mountain lad from Eastern Tennessee. She was 624 feet long. Her size was unbelievable. I grew to consider her invincible! I never knew one moment of fear from the enemy while serving aboard. I truly loved her. I belonged to her .... She was my home!

Our part in the successful invasion of the Island of Saipan was concluded on June 22, 1944. We were ordered to anchor for the night. Captain H.J. Ray requested permission to remain underway in the open sea. Permission was denied.

I was on the bridge standing watch. Our training in Quartermaster school to recognize all types of Japanese aircraft from silhouettes, which were flashed on a screen at 1,000th of a second, came to the front as I saw a Japanese "Betty", torpedo bomber. It appeared over an Island nearby, flying low to the water. It was obvious that we were it's intended target. In a few moments, it would sent it's deadly torpedo into our port bow!

A Large part of the crew who slept forward were bedded down topside, expecting a good nights rest in the cool fresh air .... but the enemy torpedo slammed into us at precisely at 7:52 PM, (That was the official time I entered it into the rough log).

With a badly damaged bow, it's plates were barely hanging in place. We steamed very slowly for Pearl Harbor, where the nearest drydock large enough to accommodate us was located. Anxiety among the crew ran high, as we were forced to reduce our speed to prevent further damage. We were extremely vulnerable, particularly to enemy submarines.

While we were in Pearl Harbor for an extended period to have our bow repaired, we were fortunate to have Bob Hope, Jerry Colona, Francis Langford and their troupe come aboard to entertain us, by invitation from Captain Ray.

Admiral Nimitz (Com Nav Pac), King, and "Bull" Halsey came aboard to inspect the damage to our bow. On one day, even President Roosevelt appeared on the dock, to review the damage, and visit the ship.

The Memoirs of William J. Haligas, S 1/C
Served aboard, March 1944- Oct. 1945

At the battle of Saipan, when the *Maryland* was torpedoed, June 22, 1944, I had lost a very close friend, Freddie Bone. He was in the Boatswain's locker at the time the destructive torpedo smashed into our bow. The Torpedo itself did not kill him, but a hatch which was his only escape route, was buckled, and could not be opened. He died of asphyxiation and gas fumes. I can still see and hear in my mind, Freddie playing his guitar, and singing western songs......

The Memoirs of Jack D. Parker, S 1/C
Served aboard Oct. 1942 - Nov. 1945

I lost a very close shipmate at Saipan, and was one of his pallbearers, when we buried him at sea. It was one of the most difficult things I had to do. I'll always remember it and the many Islands we bombarded. We saw a lot of our marines floating in the harbors ... victims of war.

I remember watching our planes in dogfights with the Japanese. That happened a lot. I also remember washing blood and parts of human bodies

The USS Maryland's 16 inch guns belch flames and destruction to enemy positions, as 20 millimeter anti-aircraft gun crews take a deserved rest. (Photo by ship's photographer 1/C, William H. Chase)

USS Maryland, BB-46 in Pearl Harbor drydock. The top portion of the bow was neatly sliced off, then placed on blocks at bottom of drydock. The lower portion of the bow was built in Pearl Harbor, transported and lowered into place with huge cranes and welded into place. Then the original top portion was lifted in place and welded—in record time! (U.S. Navy photo)

from the decks. These are things you never forget... I remember Tokyo Rose speaking though our radio system, on three or four occasions, claiming to have sunk the Battleship USS *Maryland* .... We became known as "The Ghost Ship", because we kept coming back to wreak devastation and havoc upon the Japanese!

Rendezvous In The Solomon Islands

The Battleship USS *Maryland*, sailed quietly out of Pearl Harbor on August 13, 1944, joining with a large task force headed for a rendezvous in the Solomon Islands. Our course would take us across a great expanse of the Pacific Ocean, where anything could happen. The open sea reflected beautiful royal blue hues against horizons stretched in all directions. In the distance an occasional squall would shed it's moisture into mirror like, glassy smooth waters. Yet on the opposite horizon the sun would be shining radiantly. Racing on our starboard side, schools of flying fish leaped 15 to twenty feet out of the water, to glide with their long sleek wings for unbelievable distances before splashing back into the cool blue sea.

It was a typical tropical evening, the sun sank rapidly into the sea, while hues of orange and red cast dancing reflections upon the smooth, rolling swells. A cool breeze brushed against my face as I spread my blanket upon the deck among chattering men of the sea spinning their yarns, laughing and playing cards.

A Flying Fish Story

I laid face down completely relaxed, enjoying the refreshing evening breeze. I was ready to drift into pleasant slumber when suddenly, I felt something wet flapping wildly between my legs? Startled, I leaped into the air! To my amazement, there it was: — A real flying fish had flown aboard! Our deck was a good 30 or more feet from the water's surface!

Examining the little rascal at close quarters, was most interesting. The body itself was square shaped, about one inch in diameter, and one foot long. It had two long, narrow wings that ran the entire length of it's body.

In flight, they would span into a two foot spread. Curious shipmates gathered around to view the gasping flying critter, before I cast it back into it's own environment.

Somehow, the real beauty of a flying fish was at it's best, when in it's glorious flight! After this unique experience, it was even a greater thrill to watch them launch into flight as if to challenge a battleship to race. To witness this phenomenon was a privilege only few men can claim.

As we entered the Solomon Islands, our course took us over "Steel Bottom Bay" in the Coral Sea, — the site of earlier naval battles, in which the five famous Sullivan brothers perished with hundreds of others, in shark infested waters.

We soon dropped anchor off Florida Island, and prepared for some interesting liberties ashore.

Arriving at an assembling area in Purvis Bay, off of Florida Island, it would be another few weeks before we would depart for our next target, Peleliu and Anguar, in the Palau group of Islands. But, while waiting, interesting liberties and entertainment was headed our way!

Trading With The Island Natives

Some of the natives wore bushy black hair, while others bleached theirs a very peculiar reddish orange? They appeared quite primitive and didn't seem to understand nor speak but a few words of English. They wore very few articles of clothing. Now and then, they paddled along side the ships in the harbor to trade goods such as wood carvings, and assorted shells such as "cat eyes", a favorite among crewmen. (It was a flat shell with a brownish rim and a deep green center. It polished very well, which added to it's luster and was well suited for making jewelry for wives and sweethearts). Now and then, a Japanese "Memento" would turn up, such as an enemy bayonet, etc.

An experienced trader who might hand a native a five or ten dollar bill, would often get just a pitiful three or four "cat eyes"? On the other hand, a "shop wise" sailor could hand the same Solomon Islander a handful of assorted small denomination coins and get a whole coconut shell full of "cat eyes"!

USS Mount Hood disaster. The ammunition ship USS Mount Hood, exploded violently as if she were an atom bomb! This U.S. Navy photo demonstrates it's tremendous magnitude, as you compare the size of the large supply ships near the rising cloud formation. Only one man of the entire crew and workers survived. Nearby vessels also received damage. Cause was accidental.

Even more prized than coins for trade, were such items as bread, canned food, a pocket knife, soap, after shave lotion, and especially liquid bleach. The lotion was prized by the women, to make them smell nice. The bleach would not be used for washing clothes, but was savored for bleaching native men and women's hair!

Forbidden Territory

I was told that there was a small native village nearby. Out of curiosity, I hiked about a quarter of a mile into the forbidden jungle territory alone, to see for myself how these people lived. The trail was narrow and the towering trees of the jungle were gigantic. Long draping vines flowed down into a variety of lush foliage, which at times hid the narrow foot trail. I kept a wary eye out for snakes, or other predators which might exist there. Finally, a small clearing appeared. A few "lean to" makeshift shelters surrounded a fire pit, obviously used for cooking and to provide light in the evenings.

There were only one or two natives present. They spoke a broken form of English, and I was able to communicate with them to some degree. One of the most interesting discoveries I made, concerned their village and tribal laws. I was curious about an area that to me, appeared to be a small animal pen? It was about eight feet in diameter, with a wall made up of logs

piled only two high — certainly not high enough to contain any stock? Upon further inquiry, I was able to determine that this was their jail?

"What was there to keep a man from just stepping over the logs and escaping," I enquired?

"Him would be cast out," responded the tall bushy haired native," and if we catch him, we kill him!" It was further revealed, that not one prisoner ever tried to escape!

Swimming Hazards

Swimming on a Solomon Island beach was a real experience. Since there were no ladies present, all of us went "skinny dipping!"

The water was crystal clear. The sandy bottom was filled with a variety of multicolored tropical fish of all descriptions. The smaller of the species would disappear into the safety of white chunks of coral which laid on the sandy shallows. To catch them without a net, all one had to do to was to lift the coral quickly up out of the water! The water would drain out of the crevices, but the three or four inch sized tropical fish wouldn't! We then simply picked them out of their coral trap with our fingers, and placed them into a water container!

The clear, inviting waters held other innocent looking hazards, such as an odd creature about six inches in diameter, whose long, black, needle sharp spines were poisonous. The there was an innocent spaghetti looking plant, which waved gracefully, invitingly in the current — but if you just happened to touch it, or step on it, it would stick to your body like glue! It was excruciatingly painful! The sting would leave large red welts. If you tried to pick it off with your fingers, they too would be stung!

Blankets on the beach were seldom used to lay on. Most of the time they simply provided a smooth surface for high rolling crap games! It was a veritable Las Vegas, with yelling, cheering and excited sailors winning or losing their boodles! A fight would break out here and there, now and again, but for the most part, it was a pretty well controlled recreation.

Caught With Our Pants Down!

While many of us were peacefully "skinny dipping" a PT. Boat roared up to the dock, sending a wave from it's wake through the calm surface of the swimming area. Aboard it, was a U.S.O. troupe, including actress Carol Landis, with two other female entertainers!

There we all were, standing knee deep in the lagoon, with nothing on except our birthday suits! Some simply stood there stunned, vainly trying to cover delicately exposed areas with their hands! Some dove under the crystal clear water, (It was like swimming in a fish bowl), while others simply continued about their business, exposing their "pride", while the modest of them dashed under the pier or onto the beach, and into the jungles! The ladies however didn't turn the other way, but had a good laugh, with intermittent screams, as they covered their faces with their hands, peeking through their fingers! There were a lot of red faces that day, and a lot of laughs afterwards.

The Taking of Peleliu and Anguar Islands

On the sixth day of September, 1944, the task group underway for the Palau Islands, and the invasion of Peleliu and Anguar Islands. The respite was over and it was time to get back to the business of war.

We arrived three days before "D" day. The Islands loomed up before us, appearing like huge green, round topped mushrooms! There was little beach area — just various vertical rises of lava, overgrown with lush vegetation.

While general bombardment commenced on key positions and landing areas, underwater demolition teams were dangerously clearing the beachheads for the approach of landing craft. Major attacks from enemy aircraft were not an imminent as were sudden suicide attacks from small craft loaded with explosives.

With little resistance the Islands were swiftly secured. We did not encounter any major enemy aircraft nor surface ship contact. Gun positions however were extremely well camouflaged. Firepower from the guns of the *Maryland* ferreted out and silenced enemy emplacements. Firing was continuous enough to blister the paint on the gun barrels.

From the Palau Islands, we departed for a new rendezvous in the Admiralty Islands, to assemble for another huge and very important strike. It would be one of the largest, hardest fought amphibious invasions of the war in the Pacific!

Admiralty Islands Rendezvous
For The Invasion of Leyte!

The Admiralty Island area was a small group of volcanic Islands about 800 square miles in area, located in the Southwest portion of the Pacific Ocean. They are part of the Bismarck Archipelago.

The Battleship USS *Maryland* dropped anchor Seadler Harbor, Manus Island, where we would assemble and rendezvous with other major vessels of various kinds, to take on supplies, preparatory to launching an unannounced mission of great significance. We knew it was going to be big! It could be gauged by the very heavy traffic of vessels of all descriptions which began to pour into the area.

There were supply ships, ammunition ships, all types of men of war and transports. It was obvious that something BIG was in the wind! The Japanese were among the best jungle fighters in World War II. They could exist on small rations of rice for long periods of time. Loyalty to their cause, Country and Emperor was unquestionable. Indeed, they were a dangerous and interminable adversary to be reckoned with.

USS *Mount Hood* Disaster

The water was relatively smooth and calm as we steamed out of the harbor of the Admiralty Islands. Along the shore lines, ships were taking on last minute supplies and ammunition, while waiting their turn to take their assigned position in the formation, in orderly fashion.

Suddenly, "Blam!!!," a thunderous explosion echoed across the bay! An enormous black cloud rose high into the morning sky as the thunderous death cry of the "USS *Mount Hood*, AE 11," an American ammunition ship reverberated through the early morning air!

Many ships in the immediate vicinity were damaged to some degree and a great many lives were lost that morning. Only one survivor of the *Mount Hood* crew would miraculously escape with his life!

As we continued steadily on our course out of the harbor on our Philippine mission, the mushrooming cloud of death from the USS *Mount Hood* could be seen from many miles away. It was determined later, that the explosion was the result of an accident and not an act of war.

The Turbulent Sea

As we assembled in formation at sea, we encountered a raging storm of hurricane force. Giant waves swept over our quivering bow, as it rose high out of the rough sea, only to come crashing forcibly down again, under the depths. Each time it surfaced against hundreds of tons of raging sea with shuddering force. All hands were ordered below, as we plowed on to our fateful destination. Two of our destroyers had capsized and sank with all hands, lost to the wild and violent sea, ... never to be heard from again!....

The heat and humidity became unbearable. Within a couple of days, the tempest outside began to subside somewhat. I took to topside. Though the wind had subsided, the seas were still rough, as our bow plunged back into the turbulent sea like a running dolphin! Water a foot deep sweeping down the wooden decks could still wash a man overboard to a watery grave. I climbed a ladder to higher ground, as stinging pellets of rain slapped against my face. There on the bridge, I curled in a ball against a solid steel wall which protected the walkway and filled my lungs with the cool refreshing air.

As the storm began to subside somewhat, I climbed back down to the main deck. We were still taking water over the bow. Each time she dove down into the sea and rose again, about six inches of water still swept forcibly down the *Maryland*'s decks as it rolled off back into the rolling sea. It seemed that there simply wasn't a suitable cool, dry place to rest? ....Then I remembered the ammunition hatch behind our sixteen inch gun turret number one .... The hatch was about a foot above the deck, and was sheltered from the rain, by the overhang of the big turret itself! It was about four or five feet square! I simply waited until the bow began to plunge downward. Then as the sea swept deck momentarily subsided, I dashed forward under the shelter of the turret and curled up on top of the hatch, where it was cool, sheltered, and above the river of water which flowed gently to and fro, over the deck. .... I slept like a baby!

Entering Leyte Gulf

Early on the morning of the 18th of October, out battleships streamed paravanes to cut up mines as we entered Leyte Gulf, in the Philippine Islands.

The turbulent sea.

Mine sweepers had been at work a day before, clearing as much area as possible in the time given them. Coming in however, two mines were encountered and demolished.

As we took up our position in the Gulf of Leyte, it was a clear and beautiful morning. While shipboard enjoying the sun topside, a sleek gull winged F4U Corsair Marine fighter aircraft streaked across the bay from our fantail. It flew low to the water paralleling our port bow. As it approached the *Maryland*, it zoomed by with loud menacing roar, waggling its wings in friendly gesture, then maneuvered into a fascinating vertical climb into the blue sky above. As it faded into a tiny speck, it left us with a warm feeling of pride. We felt glad that he was on our side!

On the following morning, the Battleship USS *Maryland* took up her assigned position off red and white beaches, and began bombardment of selected targets, to soften up the shore lines where the landings would take place, on October 20, 1944.

A few days later, the army had landed and established a very firm foothold. Naval bombardments on key enemy positions and strongholds were then no longer required.

The Seventh Fleet then stood by with orders to maintain and control the immediate sea. It was here in Leyte Gulf, that the first Kamikaze attacks struck their deadly blows against the 5th Fleet and other supply vessels supporting the invasion.

The Deadly Kamikaze

It was here in Leyte Gulf, where the Kamikaze was born. To the Japanese culture, it was a very honorable and noble thing to voluntarily give one's life for his country. It was in fact, a guarantee to heaven. There seemed to be no problem finding volunteers!

Leyte Gulf, November 29, 1944: Only a 13 inch hole topside (left), but the damage below decks was appalling! An upright watertight steel bulkhead (right) blows out, 20 feet from explosion. The hatchway was also blown away!

This photo illustrates the powerful impact of the armor piercing bomb which crashed through the topside and main decks, then ripped open a hole in the four inch thick armor deck, where it exploded. The compartments below, including Sick Bay were completely demolished. Thirty-one enlisted men were killed, plus 29 crewmembers and one officer were seriously injured. (U.S. Navy photo)

In order to assure a hit against their enemy, a suicidal mission was made by the volunteer. It was a one way trip. To abort or survive meant disgrace. The Japanese in fact caused very heavy damage, inflicting a terrible toll in terms of badly damaged or sunken men of war and supply ships. A great many lives were lost by the deadly effect of the kamikaze. The only way to stop them, was to literally blow them out of the sky!

There were Kamikaze raids almost every evening! Sometimes as many as eighteen raids in a single day! Most of the time they would time their arrival at dusk, when they would be more difficult to see. Some would circle in the clouds above, carefully selecting their best targets. Then suddenly they would swoop down at an almost vertical dive towards their selected target. Yes, ..they were indeed deadly and extremely effective!

Units of the Australian Fleet were now in Leyte Gulf, doing their part to protect supply ships and new American installations established on shore. I remember one gallant Australian Cruiser which had taken several successive kamikaze hits. Her skipper and half of the crew had been wiped out! They were ordered to leave the area, — but it's courageous crew and second in command defiantly refused! I had gained a great deal of respect for the unusual, exceptional gallantry displayed that day! They were finally ordered in no uncertain terms to depart, and they did.

The remaining warships in the gulf steamed in a large circle, protecting tankers and supply ships which reinforced our soldiers and marines ashore.

In one tense moment of numerous raids, a Japanese torpedo plane intent to make a hit against the "Ghost Battleship" USS *Maryland*, flew in very low to the water to avoid radar detection. The *Maryland* "splashed the enemy after it had already discharged it's deadly cargo. A quick maneuver narrowly avoided collision with the torpedo as it sped harmlessly out to sea.

Kamikaze Crashes Into *USS Maryland*!

It was a cloudy evening on November 24, 1944, just before chow time. The sun was sinking rapidly behind the distant horizon. My battle station was up near the bridge, in a 40 millimeter anti-aircraft magazine, which fed two quad-Forty Millimeter gun emplacements, one on the port side, and one on the starboard side. Our job was to pass ammunition to the gun emplacements as they were firing.

I was taking a shower at our living compartment three decks below, when suddenly a bugle sounded emergency "Air Defense", over the loudspeaker system! .

(When this happened, all anti-aircraft personnel scrambled first to their anti aircraft stations. Shortly afterwards, the General Quarters alarm would be sounded for the rest of the crew to man their battle stations.

I rushed from the shower to my locker as quickly as possible to put on some protective clothing, but all water tight hatches were already sealed. Once they are sealed, there was no opening them, until "all clear" signals were given.

This photo was taken at the exact moment of impact of the Kamikaze between 16 inch gun turrets #1 and #2 of the USS Maryland. It burst into flames as it crashed. Repair crews were on the scene immediately. Several men killed topside. The armor piercing bomb penetrated three decks, to explode on the Armor deck. Splashes of defensive antiaircraft fire rise from the sea. (U.S. Navy photo)

Kamikaze in flight, bears down upon his selected target, the battleship Maryland! The light spots are tracers (every fifth projectile) which allows the gunners to see where they are shooting. The puffs of black smoke are bursts of flak from large caliber antiaircraft fire. The vertical streaks are lines from the ship behind which took the photo. (U.S. Navy photo)

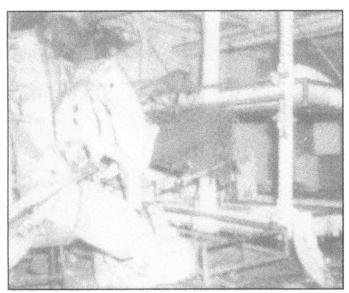

Sick Bay was thrust into total darkness when Kamikaze bomb exploded. Aftermath of explosion. (U.S. Navy photo)

Explosion aftermath. Clean up of devastated crews quarters, and the remains of those who died there. (U.S. Navy photo)

I felt that same uncomfortable enclosed feeling I had when my battle station was five decks below the water line, in the powder magazine. All I could do was wait! I cursed, and kicked a bank of lockers against the wall, indignant with myself. I should have been at my battle station where I was needed!

It was just before chow time. Tables had already been taken from their storage facilities and set up in place. There were others like myself who had been taking showers and were also trapped as I was in our living compartment. They sat there mumbling to themselves with the same concerns.

Topside, a Japanese kamikaze began it's vertical dive to the death, towards the *Maryland*! However for some unforeseen reason, he pulled back up into the clouds? A short time later, air release was once again sounded, as hungry sailors clamored to the chow lines and showers.

It was only a few minutes later, that emergency battle stations was sounded again with a note of extreme urgency! ....This time, I made it to my battle station, while many of my comrades having been caught in the showers, were trapped as I had been previously in the compartment below.

The same Japanese Kamikaze screamed downwards out of the clouds in it's vertical descent, this time intent to make his kill! Our anti-aircraft batteries pounded lead into the sky as fast as guns could be loaded. The intensity of gunfire increased, spewing a stream of tracers towards the rapidly descending kamikaze. It roar closer! ... closer! ... Heading directly for our position! It was going to hit! I ran into the magazine with my mate, slamming the steel door behind me! The deadly Kamikaze was only moments away from impact! Our gun crews fingers froze to their triggers, hoping to blast it out of the sky before impact in their midst! Suddenly the left wing ripped away, as it veered sharply left, crashing with great impact in a ball of flames a few feet away, between 16 inch gun turrets one and two!

It's armor piercing bomb crashed through two decks below, then exploded five feet from my locker on the armored third deck, penetrating it's four inches of solid steel! All those of my shipmates who had been trapped in the "F" Division Compartment, as I had been just moments before, were blown to oblivion! Not one survived the tremendous impact, with exception of a few in the nearby sick bay compartment...

Meanwhile, topside, Johnny Johnson, and Porterfield, my shipmates in the "F" Division, were outside of 16 inch Gun Turret #1 observing the action . When it appeared that the Kamikaze was going to hit, they scrambled to the hatch underside the rear end of the turret, to climb in, out of harms way. Porterfield was already inside, reaching down with a hold on Johnson's hand, pulling him up into safety, when the enemy aircraft crashed in their midst, jamming it's flaming remains under the turret! The flames shot up into the turret hatch, severely burning Porterfield's arm and face, as he fell backwards with Johnson's unattached arm still in his hands. Johnson lived only a few minutes, having lost both arms and legs, and suffering from severe burns. We had all been trained together as rangefinder operators, prior to being assigned to the *Maryland*. The memory of them will always linger in my mind. (Fifty years later in life, I found out that my shipmate Porterfield had also passed way).

A few feet away from the impact, there were two men manning a 20 millimeter anti aircraft gun mount. They had fired at the descending kamikaze until impact! One was killed. The other was blown out of his clothing and found wandering towards the quarter deck stark naked, in shock, but still very much alive!

Meanwhile, smoke billowed upwards, curling up around the bridge and on into the skies above. My companion in the magazine crouched in a corner with a handkerchief over his nose and mouth, as someone outside hollered, "Gas! Gas!" A thick acrid smell of smoke and death filled the air. I battened down the doors tightly and closed the ports from which 40 millimeter ammunition clips were passed. There was confusion outside. Voices shouted various commands as fire fighting and damage control rescue teams immediately covered the area.

We knew we were hit bad, but it wasn't until the damage control parties had fires under control and release from general quarters was sounded, that we were able to see with our own eyes the actual terrible damage which was inflicted! Chunks of human flesh had blown clear up to the foremast! We lost many of our close friends that day. It was a day that would live vividly in the minds of those who were there.

Scattered remains of the kamikaze pilot indicated that armor plate was worn as a protection against shrapnel, until he hit the target. I picked up a piece of the red "meat ball" insignia from the remains of the Japanese aircraft as a memento. I didn't want to ever forget the price that was paid on both sides, all for the sake of war!

As I proceeded to my living quarters, they were still bringing out bodies from the compartment. They were friends whom I knew well. They were stacked one upon another like cordwood and were covered with a black greasy substance from the explosion. Shrapnel wounds had cut deep, bloodless gashes into their bodies. They were blown completely out of their clothing. There were part of bodies — arms, legs — I shrank in horror. These were my friends? I felt numb. I wanted to cry, but couldn't. I walked away thanking God that the kamikaze pilot changed his mind at the last moment and pulled back up into the clouds, that I might get to my battle station... It could have just as well been me lying there instead of my shipmates who were trapped in the compartment as I had been moments before, when the Kamikaze pilot pulled out of his dive and flew back into the clouds, only to dive again trapping the others below in the showers, as I had been moments before.... Many heroic acts of unselfish bravery and leadership occurred on that terrible evening ... many of them not told until now.

Thirty one enlisted men died that night. Many more were injured. Approximately 38 men suffered from "battle fatigue". They were those who stumbled down ladders, who would not eat, who would not talk, or who simply starred into space. They were men with acute sensitivities, whose minds could not accept the tragedies of the surrounding death, and who mentally shut out the horrors or in self defense!

Sick Bay, which was adjacent to our living quarters on the armor deck, was demolished. Many lost their lives, but a few were led through flames and smoke in single file, holding hands through burning rubble, thick acrid smoke and debris, to safety. Heroes were born, and decorated deservingly for their brave and unselfish acts at the peril of their own lives.

After bodies were cleared out and the fires extinguished, those of us who had lived in that compartment were allowed to salvage what ever we could of our belongings. There was very little to salvage? ... Lockers were blown away, or crushed into a mass of crumpled metal. A shipmate by the name of "Swain", had to pry his locker open with a crow bar. Inside he saw what appeared to be a glove? He reached to retrieve it, only to discover it was a human hand covered in a greasy substance! The concussion had blown his locked locker open, as the hand flew into his locker, as the metal door then had crashed shut!

Corpsman still wondered about picking up bits of flesh and body parts, placing them in a bag. After more than 50 years, the faces of men I knew sill flash though my mind. I can see them as clear as day ... and I wonder what they would have accomplished with their lives had they lived?

As the days went by, we cleared the compartments of all the rubble, dumping it into the sea. Soon it began to look somewhat livable. Mess tables were brought in and we were able to use the area again. I remember sitting at the table eating an evening meal. I looked up to see a huge blood splashed spot on the ceiling, and quickly lost my appetite. I never again sat in that area.

The Memoirs of Wlm. P. Montgomery, FCR 3/C
Served aboard March 1944 - Sept. 1945

On November 29, 1944, we had just been relieved on the port 5 inch 25 Anti Aircraft Director. It had been a hot sultry watch that day in Leyte Gulf, with many air alerts and the manning of our battle stations at General Quarters.

"Goldie", (Morris Goldstein), who had two shiny gold front teeth, and I decided to take a shower, to somewhat ease the heat rash which plagued our bodies. As we entered the showers, I said, "You know Goldie, if general quarters should sound, we'd never make it to our battle stations in time?" (Goldie's battle station was in the plotting room several decks below, and mine was at a 40 mm. ammunition locker just aft of our number two sixteen inch gun turret).

We hadn't much more than gotten into the shower when air alert sounded! I jumped into my skivvies still wet and grabbed for my dungarees. We both took off running. The last thing I remember, was Goldie saying "See you later Moose!" By that time, General Quarters had sounded and everyone seemed to sense the urgency to get moving fast!

I had to get aft, beyond the shipfitter shop before I could go up. I knocked someone down, who was trying to shut the bulkhead door, and I made it up the nearby ladder into the superstructure, then finally through the inner bulkhead door into the ammunition locker.

The port 40 millimeter anti-aircraft guns were already firing away at the kamikaze diving headlong into us. We passed several clips through the ports. Those quad forty's could eat up a clip of four shells each in about three seconds time!

Then suddenly there was a momentary pause, followed by a shudder and then an explosive convulsion that was almost indescribable! The deck buckled under our feet and nearly knocked all ten of us down. Acrid smoke filled the locker, and we had to stand next to the clip ports to get fresh air.

Looking down, I suddenly realized that I was still in my skivvies, and next to an empty 40 mm box was my dungarees! I slipped them on, and in the twilight, we could see through the clip ports, the damage control party throwing and pitching parts of the disintegrated Kamikaze over the port side.

I can't remember how long we were required to stay at General Quarters, but it must have been four or five hours. Word had it that the devastation below in sick bay and the F Division compartments was unbelievable.

When we secured from General Quarters, most of the debris had been cleared from below decks, but the stench of death, and destruction remained. "Goldie", never 'saw me later', but I saw him ... wrapped in a sheet, along with all of the other casualties, that were placed amidships. He had been close to his locker, not far from where the bomb exploded. I still shudder at times, at what might have happened to me if I hadn't made it to my battle station? Surely, someone up there was watching over me?

The Memoirs of Lawrence E. "Larry" Dibb, CM 1/C

This story concerns the action at Leyte Gulf. *I wrote the account on Lou Berry, SF 1/C, to the lieutenant's office as a recommendation for a citation. I don't even know if he received it? But, I feel that Lou Berry, should get the recognition he deserves:*

I was alone, down the port side hatch between the shipfitter and the carpenter shops. I saw the deck in the shipfitter shop blow upwards, and I knew the explosion happened below. I opened the hatch to the second deck, wearing my RBA and with a battle lantern, I went below. The smoke and fire was so thick you couldn't see? I made my way forward to Sick Bay. Lockers had blown across the passage way, blocking the door. I cleared them out and entered. Just inside, was one corpsman laying dead. In Sick Bay, I spotted Berry sitting under a wet blanket. A lot of others were sick, or wounded. Several were dead. I asked Berry if he could walk. He weakly said no. I got a stretcher from the bulkhead, laid him in it, then dragged him to safety. I sent in my report as I felt he should have received an award for his actions during that terrible night, as he saved the lives of all of those who made it out!

What wasn't in Todd's report, was that in all the moving about, Berry had a packing of gauze in his incision that had come loose. As I was walking and dragging him, the gauze got caught on my foot. With every step I took, I pulled a little more out. Berry told me later, that he thought he was a goner, until I got there, — but with every step I took, he knew he was still with us. Every time I hear Jimmy Dean sing that song, "Big John", I think of Berry and what he did that night. Down in that hell hole of smoke, flame, and death, was a Big, Big, Man,— Lou Berry!

A Personal Testimony of Lawrence E. Dibb CM.1/C

When I had entered the compartment through the hatch, the ladder appeared stable. I found out the bottom half was blown away, when I fell to the deck. I thought I had hit a hole, with no way out, until I saw an open door way. I died many times that night. In the darkness, as I was pulling Berry out of the wreckage of Sick Bay, I had to get him past other crewmen on deck. They were all hollering for help. At the same time, a refrigerator door hit me in the back. I thought I had been stabbed! (Ha, it's funny now!)

This was the first time I had experienced the death of very close friends and shipmates. Most of the dead and wounded were in "R" Division, or closely connected to our repair party. Shipmates Evens and Riley spent a lot of time with us in the Carpenter and Ship Fitters Shops.

THE JACKPOT
By M.M. Todd, Chief Radioman

The following report was written by M.M. Todd, Chief Radioman, as the events actually took place. It is the duty of men in communications to report events as they happen and are generally typed in all CAPS. *(Submitted by Lawrence E. Larry Dibb, who had saved a copy of the following official report of a half century ago!)*

WORD GOES OUT TO MAN ALL BATTLE STATIONS. THERE ARE SUICIDE BOMBERS IN THE VICINITY.

IT IS CLOUDY ABOVE AND VISIBILITY IS NOT SO GOOD. IT IS NEAR DARKNESS.

OVER THE SHIPS TELEPHONE SYSTEM, WORD IS FLASHED THAT A SUICIDE BOMBER IS HEADING OUR WAY.

THE ANTI AIRCRAFT GUNS SET UP A TERRIFIC ROAR.

THE PLANE VEERS OVERHEAD. A WING TORN OFF. YET HE COMES ONE. THE DIN OF THE ANTI-AIRCRAFT FIRE IS DEAFENING—EVEN THREE DECKS BELOW.

ALL OF A SUDDEN THERE IS A HEAVY JAR — HEAVIER THAN ANYTHING THAT COULD BE CAUSED BY OUR GUNS.

THE LIGHTS GO OFF MOMENTARILY BELOW — NOW THEY ARE BACK ON AGAIN.

EVERYONE KNOWS WE'VE BEEN HIT AND A LOOK OF UNCERTAINTY FLASHES ACROSS EVERYONE'S FACE.

THEN AS THE SECONDS FLY BY AND NOTHING ELSE HAPPENS AN INANE CHATTER IS SET UP.

WE MUST GET IN CONTACT WITH THE NAVIGATION BRIDGE TO MAKE CERTAIN THAT COMMUNICATION CONTROLS ARE STILL IN TACT ABOVE. CONTACT IS ESTABLISHED.

WORD BEGINS TO COME OVER THE INTERPHONE SYSTEM—FLEETING APPRAISALS OF DAMAGE AND CASUALTIES. ONE OR TWO KILLED, SOME INJURED.

THE WHOLE THING BEGINS TO UNFOLD.

WE ARE HIT BAD. TWO LARGE COMPARTMENTS ARE A SHAMBLES AND ALL WITHIN, EITHER KILLED OR SERIOUSLY INJURED.

I CAME UP TO LOOK AROUND. MANY MEN WERE WALKING AROUND IN A DAZE.

OTHERS WERE RUMBLING THROUGH THEIR PITIFUL POSSESSIONS WITH A VACANT STARE ON THEIR FACES. SOON ONE FINDS SOMETHING — IT IS A PICTURE THAT HE VALUES HIGHLY. A MOMENTARY SMILE CROSSES HIS FACE.

HAVOC IS EVERYWHERE. LOCKERS CONTAINING ALL THAT A SAILOR POSSESSES ON THIS EARTH ARE SCATTERED THROUGHOUT THE COMPARTMENTS, THEIR CONTENTS STREWN FROM ONE CORNER TO ANOTHER.

HEAVY STEEL BULKHEADS ARE BLOWN AWAY AS IF THEY WERE TISSUE PAPER. A FOUR INCH STEEL DECK IS RIPPED OPEN/

STORIES BEGIN TO UNFOLD OF UNBELIEVABLE HEROISM THERE IS BERRY, THE SHIPFITTER WHO HAVING BEEN OPERATED ON ONLY THE DAY BEFORE, WAS HIMSELF IN A BED AT SICK BAY.

YET, WHEN THE EXPLOSION OCCURRED, AND HE REGAINED CONSCIOUSNESS, THE FIRST THING THAT ENTERED HIS MIND, WAS HIS FELLOW PATIENTS. HE HAD THEM ALL PUT ON THEIR SHOES FOR PROTECTION AGAINST BROKEN GLASS AND STARTED WITH THEM UP THE STARBOARD SIDE. A FIRE HAD BROKEN OUT AND BLOCKED HIS WAY. HE RETURNED TO SICK BAY AND WRAPPED THEM ALL IN BLANKETS, PLACED THEM UNDER THE SHOWERS AND TURNED ON THE WATER. HIS JOB WAS DONE, HE FOLDED UP!

WHEN THEY FOUND BERRY, HE WAS SITTING IN A HUDDLED POSITION AND COULD NEITHER LAY DOWN NOR STAND UP. YET, WHEN A LITTLE FELLOW ASKED HIM IF HE COULD MAKE IT, HE LET OUT A GROWL, THAT COULD BE HEARD ALL AROUND: "LISTEN, PIPSQUEAK, I'LL BE ALIVE WHEN YOU'RE DEAD TEN YEARS." ....AND HE PASSED OUT AGAIN.

THERE WERE MANY HEROES BORN THAT NIGHT — HEROES ALL. THEY WORKED UNTIRINGLY, THROUGHOUT THE NIGHT, MINISTERING TO THE WOUNDED AND DRAGGING OUT THOSE BEYOND ANYONE'S HELP, EXCEPT THE ALMIGHTY.

AND I SHALL NOT SOON FORGET THE LITTLE FELLOW WHO CAME UP TO US WITH A LEG IN HIS ARMS, WRAPPED IN A TOWEL, AND WITH A BLANK LOOK ON HIS FACE, POLITELY ASKED WHAT HE SHOULD DO WITH IT, VOLUNTEERING THE INFORMATION THAT HE HAD FOUND IT IN A CAN SOMEWHERE IN THAT HELLISH NIGHT MARE CALLED A COMPARTMENT.

AND THERE AGAIN, WERE THOSE STALWARTS OF DISASTER, THE DOCTORS AND PHARMACISTS MATES. THEY WORKED UNCEASINGLY THROUGH THE NIGHT — NEVER GIVING UP UNTIL

A MAN WAS BEYOND ALL HUMAN AID. MANY LIVES WERE SAVED THAT NIGHT.

AND THE PADRE — OUR CHAPLIN, EVER PRESENT, PREPARING THE REPORT SLIPS FOR THE FINAL MASS BEFORE THE GREAT — "SKIPPER"

THE SEAMAN WHO COULD BE SEEN EVERYWHERE — ANDERSON WAS HIS NAME .... FIRST SWABBING SOMEONE WITH IODINE, ANOTHER WITH ALCOHOL AND BACK TO THE PANTRY BREWING COFFEE — HOT COFFEE TO THOSE WHO WOULD NOT — WHO COULD NOT, LET UP FOR A SINGLE MOMENT.

ANOTHER WHO ANSWERED THE FINAL MUSTER WAS "BUCK" EVANS OF TURRET ONE. BUCK ALWAYS HAD A FRIENDLY SMILE FOR EVERYONE AND A CAUSTIC GLARE FOR THOSE WHO DARED QUESTION THE ABILITY OR ACCURACY OF HIS SIXTEEN INCH MUSKETS! BUCK WENT OUT TOO. IT WILL TAKE AN AWFULLY FINE MAN TO REPLACE HIM.

"IRISH " O' ROURKE, THAT REDOUBTABLE BROOKLYN IRISHMAN! ALTHOUGH HE HAD NOT BEEN WITH US LONG, HAD MADE HIMSELF A PLACE IN THE HISTORY OF THIS SHIP.

WRITINGS IN THE ONLY NEWS SHEET WE HAVE, EXPRESSED AS FINE A BIT OF SENTIMENT IN FAVOR OF OUR USS *MARYLAND*, AS EVER FLOWED FROM THE PEN OF BYRON, SHELLEY, OR KEATS. HE WAS NO BILL CUNINGHAM, AS A SPORTSWRITER, BUT HE WAS ALL WE HAD. IT WILL BE HARD TO REPLACE "IRISH"........

WE SHIPPED OUR DEAD AND WOUNDED OFF THE NEXT DAY. BUT WE DID NOT SHIP OUR MEMORIES. THEY WILL ALWAYS BE WITH US......

WE CAN ONLY HOPE THAT THEY DID NOT DIE IN VAIN. THEY HAD IDEALS AND AND PRINCIPLES FOR WHICH THEY FOUGHT AND DIED FOR. PERHAPS NONE COULD EXPRESS THEM IN WORDS, BUT THEY HAD THEM — THEY ALL DID.

IT IS LITTLE ENOUGH THAT WE CAN DO TO CARRY ON WHERE THEY LEFT OFF.

YES, THAT SON ... THAT EXPONENT OF SHINTOISM, HIT THE JACKPOT THAT NIGHT. HE WENT WITH THEM, BUT IT WAS A SORRY BARGAIN.....

The Memoirs of John A. Nelson, CPM
Served aboard, Mar. 1942 - June 1945

I came aboard the Battleship USS *Maryland*, during March of 1942, as a Hospital Apprentice 2nd class, assigned to the "H" Division, and left as a Chief Pharmacist Mate. The experience I wish to share, has to do with the perplexing mystery of fate. It focuses on a series of incidents for which there is no explanation as to why they happened as they did.....

For a period of two years, my battle station had been the area occupied by the Ship Repair Shop. Then just after getting underway for the invasion of the Philippines my battle station was changed to the boat deck. . Up I went topside, to an entirely different kind of environment....

As those who were there know so well, during the daylight hours we were under constant threat of Kamikaze attacks. The last attack of the day, usually occurred at sunset. (A definite advantage to a diving enemy aircraft bent on total destruction, because they became more difficult to see at that particular time of day.) Once the attack had subsided we would be secured from our battle stations, and allowed to return to our duty area. For me, this was Sick Bay.

On the evening of November 29, 1944, we were secured from our battle stations, and I returned to Sick Bay to prepare for the evening sick call. Preparations were just underway, when General Quarters was sounded. My immediate reaction was to ignore it, stay in Sick Bay, and continue to prepare for sick call. I reasoned that I would no sooner arrive at my battle station on the boat deck, and surely the all clear would be sounded? If I remained in Sick Bay, I could get a running start on sick call patients. Because of the constant threat of kamikaze attacks coupled with our daily firing assignments during the invasion, fatigue and stress had substantially increased the numbers of the crew requiring medical attention. So if I stayed in Sick Bay, I would be ready for them immediately after the "All Clear?" Hopefully, sick call would then be over in time for me to get caught up on some of my personal needs. However, an inner voice spoke to me which urged me to drop everything and get to my battle station!

I no sooner I arrived topside, when I saw the Japanese kamikaze diving on the *Maryland*! It's line of flight made it appear as if it were going to crash on the boat deck! I knew all along I never wanted to be there, yet there I was? I just stood there and watched. The rest is history.

The forward gun crews shot off the diving kamikaze's left wing, causing it to crash at the forward part of the ship. The armor piercing bomb it carried, find it's way between the sixteen inch gun turrets one and two, crashing through to the armor deck, (Three decks below), where it exploded. The explosive impact traveled forward, aft, and upwards! It killed most everyone in the Sick Bay area, which I had just vacated! Everyone in the Ship Repair Shop area, my former battle station, were also killed. Fate was on my side. If I had been in either place, chances are I would not be writing these memoirs!

* Note: *John A. Nelson had made no comment in reference to his receiving the decoration of the Navy and Marine Corps Medal for heroic and meritorious conduct, plus an advancement in rating when on November 29, 1944 he distinguished himself, with his heroic conduct. AFTER the kamikaze exploded, killing most of the men in Sick Bay! Nor did he mention his heroic deeds, when on the night of April 7, 1945 he again distinguished himself with unselfish devotion to duty, when the Battleship Maryland took another disastrous Kamikaze hit on top of 16 inch Gun Turret #3. Which killed 14 Marines who were strapped to their anti aircraft guns, shooting at the aircraft until it smashed into their midst, killing all but one man. John A. Nelson received another citation for call beyond the line of duty, and received a promotion to Chief Pharmacist Mate.*

The Memoirs of Harry Gabrielson, RM 3/C
Served aboard, 1942-1945

Leyte Gulf, Nov. 29, 1945 — WE were all snatched away from our comfortable surroundings, to the sinister excitement of "All hands, man your battle stations!" I rushed to my battle station up in the chart house.

I was standing outside in close proximity of the chart house, looking aft at the 20 mm, and 40 mm gun crews. How many times I wondered to myself, "How impossible it must be for a gunner to follow his own tracers, when so many other guns are shooting at the same target, at the same time?

Suddenly, from our stern, a single Japanese Kamikaze began to glide like a falling leaf out of a cluster of low hanging clouds. He must have been a very seasoned pilot, for he had to make a split second decision.

He obviously recognized that because of his limited elevation, he had less than a 50/50 chance of scoring a hit on us? At that moment in time, you could hear the distant roar of full throttle as he almost stood his aircraft on it's tail, climbing upwards back into the cover of the clouds above us. In my mind, I wondered what this mad, desperate pilot, whose last few minutes of life was to be spent in an effort to sink or severely damage our ship was thinking?

All eyes were glued to the cloud filled sky.... Suddenly, he made his move! On our port side, from the clouds above, the kamikaze emerged. "Look at this guy," I thought, "The plane is flying on it's side, so he cold get a clearer view of his target (us) below!" The obviously experienced pilot quickly executed a typical fighter wing-over, into a steep, fast dive to his certain 'honorable' death below!

The tremendous volume of deafening anti-aircraft fire pierced the air. Traders seemed to fly in at him from every direction. Still, he relentlessly continued his steep dive. I felt helpless, not having a weapon to fire back! It appeared that unless he was blasted out of the sky, he would crash into our very midst!

Instinctively, I turned, running for cover. I passed the chart house and ended up in radar plot, beside a large table. The crew members seemed to read my expression of pending doom. We all just stood there for seconds which seemed like hours, to pass. If parts of the plane or it's resultant debris didn't kill us, the fireball probably would! —

We all felt the gigantic shudder of the impact, as it crashed with thunderous speed between 16 inch gun turrets one and two!

"Dammit! He hit us! But where," we wondered? I looked at my hands palms up... "God, I'm still alive!"

After most of the initial acrid smelling smoke of gun powder and the eerie smell of destruction had cleared, I made my way back to the port side of the signal bridge. The scene was catastrophic. I kept wondering how one plane could have made such an impact? Some of the crew seemed to simply stand there bewildered for a frozen moment in time. I stood equally stunned at the sight below which met my eyes.

In short order, damage control parties and other volunteers were at the scene, doing what they could. In viewing the smooth round hole through the deck punctured by the armor piercing bomb which ultimately exploded three decks below, I thought momentarily of the pilot who must have dove full throttle all the way to his death! It was unbelievable that a bomb could go through so much steel before exploding? There was still much debris from the kamikaze strewn about the deck.

I was one of the "non essential" battle station personnel ordered to assist below. Upon arriving in the close proximity of the laundry, I was shocked into the true reality of war! There, before me on the cold steel deck lined up side by side was close to a dozen bodies covered with sheets. As I arrived at the laundry room, itself, it looked like a makeshift sick bay. Many men were sitting or laying down on benches. I was handed a cloth with an ammonia like odor to it, and told to hold it close, yet not too close to a crew member's nose, who appeared to be in a semi-conscious stare. Many suffered from smoke inhalation.

A short time later, a Chief Petty Officer pointed a finger at me and motioned several others to follow him. In another compartment, we were each handed a battle lantern. Although the fire fighting and damage control parties had put out the blaze and had the area secured, we could still see a haze beginning to build up.

The first sight upon entering the main blast area was almost indescribable. The air was still very pungent with the odor of high explosives and the unmistakable smell of death. It seemed so unreal? Everything was vividly covered in black. As I approached close proximity of where the explosion took place, the area was transformed into a forbidding surrealistic scene, as my battle lantern fell upon several bodies and the parts thereof. Everything was covered with a charred black substance from the explosion. We began the dreaded task of collecting remains, transporting them in wire mesh stretchers, blankets and sheets to designated areas.

I saw one particular individual in the devastated area shining his battle lantern upwards. A few minutes later, as I passed him again he was still standing in the same spot. He hadn't moved? He just stood there staring upwards as if frozen. Then as I looked up, an electric shock went through my scalp. It was an upper half of a body which hung head down through a gapping jagged steel hole, where the shipfitter compartment above once existed. He still wore his steel helmet and a life jacket. His arms hung downward swinging gently with the roll of the ship. He was killed instantly and certainly could not have felt any pain. The staring shipmate muttered a few incomprehensible words.

I asked, "What did you say?" He didn't answer and had a pale look on his face. Another man tried to speak with him to no avail. He just walked away as if in another world, saying nothing. I never saw him again. I suppose he must have been among the many who were taken from the ship with symptoms of battle fatigue. I'll never forget the expression on his face.

It was good to get topside again. It was an experience which continues to haunt me, — even after all of these years which have passed.

The Memoirs of Loreto L. Sinatra, MM 3/C
Served aboard 1944 -1946

On the evening of November 24, 1944, were at Leyte Gulf in the Philippine Islands, in support of our invasion forces. I had just been released from Sick Bay, after a weeks stay, which left me in a weakened condition. Suddenly the all too familiar sound of General Quarters sang throughout the ship, as a very convincing voice cried, "All hands! Man your battle stations!"

I knew I could never make it to my battle station from Sick Bay, to the aft engine room, before all the water tight doors were secured? I wasn't rally too concerned, because I supposed like so many times before, that it wouldn't be long before General Quarters would be secured. Perhaps I'd have a chance to get to my battle station when the next alert was called?

I was standing in a conversation with Shipmate Gordon Odell Ryman, S 2/C, as he laid in his upper bunk. Suddenly, the pounding of our five inch guns, and anti aircraft weapons simultaneously quickened. Instinctively, we knew we were under attack, by an enemy kamikaze bent on our destruction! We were concerned at this point, but as our 20 mm and 40 mm guns joined in, we realized that we were either had to blow him out of the sky, or take a hit!

Suddenly there was a deafening explosion and an impact which blew apart everything in its path! We were plunged in total darkness! The thick acrid smell of smoke and gunpowder enveloped us, as we were plunged into total frightening darkness! There was no ventilation nor electric power. The awesome concussion impact literally blew my body across the deck! I felt that my face had blown away? Gingerly, I placed my right hand to my chest, inching upward towards my face, to see if it was still there? .... To my great relief, it was in tact. I lifted myself from the deck and groped for a telephone to call for assistance. The phone was gone? We were trapped in thick darkness and acrid smoke, with no where to go.....

I remember the voice of my shipmate Lee Russell Jr., telling me that it was difficult to breath. I told him we had better lay down on the deck where there might be more oxygen. As I laid down, I discovered there was an inch or two of water on the deck. I was struck with an awful fear that we might be sinking! At this point, I mentally prepared myself to meet my Lord! Lee Russell Jr. and I both started to pray. I had no conception of time, nor how long we had laid in this position. We were beginning to suffocate. It seemed we waited an eternity for help to arrive. Just as I was about to lose consciousness, I heard voices! Then a hand groped for my wrist.

The next thing I remember, was being carried out of that inferno of hell, to a safer part of the ship, where we were laid on the deck. I started to breath a little better, knowing I was going to be all right. While lying there, I began mumbling and cursing the Japanese Pilot who caused such horrible death, destruction and heartaches to my shipmates.

Chaplain Francis Mc Veigh came by. He knelt over me and in his soft soothing voice said, "Son, is there anything I can do for you?"

"No Father," I said, "Go help the others." The next thing I remember was being lifted onto a bunk at the temporary sick bay, set up in the Junior and Warrant Officer's Wardroom.

I don't recall how long it was before the other wounded men and myself were transferred to the Hospital Ship U. S. S. Bountiful AH 9.

Later, I learned that my shipmate Gordon O'Dell Ryman, and thirty other shipmates were killed. Eventually, I wound up in Noumea, New Caledonia at U.S. Fleet Hospital #105.

On March 16, 1945, I returned aboard the *Maryland* at Ulithi, in the West Caroline Islands, in time to take part in the offensive operation at Okinawa.

I don't know how many of our rescuing crew members were there, nor who carried me out of that hellish inferno, (Sick Bay), that day, but I'll never forget them, nor the rest of the wonderful men who served aboard that glorious ship, the USS *Maryland*, BB-46. I shall always remember the battleship *Maryland*, particularly those who never made it home. The time I served aboard her, filled my heart with as much pride as any man could possibly feel.

The Classic Naval Battle of Surigao Straits
By Lt. Robert H. Goodell

Oct.-Nov. 1944: The great and Classic Battle of Surigao Straits would be recorded by historians, as *The greatest naval engagement in the history of naval warfare!*

The Classic Battle Of Surigao Straights..

This view of the battleship USS Maryland, BB-46, shows our two OS2U Spotter aircraft—one of which sits on launching ramp. Atop of 16 inch gun turret #3, 20 mm antiaircraft mounts which were later wiped out by a suicide plane. Just behind turret #3 is the mainmast from which our flag flies. Between the stacks are more 20 mm gun mounts manned by our marines, then the bridge and the foremast. (U.S. Navy photo, National Archives)

This freehand sketch by Fred R. Vreeken, FC 3/C, illustrates the "F" Division living compartment on the armor deck, where the armor piercing kamikaze bomb exploded. Lockers surround a 16 inch gun barbette, (a round, armored protective cylinder around the turret which went deep below to the ammunition and powder rooms). Steel beams across the ceiling supported by stanchions (steel posts), contained hammock hooks, and red night lights. Every inch of space was useable. (Petty Officers slept on cots below, while seamen slept in hammocks)

Admiral Kinkaid's 7th fleet, including six older battleships, two cruiser divisions, countless destroyers and PT boats, were under continuous daylight attack from the dreaded Kamikaze. The Battleship *Maryland* did not escape untouched!

The Japanese master plan was as follows: The Japanese fleets would converge on the American 7th Fleet from three directions, with the objective to annihilate our naval supporting forces and supply ships. Once the American Fleet had been destroyed, American forces on Leyte could be bombarded from the gulf, thus causing havoc, shutting off supplies and allowing Japanese ground forces to annihilate the invading forces.

Specifically, the Japanese fleet was to converge on the 7th Fleet from three directions: From the south, through the Surigao Straights, from the Japanese mainland in the north, and their central naval force from the west, through San Bernardino Straights.

Officers John Kelly, Ed Korr, Lt. Vernon Barnes, (Communications), and myself were aware on that morning of Oct. 24, 1944, that a possible surface engagement with the Japanese Fleet was imminent!

Our scout planes and pilots were dispatched to the beach. We turned to battle stations that afternoon. Captain Ray made a brief announcement to the crew, over the public address system, stating that a night engagement with the enemy fleet was very probable. Our targets were already approaching through the Surigao Straights! Lieutenant Buck Epperson, was on the main battery plot master control. I was on backup. Lt. Commander Warren Lowery, USN, faced all of us, directing the procedures with the precision of an orchestra leader!

Automatic gyros, head phones to top spot, the bridge, coning tower and sixteen inch gun turrets 1, 2, 3, and 4,. There were over 100 men in the "F" Division (Gun Fire Control Division), each with special training, to assure firing excellence!

At 2:00 AM on October 25th, 1944, we buttoned up to General Quarters and waited patiently. Commander Lowery said the Japanese forces consisted of at least two battleships, two heavy cruisers, and four destroyers.

About 3:00 AM, the lead battleship appeared on the radar scope, at a range of 35,000 yards. (17.5 miles) Our six older battleships were steaming at a right angle to the single file of approaching Japanese warships, which steamed steadily at 20 knots. *(This classic maneuver was known as the "Crossing of the "T"—the ultimate dream in naval warfare!)

As they neared, our PT. boats and Destroyers made their torpedo runs

first. They were then followed the 8 inch gun fire of the two Cruiser Divisions. At 3:45 AM, we opened fire at a range of 25,000 yards, or 12.5 miles. Most all of the ships of the 7th fleet were able to get in their best shots, in simultaneous rapid firing. The Battleship *Maryland* fired at least twelve 16 inch gun salvos, (96 Shells, 2,500 pound armor piercing type)!

Lt Baird of the top spotting position described it as the biggest 4th of July celebration he'd ever encountered! (4:00 AM)

In less than 15 minutes at a range of 18,000 yards, all of the Japanese ships were either sunk, or dead in the water.

At dawn, (6:AM), all eight of their men of war, were sent to the bottom! At (7:00 AM), we were at condition "one easy". Officers and men were released in small groups for hot chow, coffee, and a breath of fresh air.

Unfortunately, there was little time for celebration? The Japanese Central Naval Force consisting of five battleships and other supporting warships were advancing through the San Bernardino Straights as expected, to engage us at the entrance of Leyte Gulf!

Our submarines sank and damaged several enemy ships in their approach. Admiral Sprague's seventeen CVE's (Jeep Carriers), our air cap, was maintaining stations just a few miles east of the Leyte Gulf entrance. (Intelligence reported their central Force consisted of five battleships, 8 cruisers, plus several destroyers and destroyer escorts. (Their battleships had eighteen inch guns!)

We maintained our station just inside the Gulf, awaiting their arrival. The Japanese Task force then chased our Jeep Carriers in and out of rain squalls most of the day.

Heavy damage was inflicted to six or seven of our jeep carriers in and out of rain squalls most of the day. Heavy damage was inflicted to six or seven of our jeep carriers, which retreated back through San Bernardino Straights. Most of the Japanese task force were sunk or heavily damaged by Admiral Halsey's fast carrier air group and American submarines. Admiral Mitscher's Carriers and air group repelled the Japanese carrier force approaching from the North. All of this surface and air action occurred in less than 48 hours.

Without the threat of further naval engagements with the enemy, and after several more days of call fire from the beach, we steamed to our Manus Island Naval Base for supplies and ammunition. There, we were treated to nightly movies on the quarter deck. USO entertainers were a treat for all. As Morale Officer, I took many whale boats to some local beaches for baseball and beer busts!

Our Early Morning Sea Battle at Surigao Straights
John W. Johnson

The early morning naval engagement with the Japanese fleet took place in the pitch black darkness of early morning hours, on Oct. 15, 1944. It was a dazzling sight to see. While looking out over the splinter shield, we could see enemy tracers arching across the blackened skies. We listened to them soar over us to splash into the water, while others fell short.

The resounding sound of our 16 inch guns returning fire was deafening. There wasn't time for tension and waiting for the expectation of being hit ourselves. All hands seemed to concentrate on doing their jobs the best they could, as adrenaline flowed furiously through our veins..

There were seven tracer salvos still racing in the darkness of night, falling towards the enemy, when the order came to cease fire was given. As dawn began to shed the softness of it's light, there were Japanese survivors floating in the sea among the debris. Many would not take a line to be rescued as a prisoner of war, preferring death to dishonor. Many of them were obliged to surrender rather than to suffer further against sharks, or other ruthless perils and elements of the sea.

The anti aircraft personnel's opportunity for regular meals were limited during long hours manning their battle stations so continuously ... indeed, they were often few and far between. We lived mostly on coffee and sandwiches. Long hours on vigil watches with little sleep, tires the best of men. We went as long as 37 hours in one session of battle alert conditions.

What it Takes To Fight a War...

On the 12th of October, 1944, the Seventh Fleet under Admiral Kincaid sortied at sea for the invasion of Leyte, in the Philippines. A tally of ships present at Seadler Harbor, Manus Island in the Admiralty Islands group is listed below. The battleships, cruisers and carriers are listed by name. The remainder are listed by number of ships. The purpose is to provide the reader with an idea of how many vessels of all types it took for this one invasion. War is not only wasteful, but very expensive in time, materials, manpower, lives lost, and taxpayer dollars!

Ships Present List, Seadler Harbor
Battleships 6
   Maryland, *West Virginia*, *California*, *Tennessee*, Mississippi, and
   Pennsylvania.
Cruisers 8
   Minneapolis, Louisville, Portland, Denver, Columbia, Nashville,
   Boise, Honolulu.

Australian Cruisers 2
   HMAS Australia, HMAS Shropshire.

Aircraft Carriers 19
   Omeny Bay, Croatian, Sangamon, Santee, Kitkum Bay, Gambier
   Bay, White Plains, Chenango, Natoma Bay, Savo Island, Saginaw
   Bay, Petrof Bay, Kalinin Bay, Windom Bay Manila Bay, Marcus
   Island, Kadasham Bay, Windham Bay, Bouganville.

Destroyer Escorts 13
American Destroyers 59
Oilers 8
Tenders 7
Ammunition ships 3
Destroyer Transports 9
Mine Craft 10
Landing Ships Dock 7
Unclassified Vessels 7
Fleet Tugs 3
District Craft 4
Landing Ships Medium 5
Landing Craft Infantry 55
Landing Ship Tank 58
Total Vessels 342

The Fiercely Fought Battle For Okinawa Jima

The coming battle of Okinawa would be among the most viciously fought battles of the war. The Japanese knew that if Okinawa was taken, the next step would be the mainland of Japan itself. It would be the largest amphibious force assembled yet, by the United States of America, in the war of the Pacific. The price to pay for this real estate would come high, and we knew it! Yet, the confidence and morale of the *Maryland*'s crew was high.

It never faltered, though a few had suffered "battle fatigue" and were removed from the ship. They were those whose minds could not accept the viciousness of war, who stumbled down ladders, never spoke, and wouldn't eat nor speak and had blocked from their minds the shocking realities and horror of what they had witnessed. But for the rest of the crew, excitement ran high and we were proud to be where we were, fighting for our country!

It was February 20, 1945. Repairs had been completed from damage received at Leyte, and we had a brief period of relaxation. Now we were ready, even eager, for our next assignment. All hands turned too, loading ammunition for all batteries and provisioning the Battleship *Maryland* with food and stores. We were prepared to once again move into the forward area.

For a whole week, extensive training, and bombardment drills involving all divisions took place off of the Island of Kahoolawe, in the Hawaiian group, in preparation for the coming intense operations against Japan.

On March 4, 1945, the *Maryland* headed for Ulithi, in the West Caroline Islands, accompanied by three destroyers and an aircraft carrier. While at sea, planes which flew our from Oahu airfields, trailing sleeves, provided our anti aircraft batteries with some target practice. Other intensive drills were also held.

On March 16, 1945, we entered the huge Ulithi anchorage. In this large harbor were massed the ships of the Fifth Fleet, soon to attack the Japanese on the Island of Okinawa. The enlisted men were not told until later, as to where the operation would be. Speculation ran high, providing an exciting anticipation — not all together pleasant. The overwhelming number of ships were thrilling to view from the top of our mast, and would certainly be a most formidable scene for an enemy to look upon.

It was here that we saw the battered carrier Franklin, which had taken a savage beating from kamikaze attacks. It seemed to be a miracle she was afloat! She lost half of her crew and would set the record for the most damaged ship of World War II.

On the morning of March 21, 1945, the *Maryland* took her place in the huge disposition of ships, which were to provide gunfire for the largest amphibious operation yet in the pacific!

In task force 54, were the following battleships: USS *Maryland*, *West Virginia*, *Colorado*, *Idaho*, *Tennessee*, *New Mexico*, *Nevada*, *Texas*, *Arkansas*, and *New York*. There were also several cruiser divisions and a large number of destroyers as well.

Refueling Ships at Sea

In extremely rough weather, destroyers came along side the Battleship *Maryland* to refuel from our reserves. Signalmen busily sent signals by hand to one another, asking for such luxuries as fresh baked bread and items uncommon to smaller vessels. Huge rubber tubes joined battleship to destroyer through rough seas, as skippers skillfully maneuvered their vessels to keep just the right distance between ships, to avoid ruptures or dragging of the oil delivery tube through rough seas.. It was comforting to be aboard a battleship which did not bob like a cork, and had almost every type of convenience aboard. The Battleship *Maryland*, had a crew of approximately 2000 men!

A Special Assignment

We were within a day of our destination, when Fire Support Unite #1 was ordered to proceed independently. So the Battleships *Maryland*, and *Texas*, plus the Cruiser *Tuscaloosa*, with several screening destroyers, separated from the rest of the armada. On the morning of March 25, 1945, Okinawa Jima appeared on radar, to be 74,000 yards away. General quarters was sounded as we entered the fire support sectors to which we were assigned.

The *Maryland*'s job was to use the main battery as required to destroy shore batteries, pill boxes and other targets of opportunity. Our main purpose was to support a "demonstration" landing on the southeast coast of Okinawa. It was hoped that the action taken would distract the enemy's attention from the huge gathering of ships off Okinawa's west coast.

There were air raids on the very first day. One of the *Maryland*'s pickets (an outpost radar guard ship), the USS *Luce*, had been hit badly and was sinking. The nearest destroyer immediately moved out to rescue the crew. As she drew along side, she was also hit by a kamikaze plane and sank shortly afterwards.

For seven days, the Battleship *Maryland* ruthlessly bombarded the assigned sectors where large calibre guns were known to exist. Our spotter planes located some well camouflaged targets, which were swiftly destroyed by the *Maryland*'s ominous fire power! Each evening, the ships withdrew for the night, retiring to the safety of the open sea. We returned every morning to wreak new destruction and havoc upon the enemy. Our guns were continuously manned around the clock.

The actual landing took place on April 1, 1945 on the west side of Okinawa. A demonstration landing was effected on the southeast coast, which had received a thorough bombardment by the *Maryland* and the rest of our companion units.

Rejoining The Major Task Force

Following this action, we rejoined the major forces west of the Island, where a large calibre enemy gun emplacement was discovered. It outranged the fourteen inch guns of some of the older battleships. The *Maryland* was called upon to destroy this position.. In a headlong duel, the *Maryland* made her charge against the heavy enemy gun emplacement, waiting for just the right moment to fire. Our first salvo caused an underground explosion which terminated the enemy position. It turned out to be a huge 17.7 inch gun emplacement which could have easily outranged the *Maryland*! After the war, I had talked with marines who were there to actually see this huge piece of artillery and witness the terrible damage inflicted by the USS *Maryland* on this position!

Kamikaze Terror

After the invasion, the *Maryland* stood by, awaiting calls from the beach for main battery fire. During this time, the Japanese gave the combat ships which were standing by, the heaviest air raids of the war. Radar screens were heavily filled with enemy and friendly aircraft. There were many alerts and actual raids both day and night. Long hours were spent at General Quarters. Our anti aircraft batteries were in "Condition One" mode, most of the time.

The huge mass of ships off Bolo Point, were given a terrific pounding. Every day, ships went down to the bottom. — Every day, the Japanese scored! We watched seven of our destroyers go down in one day! One would be hit and sinking. Another would come to pick up survivors, and it too would be hit! In spite of all the danger and terrific beating withstood by these gallant destroyers, our fleet stood their ground faithfully and determined.

The Kerama Retta Rendezvous

The *Maryland*, having expended most of it's ammunition, left the area to rendezvous at nearby Kerama Retto, a small group of Islands ten miles to the west of Naha, Okinawa's Capital, to take on badly needed fuel and ammunition.

The islands appeared as if out of a story book. We were surrounded by heavily foliaged Islands which rose high out of the water, appearing very rounded at the top. It was as if they were drawn by a six year old child. Radar was constantly picking up "Bogies" (enemy aircraft).

We were tied to an ammunition ship with hundreds of metal canisters containing powder bags, (for our sixteen inch guns) lying about the decks waiting to be stored in the magazines below. While crews worked with all speed they could muster, rifle shots ricocheted off of our turrets with a resounding "ping!" Everyone simply ran around to the other side of the ship, continuing to store ammo as fast as possible..

Suddenly, radar reported "Bogies" headed our way! The lines binding us to the ammunition ship were quickly cut, as we hastily got underway! Thousands of dollars worth of gun powder and canisters were quickly thrown overboard, leaving a trail of bobbing cans in our wake! Just one spark or well placed bullet, and we could have gone up in flames!

Japanese Naval Force Foiled, as Battleship USS *Maryland* Takes Yet Another Kamikaze Hit!

It was April 7, 1945, a day the crew of the USS *Maryland* would never forget! We were once again sailing in column with other American Battleships, at Okinawa. There were reports of large Japanese naval force racing towards Okinawa from the northwest!

In the early evening, a large group of American battleships sailing in column, with many cruisers and destroyers making up the flanking forces, got underway on a northerly course to intercept and engage the enemy. The Japanese men of war were only a part of a huge force, ordered to intercept and destroy the American fleet!

Just before dusk, out fleet was attacked by enemy aircraft. While we were at general quarters, a Japanese Kamikaze, with it's 500 pound bomb dove with deadly accuracy towards the *Maryland*, amidst a hail of antiaircraft fire. The tempo of pounding gunfire quickened in simultaneous resound ... and we knew we were going to take another hit!

The enemy aircraft in it's dive of death, was heading straight for our 16 inch gun turret #3. The crew of Marines, manning four 20 millimeter anti aircraft gun positions mounted upon the top of turrets top, fired intensely into the diving enemy suicide plane, until it unmercifully crashed into flames within their midst!

The horrified gunners strapped to their weapons, with no time to escape, fired rounds of 20 millimeter projectiles into the enemy aircraft until the moment of impact!

(The remains of a 20-mm gun recovered in the aftermath contained a spent projectile in it's badly bent barrel, indicating that this marine fired his weapon until the very impact had taken place!) Heroism does not come easily!

The kamikaze smashed with a thunderous roar atop the turret amidst the pounding 20 mm gun mounts, bursting into a giant cloud of flame and black smoke, as it's bomb violently exploded against the top of the heavily armored sixteen inch gun turret #3.

The battleship USS Maryland presses on to new threats of fierce Kamikazee attacks, and adventure at Okinawa Jima. (U.S. Navy photo)

The 20 millimeter anti aircraft mounts atop the turret were completely demolished. Burning fragments of the aircraft mingled with body parts were strewn about the quarter deck. All but one of the men were killed instantly. The only surviving marine crewman was Justin Joseph David S1/c, who had literally been blown from the platform to the deck below.

Medical officers and corpsmen were quickly on the scene, evacuating wounded, and administering preliminary treatment to the wounded. Battle dressing stations and collecting stations were quickly set up to receive casualties. A sight muster was taken by division officers and a thorough search was made for the missing. Destroyers watched the waters astern for any potential survivors.

The most severely injured patients along with the bodies of the known dead were transferred to the USS Comfort, a hospital ship nearby.

Although he bomb itself did not pass through the five inch steel top of the turret, it did manage to penetrate it and damage the supporting stanchions inside! Crew members inside the turret reported being bounced around "Like a rubber ball."

As water hoses immediately played on the turret surface, it flowed with force into the turret itself, leaving some of it's crew with a false impression that the ship was sinking, causing some momentary excitement.

Only one of the gunners on top of 16 inch gun turret #3 miraculously survived! His name is Justin J. David. He lives to this day..(See his personal testimonial following this narration)

The Memoirs and Testimony of Justin David, S 1/C
Served aboard July 1943-April 1945

April 7, 1945 came upon us just as miserably as the previous six days of bombing installations on Okinawa and fighting off the determined, persistent Kamikaze.

The morning began with our "usual" call to general quarters. We sometimes remained at battle stations until well into the night. During that day, word was received that the Battleship Yamato was bound for Okinawa. News like this wasn't taken lightly, for the Yamato was armed with 18 inch guns, and was one of the newest class of enemy warships.

The *Maryland*, with other battleships, destroyers, and cruisers making up the flanking force were sent out to help intercept and destroy her! This desperate sortie by the Yamato would be her last voyage! Fortunately, she was sunk by our carrier planes before she had a chance to engage any of our surface units.

Early in the evening as the sun began to sink on the horizon, our battleship formation was attacked by enemy aircraft. While we were at our battle stations, a Kamikaze dropped out of the low hanging clouds at the starboard side. I was at my battle station on 16 inch gun turret three. There were four 20 mm guns on the turret, two on the port side, and two on the starboard side. I was the gunner on the forward gun, port side. Each gun had a four man crew. In addition, there were two "talkers" on the turret.

The kamikaze flew parallel course to our formation, low over the water. The Japanese pilot obviously determined that the *Maryland* would be his best target, as he turned and began to bore in on us. Luck was with him that day, for he had flown down the entire length of battleships in formation, with every anti aircraft battery that could bear firing away at him! He then bore down on the *Maryland*, head on! We fired at them with everything we had. I had turned my gun 180 degrees, so I could fire at him. I was actually shooting just over the head of I.W. Gist, the young man from Texas, who was the gunner on the forward 20 mm mount on the starboard side. It was truly a "down the throat" shot for many of us, but the determined kamikaze pilot kept boring in, until it crashed in our midst on 16 inch gun turret #3. I recall thinking to myself, "So this is what it's like to die!" As it was however, I don't recall that I was the only survivor? There were other casualties at nearby stations as well.

I remember walking to the ladder and climbing down to the quarterdeck. My clothing was on fire. A damage control member hosed me down with water before I even reached the deck. A corpsman was nearby. He administered morphine to me, and bandaged my lower left leg, which was hit by shrapnel. I was also struck on my left thigh. Before the plane had struck, I had neglected to put my fire retardant gear on properly, and received burns on my face and left hand. I was taken to sick bay immediately, so I had no idea of the damage which had taken place topside.

The following day, I was sent to the Hospital ship USS Comfort From there, I was left at a Naval Hospital at Guam.

I shall never forget my service on the Battleship USS *Maryland*, nor the friendships I had made, some which abide to this day. As I write this, I am 64 years of age. In retrospect, my service aboard the *Maryland* were the proudest moments of my life.

GALLANTRY IN ACTION
Release #109
ABOARD THE USS *MARYLAND* SOME WHERE IN THE PACIFIC

On April 7, 1945, the Battleship USS *Maryland*, BB-46 along with other units of Uncle Sam's fighting navy then engaged in the war at Okinawa Jima headed into the East China Sea, as ordered, to meet the enemy warships reported headed toward Okinawa.

Today it is history that Admiral Marc Mitscher and his Carrier task force, not only met the enemy, but were victorious in every sense of the word. But the actions of 18 heroic men aboard the *MARYLAND*, 17 of whom have made the supreme sacrifice for their Country are not history and never will be, except in the minds of the men on that ship who witnessed their deed.

It was on April 7th that the "Fighting Mary" was the victim of a Japanese suicide plane, and it was on that day, these 18 men became heroes in the eyes of their shipmates.

It was at sunset that the enemy plane began it's run on the "Mary", and it was at sunset that these men , members of a twenty-millimeter gun crew atop of 16" gun turret number three, opened fire, never giving in, their guns spitting flame, until the plane crashed into their midst

For this heroic action, their "skipper", Captain J.W. Wilson, U.S.N., of Clarksburg, West Virginia, has recommended each of them for the Bronze Star.

Left - A Kamikaze bursts into flame as it crashes amid 20 millimeter gun mounts on top of 16 inch gun turret #3. Tracers stream through the air. Right - Aftermath of Kamikaze explosion. Tracers and debris still fill the sky in the distance. Seventeen men manning the 20 millimeter gun mounts died instantly. Only one man survived— Justin Joseph David, S 1/C. These photos were taken in sequence from another nearby ship. (U.S. Navy photo)

The citation reads as follows: "For distinguishing himself conspicuously by gallantry and intrepidity in action as a member of a twenty millimeter gun crew on the USS *MARYLAND* during this action against a Japanese aircraft on April 7, 1945, by his incentive, energy and devotion to duty, and in the face of practically certain death, he kept his gun firing until the attacking plane crashed on his station. His conduct throughout distinguished him among those performing duties of the same character and was in accord with the best traditions of the U.S. Naval Service".

The following named men have been recommended for the Bronze Star because of their gallant "Never-say-die" spirit in action aboard the USS *Maryland*, BB-46:

* Zamor Cedillo, S 1/C .... Uvalde, Texas
* Eugene Webster Gartes, S1/C .... Trinity, Texas
* James William Gist S 1/C .... Clarksville, Texas
* Roy Petty Hargrove, S 1/C .... Hartselle Alabama
* Lawrence Loman Hill, S 1/C .... Taft, Oregon
* Arnold Leon Land, S 1/C .... .Leoma, Tenn.
* Harold Mc Clellan Lanning, S 2/C. .... Chicago, Ill.
* Harold Arie Scott, Cox .... Cheyenne, Wyo.
* William Orville Noel, Cox .... Washington
* Clyde Tennyson White, BM 3/C .... Washington
* Rex William Andrews, GM 3/C .... West Virginia
* C.H. Chambers, S 2/C .... Kirby, Arkansas.
* J.A. Consill, S 2/C .... Cleveland, Alabama
* James Breadman, S 2/C .... Alama, Tenn.
* Leslie G. Langford, S 2/C .... Gallatin, Tenn.
* Jack Edward Medaris, S 2/C .... Houston, Texas
* Edward Herbert Segraves, GM 2/C .... Illinois

The only living survivor of this action was:
* Justin Joseph David, S 1/C .... Mississippi

The Memoirs of John Halvis, PhM 2/C
Served aboard Nov. 1944—Apr.1946

On the 14th of March, we were passing the Japanese stronghold at Truk, and our watch was doubled — but no trouble ensued. Then on March 16, we arrived at Ulithe. The place was just jammed with all types of ships! I thought "Boy if the Japanese could only see us now!" We didn't have long to wait .... On the 18th of March, an enemy aircraft appeared on our screens and air defense was sounded. The enemy aircraft was shot down however by our Air Patrol, before he had a chance to get at any of our ships.

We left Ulithi at 7:30 AM. There were nine battleships in single column formation. It was a beautiful sight for an American to behold.

On March 25, 1945, We began bombardment of Okinawa. Our assignment was to knock out enemy gun emplacements, installations and anything that looked suspicious.

March 27, 1945. We were attacked by Japanese "Vals". The enemy aircraft flew off, after a few rounds of anti-aircraft fire power. Aircraft from our carrier task force bombed and strafed the hell out of Okinawa throughout the day. I saw a few our aircraft that didn't pull out of their dives.....

March 30, and 31, 1945. The *Maryland* and other ships, heavily bombarded enemy positions and installations of various sorts. While we continued, heavy bombardment of installations throughout the day. Our aircraft were coming in formations of 12 to 20 at a time, dropping bombs, shooting rockets and strafing the enemy.

April 1, 1945. Troops landed at 8:30 AM. All was quiet, until 10: AM on the 3rd of April. Japanese aircraft flew above, trying to spot us through the cover of our smoke screens. One of them got pretty bold. At 2:45 PM, he dropped a couple of flares off our starboard quarter. My heart was between my tonsils!

Suddenly, as if out of nowhere, he came screaming down at us through the smoke screen. He misjudged his distance... We had him on fire before he knew what hit him!

He crashed about 50 yards off our fantail. From that moment on, Japanese aircraft kept attacking unceasingly all through the night. It was like watching a 4th of July fire works! A big ball of orange flames, meant that we had destroyed a kamikaze. They fell like shooting stars. Our transports fired at everything that came near them. Couldn't blame them much ... they had a lot fewer guns than we did.

Damage to top of gun turret #3 from Kamikaze. (Courtesy of Fred. R. Vreeken)

Ship to Shore Duel
By John Halvis PhM 2/C

April 5, 1945: On this evening, the Battleships *Maryland*, *Texas*, and *Nevada*, plus the Cruiser *Tuscaloosa*, got underway to rake a crack at shore batteries, which kept our transports from entering Buckner Bay. Suddenly out of nowhere, Japanese shore batteries opened up on the Battleship *Nevada*. She was hit with three times. Two enemy shells missed. One of them landed directly in our path.

It suddenly dawned on me that we may be walking right into a trap? I pulled the strap of my helmet tight, and grabbed my first aid bag, keeping a wary eye on that little Island on our port side, where enemy gun flashes were numerous. Meanwhile, all eight of our big 16 inch guns continued to lob shells at enemy batteries. The rest of our companion vessels were doing the same.

The Cruiser *Tuscaloosa*'s guns were firing in very rapid succession. The cotton in our ears couldn't silence the pounding noise. Finally we were told that the guns firing at us were Army Long Toms, and that we were to take cover. They were firing over our heads, homing in on our range, but we managed to destroy the position in short order. The Japanese emplacements were transformed into rubble. The little hill which provided them cover was laid flat as a pancake.

Flames appeared in the area where enemy gun positions had lain hidden. The Battleship *Nevada* signaled us that her casualties were light, and she was not damaged badly.

Fighting Off The Kamikaze

April 6, 1945: Again, the Japanese kamikaze began their suicidal missions. A lone "Betty" torpedo bomber homed in on us. We could just make her out in the darkness, skimming low along the water in her torpedo run. Suddenly, she turned, exposing her light belly towards us. All of our port side 20 mm and 40 mm anti aircraft guns opened up a deadly hail of lead. Streaks of tracer shells swiftly found the doomed torpedo bomber, which burst into flames, and crashed into the darkness off our fantail.

As the early morning sun cast it's first rays of light towards the open sky, we could see the rest of our task force formation on the horizon. A destroyer, (which in navy slang were called "Tin Cans", was to our starboard. The Battleship *Texas* and *West Virginia* sailed peacefully to our port side. There were six battleships in the center of our formation, with destroyers and cruisers mixed in among them. Way out on the Horizon on our port side were our picket boats, which picked up the enemy on radar and reported their positions. To the starboard was the Island. We were an effective fighting team. Each vessel was concerned with the others in our group. Each had it's specific assignments.

As the sun began to rise, persistent kamikaze missions of death began one of their strongest attempts to destroy the American fleet. They came in a tenacious, dedicated effort to destroy us. Sometimes they would come alone. Other times in small groups of three or more. Though they lost many aircraft, they were deadly effective, causing serious damage, deaths, and the sinking of many ships.

A destroyer on our starboard side was firing with every gun she had at three Japanese kamikaze planes, determined to sink her. All three Kamikaze pilots crashed with deadly flaming force into the destroyer, which burned like a hellish furnace as she went down.

Suddenly, our of nowhere, came another suicide plane flying high. He headed directly toward tour battleships, particularly the battleship *West Virginia*. However, he suddenly changed his mind, climbed up, then commenced his deadly course towards the *Maryland*! I sat on top of an ammunition box, watching him, as he came closer and closer amid a hailstorm of anti aircraft fire. Our guns fired fiercely, but he kept coming in! Suddenly the plane stalled in mid-air and dropped into the drink without even catching on fire, which seemed very unusual. It narrowly missed hitting an L.C.I on our port side.

Again, another Japanese plane flying low as if in a torpedo run, sped like lightening across our bow, crashing on the top of turret two of the destroyer on our starboard side. Their turret burst into flames, but was quickly subdued. The enemy must have skidded off the destroyers turret, and into the water. No wreckage cold be seen and there were no casualties. They were very lucky that day! Enemy planes were falling like big balls of fire coming out of the sky, then

crashing into their watery deaths. I tried to count them, but couldn't look at both sides at the same time. Some crashed very close, while some to far away to be counted as being downed by a battleship. Our task force and carrier planes splashed 200 of them, while our task force 58 shot down 198 kamikaze aircraft. The majority of the deadly kamikaze aircraft were shot down by our carrier fighters before they could reach us.

A Determined Enemy Crashes Into The USS *Maryland*, BB-46
By John Halvis, Ph.M 1/C.

April 7, 1945 is one day I'll never forget as long as I live.

Just before evening chow, the public address system rang out: "Now hear this! Now hear this! Admiral Marc Mitscher reports that a Japanese Task Force has been sighted heading for Okinawa. In it, is the new Battleship Yamato. General Quarters will be sounded at 6:45 PM". As soon as we ate, we headed for our battle stations, expecting the worst. We watched, as our fleet moved into battle formation.

It was almost dark. Suddenly our anti aircraft batteries opened up! We didn't think much of it at first, but as the firing tempo became fast and furious, we knew that a kamikaze was closing in fast!

Some crewmen began leaving their gun positions, except for the ones who were strapped to their 20mm gun mounts. I ran into the superstructure, dropping my cards along the way, then backed up into a corner for protection. Since the Japanese liked to crash the superstructures if they could, we thought our goose was cooked! Then, as if by magic, all of our guns stopped firing as a thunderous explosion followed by a quaking jar, shook the *Maryland*.

There were screams and yelling. I froze in my tracks for a second. Then I ran through the hatchway where I saw the explosion and fire. Nelson called, "Have we been hit Halvis?" Doctor Canty countered, "Yes, come on, we've been hit!"

I grabbed my first aid bag and ran to the quarter deck. The kamikaze crashed on top of 16 inch gun turret #3. I attended the first casualty I saw. His face and hands were badly burned.. you could have peeled a layer of skin off. He kept telling me to get the hell out of there, because the bomb had not gone off! Fires were still burning furiously. I could hear moans, as someone called "Corpsman!"

I took care of my casualty and sent him down to the dressing station. I saw one corpsman trying to pull someone out of a 40 Millimeter gun mount.

Dr. Canty came by and said, ""Get yourself and the rest of the corpsmen out of here! (The fire surrounding us was setting off 20 millimeter shells, which were strewn about the deck!)

Finally we began to take count of our casualties: Ten killed, six missing (Blown into the sea), and twenty seriously wounded. Later it was 12 dead, 6 missing, 18 seriously wounded, and 18 moderately injured. The toll continued to mount.

The Memoirs of Horace D. Craft S1/C
Served aboard July 1943-Sept.1945

April 6, 1945 — Sky defense sounded about 1:30 AM. I woke up to the sound of anti-aircraft batteries firing away! I ran to my battle station, to see a Japanese plane burning in the water on the port side. The condition watch had just blown him out of the sky!

Air alert was secured, but another air alert was sounded at 2:30 AM. We fired twice, but they flew out of our range. We remained at condition one for the remainder of the night. It seemed like they were desperately sending everything they had at us.

Two Japanese planes, one of them a torpedo bomber, hedge hopped a full 180 degrees, with our ships firing at them all the time. Four of our fighters dove on a torpedo plane, shot it's tail off as it crashed into the sea.

We heard a plane diving. We looked up in time to see it pass over the ship. We fired from the starboard side, but it got away into the clouds. We received reports all day long that Japanese aircraft were being "splashed". Our air patrol shot down 21 enemy aircraft within a 20 minute period! .... That was some shooting!

A plane just dove on a transport, but it missed! We lost two destroyers today. One was taking survivors off of the Destroyer "Bush" after she had already been hit, by two kamikaze aircraft and was sinking. Then the second Destroyer caught two Kamikaze planes herself!

Enemy aircraft just attacked the transports! Two are burning badly. Another "bogie" just splashed into the ocean. I saw four enemy planes one after another go down in flames ... a pretty sight!

Boy, what excitement! A Plane just tried to make a carrier out of us! It went through the thickest and blackest barrage I've ever seen! When our automatic weapons opened up, he knew he wouldn't make it and tried to crash a patrol boat, but missed, splashing into the water. I can't understand how that patrol boat kept from being sunk! It was in the middle of all the flak, and I knew it was hit?

Two more suicide planes just landed on another Destroyer, setting her on fire! Then a Japanese torpedo plane made a run on it, using itself as a torpedo! It smashed into the blazing inferno, setting off the Destroyer's powder magazine with two big explosions

One of our fighter director ships was hit this morning.. Here it goes again! A torpedo plane is trying to make a fun on the Battleship USS *Colorado*, but it turned to make a run at us ... but it didn't make it in!

There's been quite a few torpedo planes coming in at us today. I don't mind those at all, ... It's the dive bombers and suicide planes that I don't like!

The count at 5:00 PM today was 92 planes destroyed, but that is just a part. There's been so much shooting and action, I can't remember it all, but our task force were supposed to have shot down 204 enemy planes today? (It later came out that 416 enemy aircraft were shot down, including the task force fifty eight count. Our fleet was made up of the Battleships *Maryland*, *Colorado*, *Tennessee*, *New Mexico*, plus nine Cruisers, and 16 Destroyers.

The Memoirs of William J. Haligas S 1/C

On the evening of April 7, 1945, a kamikaze forcing its way through a blanket of anti-aircraft fire, crashed furiously amidst the top of 16 inch gun turret number three, among the sixteen members of the gun crew stationed there. It blew them into oblivion. Only one man miraculously survived the holocaust..

One of my good friends perished atop that turret. His name was Cotton Willet. Just before he was killed, he was in the lower powder room of turret four with me. He had complained of claustrophobia, and was transferred to a 20 mm anti- aircraft gun mount atop the ill fated 16 inch gun turret three just days before it met disaster.

I recall when general quarters was secured after the kamikaze crash, I climbed up and out of turret four. As I crawled under the turret overhang, my hand landed on something mushy? On closer observation in the darkness, I discovered it was a human face detached from the head! That was a bad enough experience for anyone? The next morning, April 8, 1945, "Punch" Hydinger handed me a hunting knife and told me to climb up on a vent, to remove a human arm which had wedged, dangling grotesquely downwards! I climbed the steel ladder, and what I saw, will forever remained burned into my memory — a gold wedding band on the left finger of the hand! I somehow finally found enough courage to remove the arm... (as ordered).

The Memoirs of Richard Mosher, S 1/C
Served aboard Dec. 1944-July 1947

The most memorable even I recall while serving aboard the USS *Maryland*, took place April, 1945, during the battle of Okinawa. We were under very heavy attack from Japanese aircraft. Most of them were Kamikaze pilots destined for certain death and the destruction of American naval vessels. It did not seem to matter how bad we hit them, they just kept coming in, flying low to the water, most of the time, while still in flames. They didn't concentrate on shooting at us. They concentrated on their target until they hit us, exploding themselves an their bombs on top of us!

I happened to be a first loader on a quad 40 millimeter gun mount on the forward starboard side. The kamikaze attacked relentlessly that day, in sizeable numbers. On the gun headset, I heard that we expected there would be over 1,000 enemy planes coming in at one time. Our picket boats, (destroyers and destroyer escorts) circling around the larger ships to protect them, were really having a rough time keeping the enemy craft from coming through. They are really to be commended for the punishment they had to take in doing so.

One of our destroyers passed by that day. It was so shot up, it was difficult to really tell what kind of a ship it was? Their gallant crew still manned their battles stations, firing their remaining guns at the enemy. Half of the ship was blown away, yet they fought valiantly on, demonstrating outstanding devotion and duty to Country, while trying to stay afloat. No one attempted to abandon ship! I'll never forget them.

A day or two later, we got word to steam into battle against the Japanese fleet, heading down from Japan.

It was April 7, 1945. We were in battle formation, when more "bogies" came in. Again, we commenced firing at them, not realizing that this time one of them would make it through, to crash in the midst of our four twenty millimeter anti-aircraft gun mounts atop 16 inch gun turret number three. Three of my buddies were killed, along with all of the others stationed there, except one man ... Justin David. I was grateful to be stationed forward at that time. I felt the explosion impact, and flying debris, even up forward where we were.

To Fall In Love With a Mass of Steel!

How is it that a man could fall in love with a mass of steel, a maze of compartments, wooden decks and guns which belched flaming destruction to an enemy?

Could it be the many fond remembrances of lasting friendships? — or for the memory of shipmates who gave their very lives for everything America and free agency stood for? — Perhaps it was the adventure and excitement of risking one's very own life for the things they believed in? Maybe it was simply that we were mad, because we were caught by surprise at pearl Harbor and desired revenge?

What ever it was, — it still lingers on, in the hearts of the men who rode the stormy seas of the Pacific, hunting for an enemy to cross swords with! — To clash with those who threatened the safety of our loved ones, or who caused the tragic loss of fallen comrades? "Vengeance is mine," sayeth the Lord!

The war brought sorrow and heartbreak to many who had lost loved ones or friends. With others it brought new life long friendships with shipmates whom we shared wartime experiences with. Whatever it was, it left each man with a proud feeling inside, and memories that would remain vivid for the remainder of his days.... Yes, almost to a man, we fell in love with that great hunk of steel which we called home for so many years,—the Battleship USS *Maryland*!

Who hasn't longed to walk upon her spotless teakwood decks again, to feel the comfort of her strength and her deeds, now only a memory in history? It was the very purpose of the writing of this book — that her exploits and gallant deeds will become a valid and permanent part of American history!

It is the recording of these historic testimonies taken from the very men who walked her decks and survived to record her adventures while yet in the twilight of their lives! It is their contribution to future generations, that these deeds and experiences will live, long after they are dust! It is a sharing of that love they felt for this grand, scarred, embattled old lady they called The Battleship USS *Maryland*, BB-46.

The End of a Grand Old Lady

Years after World War II had ended, I had an opportunity to visit the USS *Maryland*, BB-46, as she sat quietly yet proudly in mothballs, tied up to a dock. Though I couldn't be aboard, it felt good to just see her waiting there quietly, standing by for another adventure which was never to come again. How I would have loved to walk her decks, to fondly stroke her mighty sixteen inch guns! In my mind I could almost hear their mighty roar and the trembling beneath my feet. She appeared majestic, even while she stood there proudly, with her gun mounts encased in a variety of cocoons.

Visions of her bow plunging into the clean blue sea, and the wind howling through her masthead filled the visions of my mind. Faces and places flashed past, as my feet itched to walk on her teakwood decks and the old haunts where fond memories were buried .... There stood quietly, majestically, as the faces, sounds and places faded from my mind. I felt sadness, yet a grateful proudness to have shared her most traumatic moments, as well as her victorious feats. It was indeed a thrilling moment .... Yet it was not long afterwards that she would be sold for scrap! ...... A menial reward for her valiant deeds, ...but her memory will be preserved herein, by those of us who were a part of her life and history.

It is fitting, in this section of the book concerning the decommission and dismantling of the Battleship USS *Maryland*, BB-46, that the following poem written in her fond remembrance, be included in this book of "Memoirs" It is dedicated to the men who walked her decks, survived her battles, shared her misery, found adventure and died with honor. She was affectionately know by many of her crew as the "Mary Maru", in bland defiance of having been reported sunk several times by the Japanese!

"Here's To The "Mary Maru"
By Fred R. Vreeken

Her bow stood tall and proud she be,
this ship which sailed so many a sea,

Mastheads rose through a cloud filled sky,
how proud I was of the flag she'd fly!

Her decks were clean and very wide,
her crew was brave and filled with pride!

If she could talk, how much she'd tell,
of roaring guns and a living hell..

Now sealed in silence..just waiting there,
with her ghostly crew and a quiet stare..

He engines rest and her screws lay still,
as she patiently waits for a mission to fill.

But the "Mary Maru" which stood so great,
was doomed to meet a degrading fate!..

Once so proud with her head held high,..
now she silently waits to die..

Sold for scrap, they saved her bell,..
but her body was cut and sent to hell!

They melted down her once proud steel..
Why Oh Lord!..How sad we feel..

Her ghosts are but a memory now,
but she'll live in glory!..and here is how!

Her crew that lives, with honor will tell,
of her scars and pride, as they touch her bell..

The "Mary Maru", we'll not forget!..
for her place in history is firmly set!

An Invasion of Japan Not Found in History Books!

By James Martin Davis

With the capture of Okinawa during the summer of 1945, the Americans in the Pacific had finally obtained what the allies in Europe had enjoyed all along — a large Island capable of being used as a launching platform for invasion!

Following the cessation of hostilities with Germany, millions of American soldiers, sailors and airmen were being redeployed to the Pacific for the anticipated invasion of Japan. The center of this immense military buildup and the primary staging area for the invasion, was the Island of Okinawa.

American military planners knew that the invasion of Japan would be a difficult undertaking. Japan had never been successfully invaded in it's entire history!

Six and one-half centuries before an invasion had been attempted and failed. That invasion had striking similarities to the one being planned by the Americans in the summer of 1945.

In the year 1281 A.D., two magnificent Chinese fleets set sail for the Empire of Japan. Their purpose was to launch a massive invasion on the Japanese home islands and to conquer Japan in the name of the Great Mongol Emperor, Kublai Khan.

Sailing from China was the main armada, consisting of 3,500 ships, and over 100,000 heavily armed troops. Sailing ships from ports in Korea was a second impressive fleet of 900 ships, containing 42,000 Mongol warriors.

In the summer of that year, the invasion force sailing from Korea arrived to the western shores of the southernmost Japanese Island of Kyushu. The Mongols maneuvered their ships into position and methodically launched their assault on the Japanese coast.

Like a human surf, wave after wave of these oriental soldiers swept ashore, at Hagata Bay, where they were met on the beaches by thousands of Japanese defenders, who had never had their homeland *successfully invaded.*

The mongol invasion force was a modern army and it's arsenal of weapons were far superior to that of the Japanese. It's soldiers were equipped with poisoned arrows, maces, iron swords, metal javelins and even gun powder.

The Japanese were forced to defend themselves with bows and arrows, swords, spears made from bamboo, and shields made of wood.

The battle was fierce, with many soldiers killed and wounded on both sides. It raged on for days, but aided by the fortifications along their beaches of which the Mongols had no advance knowledge, and inspired by the sacred cause of their homeland, these ancient Japanese warriors pushed the much stronger Mongol invaders off the beaches and back into their ships lying at anchor in the bay.

The Mongol fleet then set back out to sea, where it rendezvoused with the main body of it's army, which was arriving with the second fleet coming from China.

All over Japan, elaborate ceremonies were performed at shrines, in the cities and in the country side.

Hundreds of thousands of Japanese urged on by the Emperor, their warlords and other officials, prayed to their Shinto Gods for deliverance from the foreign invaders. A million Japanese voices called upward for divine intervention.

Miraculously, as if in answer to their prayers, from out of the south a savage typhoon sprang up and headed towards Kyushu.

It's powerful wind screamed up the coast where they struck the Mongol's invasion fleet with full fury, wreaking havoc on the ships and on the men on board. The Mongol fleet was devastated. After the typhoon had passed, over 4,000 invasion craft had been lost, and the Mongol casualties exceeded 100,000 men.

All over Japan, religious services and huge celebrations were held. Everywhere, tumultuous crowds gathered in thanksgiving to pay homage to the "Divine Wind" that would forever protect them.

The American Invasion Plans For Kyushu

During the summer of 1945, another powerful armada was being assembled to assault the same western coastline on the Island of Kyushu, where six and a half centuries earlier, the Mongols had been repelled.

The American invasion plans for Kyushu, scheduled for November 1, 1945, called for a floating invasion force of 14 army and marine divisions to be transported by ship to hit the western, eastern and southern shoreline of Kyushu.

This shipboard invasion force would consist of 550,000 combat soldiers, tens of thousands of sailors, and hundreds of naval aviators.

The assault fleet would consist of thousands of ships of every shape, size, type and description, ranging from mammoth battleships and aircraft carriers to the small amphibious craft, and they would be sailing from Okinawa, the Philippines, and the Marianas Islands.

Crucial to the success of the invasion, were nearly 4,000 army, navy and marines aircraft that would be packed into the small Island of Okinawa to be used for direct air support of our landing forces at the time of the invasion.

By July of 1945, the Japanese knew the Americans were planning to invade their homeland. Throughout the early summer, the Emperor and his government officials exhorted the military and civilian population to make preparations for the invasion. Japanese radios throughout that summer cried out to the people to "Form a wall of human flesh," and when the invasion began, to push the invaders back into the sea and back onto their ships.

The Japanese people fervently believed that the American invaders would be repelled. They all seemed to share a mystical faith that their country could never be invaded successfully and that they again, would be saved by the "Divine Wind"

The American invasion never came, however, because the bombing of Hiroshima and Nagasaki, as if by a miracle, ended the war.

Almost immediately American soldiers, sailors and airmen, in for the duration, were being discharged and sent home.

By the fall of 1945, there remained approximately 100,000 soldiers, sailors and airman still in Okinawa.

Okinawa, which would have been the major launching platform for the invasion of Japan, was now peaceful.

In October, Buckner Bay, on the east coast of the Island was still jammed with vessels of all kinds, from victory ships to landing craft.

On the Island itself, 150,000 soldiers lived under miles of canvas, in what were referred to as "tent cities." All over the Island, hundreds of tons of food, equipment and supplies stacked in immense piles, laid out in the open.

During the early part of October, to the southwest of Okinawa, just east of the Marianas Islands, the seas were growing restless and the winds began to blow.

The ocean skies slowly turned black, and the large swells that were developing began to turn the Pacific Ocean white with froth. In a matter of only a few days, a gigantic typhoon had somehow, out of season, sprung to life, and began sweeping past Saipan and into the Philippine Sea. As the storm grew more violent, it raced northward and kicked up waves sixty feet high!

Navy meteorologists eventually became aware of the storm, but they expected it to pass well between Formosa and Okinawa and disappear into the East China Sea.

Unexplainable, on the evening of October 8, the storm changed direction and abruptly veered to the east. When it did so, there was insufficient warning to allow the ships in the harbor to get underway in order to escape the typhoon's terrible violence!

By early morning on 9th of October, rain was coming down in torrents. The seas were rising and visibility was zero. Winds now over 80 miles per hour, blowing from the east and northeast, caused small craft in Buckner Bay to drag their anchors.

By early afternoon, the wind had risen to over 100 miles per hour! The rain coming in horizontally now, was more salt than fresh, and even the larger vessels began dragging their anchors under the pounding of 50 foot seas!

As the winds continued to increase and the storm unleashed it's fury, the entire bay became a scene of devastation. Ships, dragging their anchors, collided with one another. Hundreds of vessels were blown ashore.

Vessels in groups of twos and threes were washed ashore into masses of wreckage that began to accumulate on the beaches. Numerous ships had to be abandoned, while their crews were precariously transferred between ships.

By mid-afternoon, the typhoon had reached it's raging peak, with winds now coming from the north and the northeast, blowing up to 150 miles per hour!

Ships initially grounded by the storm were now blown off the reefs

52

and back across the Bay to the south shore, dragging their anchors the entire way. More collisions occurred between wind-blown ships and shattered hulks!

Gigantic waves swamped small vessels and engulfed larger ones. Liberty ships lost their propellers, while men in transports, destroyers and the Victory ships were swept off decks by 60 foot waves that reached the tops of the masts of their vessels.

On shore, the raging typhoon was devastating the Island. Twenty hours of torrential rain washed away our roads and ruined the Islands store of rations and supplies. Aircraft were picked up and catapulted off the airfields. Huge quonset huts went sailing into the air. Metal hangars were ripped to shreds, and the tent cities housing 150,000 troops on the island ceased to exist!

Almost all of the entire food supply on the island was blown away. Americans on the island had nowhere to go, but into caves, trenches and ditches on the island in order to survive. All over the Island there were tents, boards, sections of galvanized iron being hurled through the air at over 100 mph!

The storm raged over the Island for hours, and then slowly headed out to sea, doubled back, and two days later, howled in from the ocean and hit the Island again!

On the following day, when the typhoon had finally past, dazed men crawled out of holes and caves, to count the losses. Countless aircraft had been destroyed. All power was gone, communications and supplies were non-existent. B-29's were requisitioned to rush in tons of new rations and supplies from the Marianas Islands.

General Stillwell, the 10th Army Commander, asked for immediate plans to evacuate all hospital cases from the Island. The harbor facilities were useless.

After the typhoon roared out into the Sea of Japan and started to die its slow death, the bodies began to wash ashore. The toll on ships were staggering. Almost 270 ships were sunk, grounded or damaged beyond repair. Fifty three ships were in too bad a state to be restored to duty and were decommissioned, stripped and abandoned!

Out of 90 ships which needed major repair, the Navy decided only 10 were even worthy of complete salvage, and so the remaining 80 were scrapped.

According to Samuel Eliot Morrison, the famous Naval historian, "Typhoon Louise" was the most furious and lethal storm ever encountered by the United States Navy in it's entire history! Hundreds of Americans were killed, injured and missing. Ships were sunk and the Island of Okinawa was in havoc.

New accounts at the time disclosed that the press and the public back home paid little attention to this storm that struck the Pacific with such force. The very existence of this storm is still a little known fact!

Surprisingly, a few people then, or even now, have made the connection that an American invasion fleet of thousands of ships, planes, landing craft and a half million men might well have been in that exact place at that exact time, posed to strike Japan when the typhoon enveloped Okinawa and it's surrounding seas!

In the aftermath of this storm, and with the war now history, few people concerned themselves with the obsolete invasion plans for Japan. However, had there been no atom bomb for only a matter of months, history might have repeated itself!

In the fall of 1945, in the aftermath of this typhoon, had things been different, all over Japan there would have been religious services and huge celebrations held.

A million Japanese would have been raised upward in thanksgiving. Everywhere tumultuous crowds would have gathered in delirious gratitude to pay homage to a "Divine Wind" which might have once again protected their homeland from foreign invaders: *A "Divine Wind" they had named centuries before ... the "Kamikaze!"*

USS *MARYLAND* STATISTICS

Launched— 20 March, 1920, Newport News, Virginia
Commissioned — 21 July, 1921
Tonnage—32,500 tons
Length—624 feet
Beam— 108 Feet
Draft—32 1/2 feet forward: 33 feet aft.
Wartime Compliment—107 Officers, 1,988 enlisted men, 67 Marines

Total: 2,162

Armament— 8, 16 inch 45 caliber.
  16, 5 inch 38 caliber.
  48 barrels — 40 mm.
  44 barrels — 20 mm.
Rounds of Ammunitions Fired:
  16" / 45 Caliber 3,479
  5" / 51 Caliber 6,786
  5" / 25 Caliber 7,186
  40 mm Caliber 4,093
  20 mm Caliber 10,500

Miles Steamed:
  1942 39,073
  1943 31,095
  1944 61,355
  1945 21,174
  Total 152,679

Damage Sustained:
  Bombs ....7th December, 1941
  Aerial Torpedo .... 22 June, 1944
  Kamikaze .... 29 November, 1944
  Kamikaze .... 7 April, 1945

Combat Casualties:
  Killed 53
  Wounded 68

DEDICATION

The preceding "Memoirs" section of this book is dedicated to the gallant men who served aboard the USS *Maryland*, BB-46, during the World War II Conflict with the Japanese, in the battle for the Pacific.

To those who were wounded in battle or unselfishly gave their lives for the preservation of our American Heritage, we will be forever grateful.

To the surviving Veterans who live today and for those who have gone beyond into the next life, it is a salute of gratitude and everlasting comradeship. What you are about to read, are the true personal testimonials of individual surviving crewmembers of the Battleship USS *Maryland*, BB-46, as they witnessed and remembered these incredible historical events as they happened.

Their original testimonial manuscripts, written in their own hand, which document these documented these printed testimonies, are preserved as a part of America's great naval history and heritage.

World War II brought great suffering to the families and loved ones of those who would never come home again. To them, we offer this tribute.

"They were heroes all and will live forever in their glory, to once again be with those who loved them."

We must always remember the events of these great times in our history ... especially that catalyst which pulled the American people together in absolute unity, to prove their steadfastness, determination and willingness to sacrifice in so many ways to build the mightiest, most powerfully equipped force for peace, the World has ever seen

They demonstrated an uncommon love for their Country with a spirit of willingness and unity, unparalleled in American history. They were among the unsung heroes ... the backbone of an unfaltering American Spirit, which bound our nation strong! **God Bless America!**

We gratefully acknowledge the survivors of the crew of the USS *Maryland*, BB-46

Who contributed their testimonials and manuscripts for this special publication. Editing was limited mostly corrections of grammar and spelling, otherwise each testimonial was in the words of those who authored them. The original hand written or typed manuscripts and a notarized certification of this edition, have been donated for preservation and validation, to the Maryland Historical Society, Department of Valuable Historic Documents, 201 West Monument Street, Baltimore, Maryland 21201.

(Courtesy of Walter J. Mycka)

USS Maryland (BB-46)
Special Stories

USS Maryland, San Francisco, 1940. (Courtesy of Glenn H. Conner)

Four of the Maryland's 16-inch guns, taken 1934. (Courtesy of Norman Morton)

Mycka's Tribute

by Walter J. Mycka

Fifty-four plus years after the attack at Pearl Harbor, local survivor verifies events resulting in the death of his battle station replacement.

Walter J. Mycka, age 77, Treasurer of Colorado Mile-Hi, Chapter #1, Pearl Harbor Survivors Association, describes circumstances relating to discovery of the tragic events so many years ago.

I served aboard the USS *Maryland* (BB-46) from December 1940 through June 1944. I was assigned to the 6 AL Division (50 caliber machine gun and 20 mm antiaircraft defense). My General Quarters battle station was a gunner on a 50 caliber machine gun atop the main mast (port side) on the USS *Maryland*. I recall in May of 1941 Sea 2/c Warren McCutcheon reported for duty aboard the *Maryland*, assigned to our division and later as a loader on my battle station. On November 29, 1941 (a week before the Japanese attack at Pearl Harbor) The Navy saw fit to temporarily transfer me for a two week training course at the Fleet Machine Gun School located at Puloa Point on the Island of Oahu, TH. Upon my return to the ship (December 15, 1941) I discovered that during my absence, Warren had replaced me on my battle station. My shipmates also informed me that Warren was killed as a result of the Jap attack. This I was so sorry to hear, not only because Warren lost his life, but for the Grace of God and the Navy's infinite wisdom, could very well had been myself. Except from what I was told of Warren's fate, I had no visible evidence of what occurred, nor have I ever seen his name appear as being killed in action. This bothered me and was frequently on my mind, but with passing of time and ensuing events this also faded to some extent from my memory.

At the eighth annual reunion of the USS *Maryland* in 1982, at Santa Rosa, California, one of my shipmates made a comment to the effect that it seemed strange to him that he had never heard or seen any publication, or on a memorial, Warren McCutheon's name being mentioned as killed in action and yet he was sure that there was a VFW Post in California named in his memory. At an ensuing executive business meeting I brought this subject to the attention of the membership and after some discussion, the result left me somewhat disappointed and with the impression that there isn't much we can do about it now, not even to enter his name on our association memorial plaque.

In 1989, at the 15th reunion in Denver, another of my former shipmates (Division Petty Officer) stated that Warren was definitely killed in action, that he had helped remove his body from the main mast and had packed Warren's personal possessions for shipment to his next of kin. At our San Diego Reunion in 1994 I spoke with our historian. After checking with the material that was available to him, he found no information that could shed light on this.

Early in June 1996, while at breakfast and scanning through our local paper (*Rocky Mountain News),* there appeared to my complete surprise, an article (*1st Pearl Harbor Victim Honored),* by John Howard of the *Associated Press.* I was elated. This confirmed everything I suspected these many years and indeed was true. A few days later I discovered this newspaper article, I received a copy letter from our association president, that was sent to him from another shipmate (L.E. Dibb), who also read this same newspaper article concerning Warren. Mr. Dibb initiated some research revealing serious omissions on the memorial plaque of shipmates who had lost their lives. He also checked a copy of the (the ships log) of December 7, 1941 (The ships log is a detailed report made out by the duty officer of the deck of all events that have taken place while he was on duty.) This research revealed that Warren's name was never entered as being killed in action in the ship's log.

Further research revealed many facts heretofore unknown as to events that occurred on that fateful day. This accumulated information was presented to our governing board at our reunion in Annapolis, Maryland on October 9 of this year. Their support was unanimous to take necessary steps correcting this serious omission and to enshrine, Warren as well as our other fallen heroes, (who sacrificed their lives for our country) and to restore their rightful place of honor on our memorials. The board authorized $250.00 for an appropriate plaque from the surviving members of the crew of the USS *Maryland* (BB-46). With the permission and approval of those responsible for Warren McCutheon's Memorial in Gridley, California, we hope to have a representation of members from the Maryland Veterans Association to present this plaque and to honor Warren's memory at the cemetery. This we hope to accomplish in 1998 before or after our 24th annual reunion in Monterey, California.

Ship's Log
United States Ship *Maryland* Sunday 7 December 1941

Zone Description Plus 10 1/2

Remarks

00 - 04

Moored starboard side to Berth Fox-5, Pearl Harbor, T.H., with the following lines: Bow line, 4 parts 1-5/8" wire; forward bow spring, 6 parts 10' manila; bow breast, 9 parts 8" manila; after bow spring, 7 parts 8"

manila; forward quarter spring, 7 parts 10" manila; after quarter spring, 12 parts 8" manila; stern line, 4 parts 1-5/8" wire. Using #3 boiler and after machinery space in use for auxiliary purposes. Ships present: U.S. Pacific Fleet less various units. Admiral H.E. Kimmel, USN, in Submarine Base, S.O.P.A. USS *Oklahoma* moored to port. 0145 The following named men returned aboard having completed temporary duty as shore patrol, Honolulu, T.H., - Puckett, H.W., 336-72-33, BM1c; Wilsey, H.F., 316-08-14, WT1c; Klimcak, J.T., 341-95-34, GM2c; Coleman, F.H., 346-69-33. The following named men returned to the ship AOL since 0100, a period of forty-five (45) minutes, (name censored), MAtt 2c; Segen, C.; Sea1c; (name censored), Sea2c; (name censored) MAtt 3c; (name censored) MAtt 2c; (name censored), Sea1c; 0230 (name censored), Sea2c returned AOL from 0100 to 0230, one hour and thirty minutes. 0315 the following named men were returned aboard by the shore patrol for their own good, patrol report not to follow AOL from 0100 to 0315 a period of two (2) hours and fifteen (15) minutes; (name censored), BM2c; (censored).

/s/ J.D. White, Jr.
Lieutenant (jg), USNR

04 - 08

Moored as before. 0640 Received aboard from Oahu Ice and Cold Storage Co., of Honolulu, T.H., 2000 lbs. of ice for use in ships ice boxes. 0750 Japanese planes commenced bombing attack on yard. Dive bombers. 0752 Sounded General Quarters. USS *Oklahoma* hit by unknown number of torpedoes. Control shifted to Conning Tower.

/s/ J.B. Thro
Ensign, US Navy

08 - 12

Moored as before. Commanding Officer restored Lieutenant (jg) Nelson H. Randall, C-V(S), USNR; and Ensign James A. Parks, Jr., D-V(g), USNR, to duty. Commenced getting up steam and making all preparations for getting underway. 0805 Opened fire with 1.1" battery, the 50 caliber machine gun battery, and the 5"/25 caliber battery had opened fire in that order shortly before. 0810 USS *Oklahoma* alongside to port listed to port until lying on starboard side with keel showing. 0815 Conning tower took steering and engine control. 0838 Received report that an enemy submarine was inside Pearl Harbor. 0848 USS *Neosho* underway

USS Maryland Division "A" July 1942. (Courtesy of Charles Staggs)

from fuel oil pier directly ahead of this vessel. Various destroyers standing out of harbor. 0855 Commenced firing with 5"/25 caliber battery. 0857 USS *Nevada* getting underway, USS *Oglala* getting underway. 0858 USS *West Virginia* setting, fire appeared on or near USS *Tennessee*. 0859 USS *California* listing to port. 0900 Opened fire with remaining AA batteries. 0909 Received one and possibly two bomb hits on forecastle on amidships line about frame 10, detailed report of damage to be given later, and about three near misses on each side and ahead of bow. 0914 Received report of large number of enemy bombers over Pearl. 0924 Torpedo air compressor reported out of commission, lost air pressure on port 5"/25 caliber battery. Burning enemy plane, fell on USS *Curtiss*. 0925 Recommenced firing. 0928 Slight fire on forecastle and signal bridge out. Received report that Rear Admiral W.S. Anderson came aboard at 0905. 0930 Lull in attack. 0936 USS *Phelps* standing out. Japanese submarines reported inside and outside of Pearl Harbor. 0940 USS *West Virginia* abandoning ship. 50 caliber magazines flooded. 0941 Turret three covered with flames from burning oil on water. 0945 Received report that enemy planes massing south of Pearl Harbor. 0947 Received from CinCpac all battleships remain in Pearl until further orders, channel probably mined. 0949 Catalina patrol bombers taking off. 0950 USS *Oglala* sank alongside 1010 dock. 0955 Fire under control around quarterdeck. 1005 USS *Solace* underway, USS *Shaw* in floating drydock enveloped in flames. 1009 Commenced firing on enemy aircraft. 1012 Commenced pumping in forward trunks. 1022 Floating drydock sinking, explosions on USS *Shaw*. 1029 Report of casualties, one officer dead. One enlisted man dead, one enlisted man wounded. 1025 Parachute troops reported near Barbers Point. 1034 Submarine reported 10 miles south of Barbers Point. 1039 USS *Cummings* underway. 1040 Explosions of USS *West Virginia*. 1044 USS *California* settling. 1051 Enemy submarine sighted by USS *Solace*. 1055 Commenced firing on enemy aircraft coming from port side. 1100 Enemy reported approaching towards Pearl from South. 1150 Commenced firing. 1101 USS *Phoenix* standing out. 1105 Cruiser and Destroyer standing out. 1106 450 rounds of 5"/25 caliber expended up to this time. 1107 Commenced firing on enemy planes off starboard beam. 1112 Enemy tanker reported to southward. 1114 Commenced firing on enemy planes. 1119 Oil fire on water around USS *West Virginia* getting worse, approaching stern of this vessel. 1124 Opened fire on plane on port quarter. 1127 Eight enemy ships reported at Latitude 21 10" N, Longitude 160° 16" west 1127 Commenced firing at enemy planes, expended 15 rounds 5"/25 caliber. 1137 Parachute troops reported landing on North Shore. 1143 Report received enemy troops wearing blue coveralls with red emblems. 1145 Called away fire and rescue party to assist in rescue of USS *Oklahoma* personnel.

/s/ H.W. Hadley, LtComdr, USN

12 - 16

Moored as before. 1201 Parachute troops reported landing at Barbers Point and enemy tankers reported four miles off Wainae. 1204 Flames from oil fire coming forward along port side. 1229 Sighted enemy planes on port beam, enemy submarines reported south of Pearl. 1327 Sent 400 rounds 5"/25 caliber ammunition to USS *California*. 1350 Oil fire astern of USS *Tennessee*. 1355 Commenced firing on enemy planes. 1400 No change of draft of ships in last four hours, 7 feet down by bow 3 1/2° list to starboard. 1428 Secured boilers #5-6-7-and 8. 1441 USS *California* reported settling with list to port; USS *Helena* down by bow. 1445 USS *Boggs* standing in. 1446 Received 15000 rounds of 50 caliber ammunition from West Loch. 1458 USS *Dewey* standing out. Pumping in forward trunks not showing progress. 1501 Planes reported overhead, very high. 1508 USS *Curtiss* reported sighting submarine. 1525 USS *Benham* dropping depth charges to north channel. 1523 Two unidentified planes sighted on starboard beam. 1529 Unidentified plane sighted on starboard bow. 1538 Three Navy bombers landed at Ford Island. Various friendly planes taking off and landing at Ford Island and Hickam Field. 1551 Mines reported between Diamond Head and Barbers Pt. 1553 Two battleships and many destroyers reported sighted at Latitude 21°21' Longitude 158°37'.

/s/ H.W. Hadley
Lieut-Comdr., US Navy

16 - 20

Moored as before. Dead reported as Ensign H.D. Crow, USNR, and Lutz, C.S., Sea1c. 1635 Sent diver down on starboard side of forecastle to check on hull damages. 1655 Received OpNav dispatch that 'U.S. at war with Japan, darken ship at night'. 1656 Air pressure on port battery

resumed. 1700 5"/25 caliber guns #8 back in commission. 1701 Diver found several small holes in hull on starboard side of hull between frame 12 and 15. 1720 Sunset darkened ship. 1722 USS *Neosho* standing out from Merry Point. 1729 Lost air pressure on port 5"/25 battery. 1816 #4 searchlight out of commission due to gunfire. 1822 Water at Ford Island reported contaminated. Numerous friendly aircraft landing and taking off. 1854 Submarine periscope reported south end of Ford Island. 1905 Posted special security watches on forecastle and quarterdeck. 1915 Rescue work continuing on USS *Oklahoma*, sent reliefs, men reported rescued after cutting through hull, number not known. 1920 Divers reported bow is clear of bottom. 1930 Set condition of Readiness Two, material condition Zed. 1958 Secured boilers #3 and 4. Various unidentified aircraft reported.

/s/ H.W. Hadley
Lieut-Comdr., US Navy

20 - 24

Moored as before. Various unidentified aircraft reports being received. Own aircraft landing at Ford Island. 2053 Received dispatch from Com 14 'prepare for air attack at dawn'. 2054 Moonrise. 2101 Aircraft with running lights approached ship in bombing position and not in landing position for Ford Island. All ships opened fire; about three planes observed brought down. 2108 Received report Hickam Field attacked. ComPatWingTwo ordered cease firing. 2110 CinCpac and ComPatWingTwo directed 'Disregard cease fire'. 2118 Hickam Field reported being bombed. Various aircraft reports continuing to be received. 2227 Mustered officers and crew. 2240 Diving party Submarine Base arrived. 2301 Enemy vessels reported north of island. 2354 USS *Pennsylvania* opened fire and ceased at 2355.

/s/ H.W. Hadley
Lieut-Comdr., US Navy

Approved: Examined:
/s/ D.C. Godwin   /s/ H.W. Hadley

A Funny Thing At The Battle of Okinawa

By Homer Moore

We had a new Captain Wilson in his first battle. About midnight every night, we had an enemy plane (dubbed piss call Charlie) come over as we were in a smoke screen. This one night a lieutenant was standing to my left and I was buckled in my gun, a 20mm. The lieutenant was talking to the captain through the open of the captain's shack. About that time, the enemy plane came out of the smoke cloud, I opened fire right in his face. When I fired, this lieutenant, who stood about 6'8", 250 pounds jumped through the window and rode the captain to the deck. After that we never saw P.C. Charlie again. I'm sure the lieutenant never forgot that night.

Personnel Office L to R: Bryan Y3/C, Joe Minitti Y1/C, Anderson Y3/C, Donald H. Blimling (Blimp) Y2/C, Lt. Murphy, Robert Bails Chief Yeoman. (Courtesy of Donald Blimling)

Remembering *Mary*

By Warren Lowerre

Late in 1946 I left the *Maryland,* headed for civilian life, after helping to put her in "mothballs" in Bremerton. After having served 6 1/2 years aboard her, I assumed I was taking my last look at her. I was wrong.

Many years later, while attending a convention in San Francisco, my wife and I looked out our hotel room one morning and there, big as life, was the *Mary* being towed across the bay to the site of her final ignominious dismemberment. A sad moment indeed — but tempered by a flood of memories of events and people — mostly of people with whom I had shared the *Maryland* as home during those long-ago years. Or were they long ago? Just at that moment I remembered them as yesterday — or certainly no longer than two or three months ago!

The Revenge Of A Seaman Deuce On A Commander—and How He Got Away With It!

By William "Bill" Haligas S1/c

As a small boy growing up in Northern Illinois, I would occasionally catch a cold, accompanied by a fever. It seemed that every time this could happen, I would become delirious, screaming and thrashing around repeatedly, until the fever subsided? The doctor told my worried parents that this was an unusual symptom, but normal in my case, and not to worry. I would outgrow it.

When I was seventeen, I joined the navy and was assigned to a naval training base in northern Idaho. I started my training at the USNTS, Farragut, in January of 1944. (The coldest place in the USA in the wintertime). I was assigned to Camp Ward, Company 41-44. A few days after being assigned to my barracks (with over 100 other apprentice seamen), I became ill, with a bad cold. During the night, my temperature soared. Unbeknownst to me, I began screaming at the top of my voice and ran through the barracks like a mad man, scaring the living hell out of over 100 sleeping boots! I finally came out of it, and was escorted to sick bay, and for 48 hours, was examined, observed, and questioned. I told the doctors of the childhood occurrences of these spells and provided the name of my childhood doctor. When my fever had subsided, I returned to my barracks.

I graduated from boot camp without hearing anything further of the incident. After boot camp, and a short leave, I was assigned to sea duty in the South Pacific aboard the USS *Maryland* (BB-46). I was placed in the 4th Division. My battle station was in the lower powder handling room of 16 inch gun turret #four.

Not long after we got underway, we learned that our next engagement with the enemy would be at Saipan, in the Marianas Islands.

One evening on the high seas, while serving supper at my work station on steam table #4, Petty Officer First Class Master at Arms, Mason came through the line and stopped where I was serving the meat. I served him one piece. He insisted on having another? I explained to him that my orders were "One piece of meat per man, regardless of name or rank!" Becoming quite frustrated, he ordered me to report to the Master at Arms Office the next morning at 0800, (which I did?)

He commenced to lecture me on the subject of insubordination, and failing to follow orders. He then escorted me to the Officer's Quarters. He knocked on Commander Goldman's cabin door. The door opened. The Commander towered in front of me, and as he commanded us to enter, my knees went weak! (I later found out that Mason and Goldman were very close friends, and that our three way meeting was prearranged by Mason to get "revenge" because I refused to serve him extra meat!)

Commander Goldman gave me a stern scolding, then saddled me with many hours of extra duty for doing my duty? My side of the story was never heard!

On June 14, 1944 soon after my confrontation with our Commander, I took my battle station five decks below the water line in the lower powder handling room of sixteen inch gun turret #four, along with the editor and publisher of this book, Fred Vreeken, and several other shipmates. We commenced bombarding Saipan's coastal defense positions in preparation for the invasion.

On the evening of June 22, 1944, the USS *Maryland* was torpedoed in the port bow, taking the life of one of my best friends in the 4th Division, Freddie Bone. During the concerted efforts to keep the sea out of our struggling ship, and with two lonely destroyer escorts bravely shielding us from enemy submarines, we slowly made our way to Pearl Harbor.

Halfway between Saipan and Pearl Harbor I became sick . . . and you guessed it! I started to run a fever that evening! I made my customary bed on the quarter deck—one shoe for a pillow, the other under the small of my back. I slept in my dungarees. The rule was no bedding topside while underway. During war time, our compartments were much too hot to sleep in. The best alternative was to find a spot to rest topside.

After I had lain down with my raging fever, I looked toward the fantail. There were several officers, including Commander Goldman, shooting the breeze. I quickly drifted off into a peaceful slumber . . . Then Oh boy! It only seemed a second later that I heard someone yell, "Get him off me! Get him off me!" As I woke up, I was being held down to the deck in the officers area of the fantail. At least six officers were on top of me! I glanced at Goldman's face—it was ashen white. I was being held down near the lifeline.

Soon a group of medics appeared with a straight jacket and a stretcher! They put me on, and swiftly carried me to sick bay, where I was placed in a rack.

The next morning my fever had subsided, but I was still in the straight jacket! I was questioned thoroughly. I gave the same information that I had given at boot camp. Then two days later, I was released back to duty.

Upon my arrival back to the 4th Division, my shipmates filled me in on the part of the story I could not remember. I was told that I started screaming like a wild Indian, ran back and forth, then singled out Goldman from a large group of officers, picked him up bodily and ran for the lifeline, attempting to throw him over the side! That's when I became conscious, when Commander Goldman was screaming, "Get him off me!" That's when the officers floored me! I was never an offensive person and never would have attacked anyone in my right mind, *especially the executive officer!* The extra duty Goldman gave me must have lingered in my subconscious.

We arrived in Pearl Harbor, received a new bow, left Pearl Harbor for the Battle of Palau. I remained aboard the *Maryland* for the duration of the war, and never heard anything further concerning this incident. (They must have checked with old Doc Abbot in Elgin, Illinois. I was then eighteen years old. Today I am sixty-three, and have not experienced any further form of deliriousness since my attack on Commander Goldman. Old "Doc Abbott" was right. I did outgrow it.

I was discharged on April Fool's Day, 1946.

P.S. After being released from sick bay, Seaman Hollis O'Quin of the 4th Division, who loved to fight with his fists, insisted on sleeping with me every night because he informed me that if I had another fit, he would belt me in the jaw, and that would cure me forever! I'm really happy it did not occur, but poor Hollis was deeply disappointed. Mason changed steam tables because I still refused to serve him more than one piece of meat!

General Quarters

11/29/44 Approx. 5:45 p.m.
An eyewitness account by Harry (Gabe) Gabrielson

Thirty-one enlisted men were killed. One officer and twenty-nine enlisted men were seriously injured.

We were all snatched away from our comfortable surroundings to the sinister excitement of battle.

My battle station was up in the charthouse. It was a small compartment and the confinement drove me crazy for there was nothing to do. I either had to sit, read, or best of all walk five feet or so and watch the outside action. If only I had a camera to catch part of our personal history and to record the crew in battle.

I was in charge of an old fashion D.P.E. (Direction Finder) D/F 100 to 1500 KC which was totally useless in battle. For the arrival of radar and loran it made it almost completely obsolete.

The charthouse was on the portside of the ship next to the flag "signal" bridge. It had two passageways that for some reason always seem to be open. "Due to the heat I guess". On the portside you could always step out for a welcome breath of fresh air. The starboard passageway led into radar plot.

I was standing outside in close proximity of the charthouse looking aft at the 20mm and 40mm gun crews. How many times I thought how impossible it must be for a gunner to follow his own tracers while viewing hundreds of other roman candles going off at the same time. What if they each had a different color pattern?

Suddenly far astern a single engine fighter plane (Oscar) came gliding like a falling leaf out of a cluster of low hanging rain clouds. He must have been a seasoned pilot for he had to make a split second calculation. He immediately recognized that because of his height and speed he had less than a 50/50 chance of hitting our ship. At that instant you could hear the distant roar of full throttle as he almost stood the fighter on its tail and climbed vertically back into the stanchion of the clouds above.

A few 20mm and 40mm fired a few rounds into the clouds. You could now hear the low drone of his engine regaining altitude and slowly over taking our position. I kept thinking why don't we take evasive action! Turn, dammit, turn! He's no fool! He'll soon be on top of us! The drone of the engine became louder and louder.

I thought this maddened and desperate pilot whose last few minutes in life was to achieve a fanatical desire to be a true kamikaze pilot. To sink our ship or knock it out of action and take with him as many men as possible. Well buddy you got yourself a one way ticket to Hell for a bee can only sting once.

I looked around and began to feel a little ridiculous and stupid standing out in the open. What if he begins to strafe on the way down? Everyone else had on helmets and life jackets. Even that 20mm has a shield on it.

All eyes were glued to the sky, suddenly on the portside from a cloud above the plane re-emerged. Look at this guy! The plane was flying on it's side, so he could have a clearer view below! I was impressed by his aerobatics and dead reckoning. The pilot quickly executed a typical fighter wing over to attack his prey below.

A tremendous volume of deafening anti-aircraft fire pierced the air. Tracers seem to be flying in every which way. I wanted to join in the firing! No weapon! I felt so helpless, nothing to fight with!

It looked like he was headed right for me! That's it! The Pilot House? Instinctively I turned and ran for cover, passing the charthouse and ended up in the radar plot beside a large ploting table.

As several shipmates looked up at me they must of read my expression of impending doom. We all just stood there with blank expressions, waiting, staring at one another. I had seen before what happens when a plane hits a ship. If parts of debris or a bomb doesn't kill you the fireball will.

Then at that moment we all felt a gigantic shudder. "Dammit! He hit us; but where?" I slowly looked at my hands; "God, I'm still alive!"

After most of the acrid smelling smoke had cleared away, I finally was able to make my way back on to the portside of the signal bridge. Although it was a catastrophic event I kept remembering how one plane could have made such a heavy impact.

On my first view crewmembers were still obviously in a state of shock. I stood transfixed, stunned by the sight below. In short order the damage control parties and other heroic volunteers had the situation well under control. I was amazed at the small amount of damage topside. I kept looking for a large hole in the deck. Not until later did I learn that an armor piercing bomb had exploded two decks blow, blowing men to bits and choking them with fumes. Solid steel deck and compartment had buckled like paper.

Then at this time and long before General Quarters was sounded I was one of many nonessential battle station personal ordered to assist below.

Upon arriving in close proximity of the laundry I was shocked into the true reality of war! There before me on the cold steel deck lined up side by side was close to a dozen bodies covered with sheets. I couldn't believe it and I remembered I didn't want to. I couldn't understand where all the bodies were coming from. I was told that a bomb had penetrated the ship down to the armor deck and had exploded between turret one and two.

When I arrived in the laundry room it looked like a makeshift sick bay for many men were sitting and laying down on benches. Someone; a Corpsman? Handed me a cloth with ammonia (or something) for I remember it had a strong smell to it. I was told to hold it close, but not to close to a crewmember's nose. He was almost in a semi-conscious state.

Signal Gang USS Maryland 1942. (Courtesy of Ed Swanson)

Outside of the wounded many crew members were suffering from smoke inhalation.

A short time later a chief petty officer pointed a finger at me and several others to follow him. In another compartment we were each handed a battle lantern.

Although the fire-fighting and damage control parties had put out the fire and had the area secured. As we approached the forward compartments we could still see a haze beginning to build up.

The first sight upon entering the main blast area was almost indescribable when I entered the C.R. Division compartment (this is where I slept and ate) The C.R. Division compartment was only a stone throw from where the bomb had exploded.

The air was still pungent with the smell of high explosive and sickly with smell of unburied dead. It seemed so unreal everything vividly colored in black. As I approached in close proximity of where the explosion occurred the area was transformed into a forbidding surrealistic scene.

The light of my battle lantern fell upon several bodies. At first I thought they were from the officers mess crew for they appeared to be of Negro descent.

I was later told that this was a battle station location for a small damage control party and in addition to the group there were other crew members who were unable to make it to their battle station.

So began the dreaded task of removing our deceased crew members. It's gruesome to say this, but in placing bodies you had to be careful it was all of the same person. Almost all of the bodies had to be transported in wiremesh stretchers, blankets, sheets and even hammocks!

The touching of peeling flesh is somewhat indescribable. I remember of one particular individual. It was if his feet had been bolted to the deck for when the blast occurred his body went forward like a hinge on a trapdoor. The explosion had pivoted his whole body face first on the steel deck. His head had opened up like a ripe watermelon.

I had viewed a shipmate earlier shining his battle lantern upwards. A few minutes later I still saw him standing in the same spot, he hadn't moved. He seemed frozen. The way he was staring upwards was as if whatever he was viewing was beyond his normal comprehension. I looked up to the sight, an electric shiver went through my scalp. His battle lantern was shining on to a dead crew member who was hanging face down from the shipfitters shop above.

The terrific force of the explosion had split the shipfitters deck above in between the two barbettes turrets one and two. Unfortunately this unlucky shipmate was at the wrong place at the wrong time for he was wearing a life jacket and steel helmet.

He apparently had been standing in the shipfitters shop. Then when the blast blew the deck apart, a portion of it had curled into his midsection lifting him upwards, and finally he fell forward in the position that we now saw him.

An eerie sight that I will never forget. His body ever so slowing moving back and forth with the motion of the ship. His arms and hands were out stretched as if he was going to break his fall. From each finger tip you could see dripping of body fluid.

When I turned away I still saw this same shipmate still staring at the hanging crew member. I shined my light at him. He said a few incomprehensible words. I asked him, "What did you say?" He didn't answer. Then a few moments later when he turned I saw this sardonic smile on his face.

How pale his cheeks looked! And those eyes dare the eyes as of one dead. He seemed to be in another world. Someone else tried to talk to him but he just kept walking. That was the last I ever saw of him. Battle fatigue? I never did find out. To this day I can still see that look on his face.

By the time I left they still hadn't removed the hanging crew member. Several of us were told to take some bodies aft. It was beginning to get to me, that appalling, sweet sickly stench of burned flesh. I was never so glad to leave for now we had plenty of help.

When we sat down the stretcher we were carrying the three of us must of looked sick. It was also about this time General Quarters had been secured. Words I was never so glad to hear, "Go on up and get some fresh air".

It was so good to be back on topside. I gave thanks to the anti-aircraft crew, for I was told indeed the plane would have hit the superstructure had it not been for a wing being shot off at the last moment.

I made my way forward to where the plane had hit. A shipmate told me that a mercury bomb had hit us for he had seen some on the deck. Another shipmate said no. That the mercury came from inside that damaged paravane. We had two paravanes stored forward topside; one on the portside and the other on the starboard side of number two turrets barbettes. I didn't know who, or what to believe.

In viewing the hole made by the armor piercing bomb, I thought the pilot had to have had full throttle all the way down, for it was hard to believe that a bomb could have gone through so much steel before exploding.

There was still a lot of aircraft debris about the deck. I walked around picking up different parts here and there.

In the pictures I am holding a letter opener. The handle is made of teakwood from the deck of the USS *Maryland*. Where upon I wonder how many men had once walked upon it?

The letter opener is pointing at a piece of the planes fuselage. It has dried up now but you can still see the remaining stains of the pilots flesh that was on it when I first picked it up. The Navy T-shirt is the same original one that I used to wrap up all the plane parts. The shell casing had not been fired and still has gun powder in it.

There are many stories to be told by many crew members and I could go on and on about the many battles I have viewed from topside. I for one feel very fortunate, for I was always able to be above deck to see the majority of the action.

At the time of Pearl Harbor was attacked, I was still in boot camp in San Diego, California. In January of 1942 I went aboard the USS *Maryland* in Bremerton, Washington and was assigned to the L Division for awhile, then later transferred to the C.R. Division.

The thrill of a lifetime was to have witnessed the firing of a broadside in the night action in Leyte Gulf in the Philippine Islands. "The crossing of the "T" in Surigao Straits. Although I did miss a major event when a kamikaze hit turret three in Okinawa.

Paladium, Hollywood taken June 1942 L to R: Swanson, Wilson, and Whitley. (Courtesy of Ed Swanson)

G.L. "Salty" Mountz, unknown, Johnny Wilson, John L. Wilson, Howard Whims, and Nathan Fox.

Shining the Tompkins M.B. Vann, left, and Mike Cotter, right, turret four gunners mates.

Fishing party, South Pacific, 1943, L to R: Dental Officer, CDR Claude Ricketts, CWT Preston and Lt. "Pete" Batchelle.

It was just prior to this that my battle station was changed aft to the transmitter room, which was close to turret three. One could not help think, maybe your days were numbered. A coma we all have of danger.

Then a week or so after this action we left the forward area for Guam, on to Pearl Harbor and then to the Navy Yard at Bremerton, Washington. We timed it just right for when we arrived the war had ended in Europe.

Along with a thirty day leave I received orders to report to the Alameda Naval Air Station, California. One wise guy said he heard I was being transferred because of "battle fatigue". When I inquired about it, I never did get a straight answer, for after my leave was up I had wanted to return to the *Maryland.*

A few months later Japan surrendered, ending the war. I was on the list for another rating. Now I wish I had reenlisted, instead I was caught up in the tide for everyone else wanting back into civilian life. Being high on the point system, I was one of the first groups to be discharged.

War is a nasty thing that has always proved disastrous for one side or the other, many times both. I hope that we never have another major war because with all these sophisticated weapons we could obliterate ourselves.

This book marks a rather significant even in our personal history. A record of historical outward facts they are eminently precious, not as a record of outward fact, but as a mirror of ourselves aboard the USS *Maryland,* and an extension of a persons self. The vigilant, the active, and the brave.

Wartime
Honolulu, Hawaii
Witnessed by, H. (Gabe) Gabrielson

A dramatic event occurred one afternoon while returning to the USS *Maryland* from a Honolulu liberty. You always payed a price when you waited until the last minute to get transportation back to Pearl Harbor, for liberty was up at 1800 hours.

The three of us were short of cash, so instead of taking a taxi for 50¢ a head we had to take the 25¢ sardine can, "The Bus". This time I was lucky for I had a portside window seat, complete with fresh air. They always overloaded the bus by jam packing the isle. Every time we hit a ground swell the rear tires sounded like they were coming up through the frame.

A soldier who was sitting two seats behind me seemed to have had more than his share of drinks. He kept saying over and over again, "I can't hold it! I can't hold it! I'll never make it, stop the damn bus! I've got to go now." Another voice said, "You crazy S.O.B. you can't do it in here!" Others said, "Stick it out the window, do it out the window!"

How he ever got into a position to do it, I'll never know. It was a bad decision for low and behold in the oncoming traffic the last person you had wanted to see, a police car. Suddenly in the background "Oh . . . My . . . God!" Other mixed voiced exclaimed, "Bullseye! Good shot! Right on target! You got him good!" A roar of laughter filled the bus.

The laughter was short lived for in a few minutes the bus was pulling off to the side of the road. We were all told to get out of the bus and then ordered by two policeman to sit by the side of it.

One police officer was still holding a white handkerchief. You could clearly see the telltale urine splatter on his shirt. I remember he was an old timer for I had seen him several times in town. His eyes were squinted and canny, square jawed, a rugged looking bully. He was mad, furious to say the least. The other officer was younger. He just stood by trying to look tough and let his partner do all the talking.

"O.K! . . . Now! Which one of you urinated out of the window?" A long pause. "All right! if that's the way you want it! Nobody is going anywhere until the jockey steps forward who did it!"

The word jockey didn't set too well for over half of the men on the bus were sailors. Then one sailor, he must of been at least six foot two or three, stood up and began to brush himself off. He was followed by a buddy next to him.

The officer bellowed, "So your the one!" and the sailor said, "Hell no!" so the officer said. "Then the both of you sit down!" The sailor said, "I'm not going to; it's dirty. "The officer asked, "What did you say?" A sudden revulsion, before he could finish, the whole group stood up.

The officer said, "Now hold it right there! No one is getting back on the bus until I have the man's name, rank, and serial number!"

In the front of our group stood a first class boat'swan mate. In a firm voice, he said, "If you like it or not, your not going to hold our bus up just because you can't identify the person who did what you said he did. If any of us are late reporting in, it will be because your abusing your authority. Then your tail is going to be on our carpet. Your treating us like a bunch of kids. Were not civilians, were in the military. You made your point now don't get the rest of us all riled up."

A tense moment, after a few cat calls. The group started to move forward; both officers quickly backpedaled. The officer said, "All right, All right, on your way." Everyone back on the bus!" As both officers turned to leave, "Mark my word your commanding officer will hear of this!"

It was the highlight of the day, everybody's morale went up 50 points. A happy singing bunch on the way back to the base. One for all and all for one. A single voice carries no clout; many voices get action.

Memorable Experience
By M.J. "Mike" Cotter

One of my experiences occurred concerning the firing lock MK XIV Mod. 5 which is attached to the breech plug of the 16" guns. Our Chief Turret Captain, F.J. Longtin was a perfectionist and insisted that the Gun Captain of each 16" gun completely disassemble, clean and lubricate the firing lock even if only one salvo was fired. The cleaning solution we used was alcohol, but Longtin insisted that pink lady (the only alcohol we had access to) might harm the firing locks so under his supervision we made a small still out of a Bright Work Polish Can (approx. 1 pint), some copper tubing and a hot plate. They still worked perfectly and took all of the pink out of the pink lady and we then had good, clear, 180 proof alcohol. After that we didn't mind cleaning the firing locks but the only thing we could cut the 180 proof with was grapefruit juice which one of our friendly storekeepers gladly provided. We used a lot of alcohol after the still worked so good.

Another thing the chief was particular about was the maintenance of the 16" shell hoists. I don't remember the size or quantity but for disassembly on the shell deck we had to remove a group of identical stud bolts. As we removed them, we had to mark which hole each one was removed from and place them in the same bolt hole on reassembly. We tried to say it made no difference which hole they went back in but he let us know that there might be a slight difference or a burr on the threads etc. Also he was the man in charge and of course we didn't argue with the ex Pacific Fleet Heavy Weight Boxing Champion.

Another thing the chief was very particular about was that after a salvo was fired, the Gun Captain would continue to wipe the mushroom on the breech plug with the wet toweling wrapped around his arm from wrist to elbow until the 150 pounds of compressed air had forced all of the smoke and gases out of the 720 inches of gun barrel and the gun captain gave a bore clear and only then could a reload be started.

At Tarawa under continuous prolonged firing, the Hot Mushroom (front part of the breech plug) caused the wet toweling to steam through to the gun captain's arms and in turret four, Robert Jurovich, the other gun captain, and I both had a continuous blister from wrist to elbow. In gunnery practice we had never fired that many salvos in succession so had not experienced that problem. The chief didn't want us to go to the sick bay as he was afraid it would reflect on him. We did get first aid and thought no more about it as some one came up with a solution by placing asbestos under the wet toweling and that solved the problem. About five months later at Morning Quarters, Jurovich and I were presented with a Purple Heart. We didn't know it had even been turned in.

There was no problem with the cleaning of the Mushroom and giving the bore-clear, only a problem of preventing the steam from reaching the arm.

Other battleships have had turret explosions and possibly could have been caused by giving a premature bore-clear to save time.

Personal Story
By Arthur Eresman

Pictured (above right) is a photo of the scale model of the *Maryland* Eresman constructed from Navy drawings. Everything above the weather decks is machined and fabricated brass and the hull is laminated basswood. The scale is 120:1 (1/10" to the foot) which translates to a length of 5'3". The model has been on display for the last five years at the Louisiana Naval War Memorial Museum in Baton Rouge, Louisiana and is slated for permanent display in the *Maryland* statehouse in Annapolis.

Fishing in The South Pacific
By James H. Pete Batchelle

In 1943 the USS *Maryland* was working her way down to the South Pacific via Suva, Fiji and Efate, New Hebrides. I had been designated the ships fishing officer and arranged fishing trips from before sunup until around 9 a.m. with other junior officers and enlisted men.

One morning upon returning to the ship the First Lt-Damage Control Officer Claude Ricketts looked over the side and asked if that was the bait we were unloading or the little fish we had caught. I knew he was dying to go fishing but was hesitant to push himself - a senior commander, head of department and responsible for the ship's boats. I asked him if he would like to go out with us the next morning and show us how to fish. He jumped at this invitation as I knew he would.

On board the next morning he said I was "In Charge" and we all gulped. How was this going to work out? We only had two rods and two hand lines. He took one of the hand lines and stationed himself in the bow as we trolled out to the reef. About 200 yards from the reef he got a hook up that jerked him to his feet and as the white line burned through his hands he ended up in the stern with bleeding hands and asked what the devil we were fishing for. He had obviously hooked a big tuna or marlin. On the reef the water was so clear one could not tell if it was six inches or 60 feet deep. Naturally we found the six inches and grounded on a coral head. Ugh!

About that time the men began patting their pockets and I told the commander that after sunrise I had allowed the men to smoke in the forward compartment even though this was against regulations. He replied "Carry On". Shortly after this I hooked a three foot barracuda and skillfully brought it up to and into the boat. Whereupon he threw it overboard and he said never bring a live barracuda into a boat he was in and drew up his trouser leg to display scars on his calf from a thrashing barracuda.

Arthur Eresman with his scale model of the USS Maryland.

He caught the biggest and the most fish and stayed in the boat and helped clean it up claiming most of the mess was from his fish. He never missed a fishing trip.

What a guy and what a fisherman - no wonder he made Admiral and even has a building at the Naval Academy named after him - Ricketts Hall.

Pearl Harbor December 7, 1941
My Day Aboard the USS *Maryland* (BB-46)
By Stan J. Van Hoose

I was awakened about 7 a.m. by a shipmate for breakfast. As it was Sunday and holiday routine, if you didn't have the duty. Since I didn't have any duties until noon, I planned to sleep in, up in the wheel house, my normal cleaning station responsibility. I was to become third class quartermaster January 1, 1942; On my way to 20 plus years, and to chief some day. The depression years behind 1940, entry date, were not too rosy for a coal miners son. I turned 21, November 12, 1941. Besides my friend said the breakfast was mincemeat on toast and that was the proper name in mixed company, there were other names too.

I did go back to sleep. About 0755, there about, all hell broke loose. I was awakened by a 50 cal. machine gun just below the conning tower. I raised up and looked out the bridge drop down windows (port). Planes were flying in all directions, I looked over towards the navy yard area, beyond was Hickam Field, explosions, buildings on fire, my attention was drawn to starboard at Ford Island; hangars and planes on the runway, all on fire and being bombed, at first I thought a practice raid, as we had been having such often for about a month. But then I saw two planes to port coming from the fleet landing area, dropped torpedoes into the water toward the *Oklahoma*, tied up to our port side. When the planes banked out their run, I could see they were Japs, and then the explosion in the *Oklahoma* raised her out of the water about four feet or so. The tail gunner was strafing everything he could. Then I realized we were really being attacked and it was war.

As my battle station was in the conning tower to man head set phones for the navigator, I was there in quick time. In following the navigator about the area I got to view the harbor activities. The *Arizona* blowing and burning, the *Oklahoma* capsizing, and our sister ship *West Virginia* settling and fires. They never touched the tanker *Neosha* just ahead of our bow, that would have been a hell of a fire. She was loaded with aviation fuel for Ford Island. If the Japs had waited until 10 a.m. an ammunition ship would have been along side the *Nevada* and *Arizona*. The whole area would have been destroyed, seeing the *Nevada* as they passed us, get bombed like bees attacking. They were able to go aground to save sinking and plugging the harbor.

The dive bombers did one big number on the navy yard ships, drydocked and moored. Then I was sent down to central station for the rest of the battle to relieve some man for whatever reason. It was past noon time before we secured from general quarters and I came to top side and what a mess. Feeling the weight of war was a terrible phase. Not knowing what will happen next.

We had anti-aircraft 4, 1.1 quads of four guns, they were very good at low level protection. Had like funnels at mussel ends. Favored the

British A.A. I always felt they helped keep the dive bombers away from the *Maryland.*

We had men going in all directions to help wherever needed. I was sent to the bridge for any stand by service that I could do. I remember we had sandwiches and coffee brought up to us. There was a messed up routine of all normal activity for three or four days. We lost two officers and two enlisted men. We were very lucky. I think that every man felt we had been dealt a dirty hand by both the Japs and Washington, D.C. Washington knew and did not prepare for the battle. They did not inform the armed forces of the coming attack, so as to get the American people mad enough to go to war to save Russia and Communism. I read and studied a lot before the attack and have a big collection of Roosevelts deals and closeness to Russia. Some president! He is still a traitor in my mind.

I left the *Maryland* after the Midway battle, went aboard a survey ship, USS *Pathfinder.* It did survey of all sorts, for new maps, harbors. We did some advance activity in small groups before some invasions in the Solomon Islands from beginning to New Georgia (Munda) group. Then back to the States in October.

Out again on a transport AP-160, *Prince Georges,* for Tarawa, then Kwajalein, Eniwetok, Saipan, Guam and Palau. Made CPO July 1, 1944. Then to New Caledonia, got orders for stateside for reassignment. Was assigned to Mare Island Navy Yard as a tug dispatcher.

Reenlisted August 20, 1946 and went back to sea on the USS *Monongahela* (AO-42). Served aboard her as navigator and discharged August 21, 1948. That tanker hauled oil from the Persian Gulf, all over three oceans and seven seas. What a ride. "Join the navy to see the world," and I got to navigate it.

Finished college in San Francisco, California, came to Beloit, Wisconsin, opened a business as paint distributor (OBrien and Pratt Lambert). Distributor for Kirby and Hoover vacuum cleaners; Custom picture framers, art supplies and gallery. My wife is an artist with her work in some 40 states. We semi-retired from that in 1978, went to work for Mautz Paint Company, as branch manager of Beloit and Janesville stores, January 1981. Retired April 25, 1996.

Now I've started into guitar and banjo, The People's Network (T.V.) and hope to hunt, fish, and travel as long as God lets me be in this old world.

I feel blessed that I served my country, and proud of my countrymen for the job we've done to preserve our nation and our freedom. I logged 32 months of World War II in a combat area, got a $500.00 bonus check in 1961 from Kentucky. I'm proud to be a coal miners son from Kentucky. I thank God for a great wife of 52 years, (November 6, 1943), great health, friends, and a great country. God Bless the USA.

Aboard the USS *Maryland* in 1945
By Julian J. Smith BM3/c

At the end of World War II the *Maryland* was assigned duties to transport Navy, Marine Corps and Army men back home from Pearl Harbor. With the extra load of passengers, we ran low on potable water and were forced to shower with salt water. About halfway across the Pacific, heading to Seattle, Washington, we were working on one of the eight boilers when we noticed severe shaking and swaying of the vessel. We were notified by our pipe communications that we were going through a typhoon. After several hours after completing our job on the boiler, we were able to go up to the main deck and survey the damage caused by the typhoon. We were told that one ship accompanying us was sunk and lots of damage was noticed on our ship, including broken winches, booms and plane launcher. We did make it to Pier 90 in Seattle, where due to plans to mothball the *Maryland,* I was sent to the naval hospital for dental work prior to receiving my discharge in April 1946.

Steve Ross
Anecdote about as told by shipmate Walt Obermeier

In our very early Navy days, late 1940, Ross and I were standing on the dock in Long Beach waiting for a liberty launch to return us to the ship. A full lieutenant detached himself from a group of fellow officers and approached us, making me extremely nervous - Naval officers do not casually associate with enlisted men, especially raw boots.

"E" Division Fire Control Shop 1944. Back row L to R: Lavar Young, James "Windy" Newman, L.A. Eck, George E. Prue, Clarence A. Lowe. Middle row L to R: R.A. McBeth, Fred Koerner, J.P. Quinn. Front row L to R: Rhea Starr Jr., Richard Jacobs, Erwin Jendrziczyk, Robert Morris. (Courtesy of Fred Koerner)

He addressed Ross, asking if we were waiting for a *Maryland* boat. "Yes, Sir", says Ross. "I understand that's not much of a ship", the lieutenant then said. I could see that Ross was instantly angry and I'm about to pass out. "You have been badly misinformed, Sir," says Ross, with a lot more heat than necessary according to my thinking, "the *Maryland* is the best ship in the U.S. Navy." The lieutenant grinned; "Good for you, Son, that's my ship, too."

The lieutenant's name was Gore and I believe he was from Tennessee. Later, standing messenger watches while he was OOD, we learned that there was no humor in Lt. Gore when he was on duty. I guess he was just checking out what the lowly ones thought of their ship. And Ross was everyone's friend, but he wouldn't be walked on.

His family and mine are friends to this day, but sadly, Steve passed away in 1980 and earth is poorer for it.

Denver Man's Battle Replacement First to Fall
By Lisa Levitt Ryckman
Rocky Mountain News Staff Writer

Walter Mycka almost became the first American serviceman killed at Pearl Harbor.

On that morning 55 years ago, a Japanese torpedo exploded on the bow of the USS *Tennessee* and shrapnel rained down on the nearby USS *Maryland.*

Seaman Second Class Warren McCutcheon, a 17-year-old from Gridley, California, caught a piece in the neck and died instantly.

At that moment, he was filling in at Mycka's battle station atop the *Maryland* mainmast gun.

"But for the grace of God and the Navy's infinite wisdom, that could very well have been myself," said Mycka, 77, who had been temporarily transferred to the fleet machine-gun school on Oahu for training earlier that week.

As the Japanese bombers flew in, the Marine sergeant in charge of the school ordered Mycka and the others to man their training weapons.

For the next 30 minutes, Mycka loaded a .50-caliber machine gun aimed at the incoming Japanese bombers.

"They flew directly over the school at no higher than 500 feet," he said. "You could very definitely see the Japanese insignia, the rising sun. You could see the pilot and the gunner.

"You could almost see the expressions on their faces, they were so low."

Mycka and his classmates brought down several planes in the first wave. For the rest of the day, they waited at their guns for the next attack.

It never came.

When the smoke cleared, more than 2,400 men were dead, McCutcheon among them. But somehow, the USS *Maryland* duty officer never recorded

McCutcheon's name in the ship's log that day, a fact that haunted Mycka, then 22.

"I wasn't aware Warren McCutcheon had taken my place until I returned to the ship," he said. "My shipmates informed me then that Warren McCutcheon had lost his life at my station. But except for what I was told, I had no evidence of what occurred, nor have I ever seen his name appear as being killed in action."

McCutcheon was still on Mycka's mind several years later when he survived two Japanese bomb attacks on the USS *Randolph,* an aircraft carrier.

"I felt it was something more than just luck or fate or whatever, because of what happened on the *Maryland* and what happened later on," he said.

"I had just left a place aboard (the USS *Randolph*) that was bombed. Had it not been for a period of about 30 seconds or so, I would have been at those particular spots — twice — where enemy planes had hit and killed a lot of my shipmates."

After the war, Mycka became a correctional officer. In the 1950s he transferred to the Federal Correctional Institution in Jefferson County. He and his wife, Helen, now 75, had three children and lived in Denver. Mycka retired in 1971.

As the years passed, the war memories faded. But the unresolved story of McCutcheon nagged at Mycka.

"It was always on my mind." he said, "And it bothered me."

At reunions of USS *Maryland* survivors, Mycka's shipmates confirmed that McCutcheon had died on the mainmast. One told Mycka he had helped move the body and had packed McCutcheon's possessions for shipment to next of kin.

In June, Mycka was elated to learn that Gridley, California, had erected a nine-foot-high, black granite monument to the young man who had died in his place.

"The First to Fall," reads part of the inscription on McCutcheon's memorial. "He had no warning — He had no chance."

In 1998, surviving *Maryland* crew members, Mycka among them, plan to place a plaque in McCutcheon's memory at the Gridley cemetery.

And at least one mission in Walter Mycka's long life will be complete.

"I know as a fact that it must have been intended for me to be here, to accomplish a certain goal in my life. Otherwise, I probably would have perished with the rest of them," he said.

"Maybe I still have that goal to accomplish, whatever that was intended to be."

Meritorious Conduct of a Seaman
by D.C. Godwin

Though the conduct of all hands aboard this vessel during the air raid on the morning of Sunday, December 7, 1941, could be classified as meritorious, outstanding was the action of Leslie Vernon Short, Seaman First Class, USN, Service No. 342-29-54, enlisted September 25, 1940, at Garden City, KS, and whose present home address is Noel, MO.

Short, a machine gun striker, 22 years old, truly demonstrated the spirit of men behind the Navy guns. Though he had not been called to duty at his gun station, upon seeing our country being attacked, he immediately manned a machine gun, opened fire on the approaching torpedo planes, downing the first one and injuring the second.

Short's action is best described by his own statement: "After breakfast on Sunday morning, I came to Group A Machine Gun Station to write some letters home and address some Christmas cards. Suddenly, I noticed planes diving on the Naval Air Base nearby. At first I thought they were our planes just in mock diving practice attack, but when I saw smoke and flames rise from a building, I looked closer and saw that they were not American planes. I broke out ammunition nearby, loaded my machine gun and opened fire on the torpedo planes coming in from the east, which had just dropped two torpedoes. Flames and smoke burst from the first plane I aimed at, and it veered off to the left falling toward the hospital; I think I also hit the second plane which I aimed at immediately after shooting at the first one, but by then I was so busy that I cannot say for sure."

Sailor's Pearl Harbor Diary
by Howard Rector

It was the starting moments of WWII at Pearl Harbor, Territory of Hawaii. I was stationed aboard the battleship USS *Maryland.*

The morning of December 7, 1941, I had finished breakfast and went forward to the low area where the seaman's washrooms, showers and toilets were located.

There were approximately 2,000 men aboard and water hours were in effect. I had a suit of inspection whites that needed washing and the early water hours 0530-0730 a.m., as a rule left a little space in the washroom (especially on Sunday morning) and I intended to take advantage of that uncrowded luxury.

USS Maryland, 1943. (Courtesy of Norman Morton)

On a normal workday, and at quitting time, the washroom was so packed with seamen trying to get cleaned up for liberty ashore - well somebody one day yelled out (to no one in particular) that he had scrubbed 16 fannies (a polite phrase I am inserting) before he could possible find his own. When you think of that phrase in the proper perspective, the seaman who uttered it could have been deemed a hero. It relieved a lot of tension in lots of slippery, soapy young bodies jammed together and naked as the day they were first born.

Getting back to the part where I came close to being a hero, as I said, I was up in the seaman's' washroom scrubbing my whites along with a seaman from another deck division whom I will refer to as "Mac" (all other males not known by most USN sailormen are referred to as Mac). In the same vein, anything that is unknown or whose proper name cannot be recalled at the moment is referred to as a "Gismo."

I was really involved in my chores and didn't pay too much attention to distant rumbles as planes were always flying around and/or taking off from ford Island (in the center of Pearl Harbor).

Couldn't see outside as the portholes had plates welded over them many months prior to the actual start of the war. I think maybe somebody knew something long before I did.

The click of the intercom speaker alerted us to the fact that the boatswain's mate on watch was about to give the word. The word was "all hands in the fire and rescue party, starboard watch report to the quarter deck on the double." I turned to Mac and stated emphatically that I was not going to report for another damn drill, and closed with the statement, "to hell with em!"

Aside from the fact that I was naked and all wet, I was sick of attending drills at all hours of the days and nights for the past two weeks, both at sea and in port.

You see, we were just completing our annual fleet fitness inspection and there had been a stream of battle drills, target practice, general quarters day and night.

That's why I was washing my inspection uniform so as to be prepared for the next one. Yeah I was not only a Seaman 1st Class, I was a real first class seaman getting paid the great sum (it really was in those days!) of $54 per month.

At about the same instance that I ended my exclamation "to hell with em" the steel deck under my butt lifted me what seemed to be at least one foot upwards.

When it settled back, still trembling (both me and the decks), I can't remember whether I said it out loud or just thought, "The after 16 powder magazines are exploding, this is no drill! They really need me."

I grabbed a wet pair of shorts I had just laundered and headed off jumping into one leg at a time, and never breaking stride.

Before I could reach amidships (I was on the main deck) the voice again came out of the ship's speakers and these were the exact words as I heard them.

"All hands man your battle stations on the double. The Japs are attacking. This is no s...."

I wish I could remember that boatswain's mate name, because he was a hero and no doubt about it. One man with a few chosen words started adrenaline pumping in a thousand plus hearts, preparing them for survival or anything else.

This announcement changed my direction to the midship ladder and heading for my battle station which was operating a 50 caliber machine gun (part of our anti-aircraft weapons system) located in the superstructure forward of the bridge and conning.

I had just reached the first step of the ladder leading upward to the open boat deck and again the word was urgently passed "Take Cover, take cover, strafers, strafers."

The Japanese fighter planes were roaming freely up and down battleship row.

This action was repeated several times in the next few moments, with men surging up then dropping back to hide.

I glanced up through the open hatch and saw one lone man sitting in the pointers seat of an anti-aircraft gun desperately firing an empty gun, with nobody to train it, nobody to load it and no ammunition even if the whole gun crew had been present.

Now that one lone guy was a real, full blown, died in the wool, hero and I know he must have been squeezing that firing key with all his might and not a thing happening. Did he let this take him from his duty assignment at general quarters?

Hell no! He wasn't hiding from strafing planes, he was manning his battle station as every man Jack of us should have been doing.

That lone sailor (may God bless him wherever he may be) did something for me, he made me a hero also.

My heroic action (after seeing him) was to yell out in a loud clear forceful voice, "Let's get out of this hole. If we are going to die, let's die at our battle stations."

It was that simple, the men blocking the ladder scrambled up on decks and we all followed, everyone striving to reach their assignment station.

I had just climbed up two rungs of the ladder welded to the starboard side of the bridge superstructure, glanced up to see my division officer (Lt. Manning) hurrying down the same ladder. I dropped back to the boat deck to see what his orders would be.

On touching the deck he turned and asked me where I was going. I said to my battle station on the forward 50 caliber guns. Mr. Manning said, "Come with me."

I followed him back down into the ship, down to the ammunition hoists located on the 2nd deck. In retrospect, going down into the bowels of the ship must have taken a tremendous amount of courage on Mr. Manning's part.

I'm sure as he was coming down from the superstructure he witnessed the horror going on around the harbor as helpless ships were bombed, sinking and burning.

Closer to home, the battleship USS *Oklahoma* which was moored to us on the portside was listing about 45 degrees to her port and tipping fast. It was the Japanese torpedoes striking her that made our ships leap skyward and I had mistakenly thought it was our aft magazines exploding when I was forward in the seamen's washrooms. I had a brief glimpse of the listing *Okie* and a Japanese plane trailing smoke going down to our starboard across Ford Island.

For the lieutenant, I guess it was the Annapolis training, or duty to God and Country. For me it was obeying orders with no thoughts of what could happen, probably, in either of our minds.

Upon reaching the head of the hoist at the second deck level we found a beehive of activity.

The lower deck magazines had already been opened and boxes of anti-aircraft ammunition were being grabbed by many willing hands.

The ammunition had to be moved from below decks to "clipping stations" where other sailors had to lug the heavy rounds into eight-shot clips, that could then be loaded into gun cradles and fired at our tormentors.

Mr. Manning grabbed me and some other sailors and took us to a clipping room to begin preparing the ammunition for firing.

I don't remember the exact route we took from the third deck to the aft clipping room, but the five of us didn't waste anytime as daylight and open decks were something we all cherished after a time literally trapped below decks with all the noise of high explosives shaking the ship. It sort of gives one the feeling that submarine sailors must get being depth charged in a submerged sub.

In the clipping room, there were already more sailors than needed to clip up the ammunition.

There were sailors from the *Oklahoma* who managed to scramble aboard our ship before the *Okie* went over on her portside with only part of her bottom in the open.

Some sailors were pulled out of the harbor soaked with heavy fuel oil, eyes closed to keep out the oil running from their hair.

Nonetheless, they stood shoulder-to-shoulder with others guiding them as they clipped the ammunition.

Soon they had ammunition stacked high at the gun mounts. I wasn't really needed in the clipping room but stayed there awaiting further orders from Mr. Manning and hoping to get on the open deck again.

Someone from gun mount three yelled in that they needed a first loader and I really scooted out to get the position as I was experienced in the first loader position on the anti-aircraft gun.

The gun consists of four separate barrels all mounted side by side in a horizontal framework. The crew consisted of a pointer at the left side and a trainer on the right side, both seated. There were four first loaders standing, but moving right or left as the trainer swiveled the gun either direction keeping in line with the barrel and ammunition cradle each loader was servicing.

There were four second loaders on the decks below the gun mount handing up clips of ammunition to the first loader assigned to them.

This gun, with a well-trained crew, could fire 600 rounds per minute. It was fixed ammunition, exploding on contact, with a 2,000 yard range. Unfortunately, we had a tremendous amount of faulty ammo and it seemed as if one of the four barrels was constantly jammed or misfiring.

My biggest concern during the early firing was to keep my bare feet off the hot shell casings being ejected onto the floor of the gun mount as I was still only wearing my under shorts. Somebody, bless his heart, was alert to my problems and produced a pair of rubber knee boots thrusting them at my feet and I scrambled into them between clip loadings. I guess my frenzied feet shuffling probably looked rather comical in retrospect.

Anyhow that's where I stayed for the remainder of the day, December 7, 1941.

I think there were 3,500 Americans killed at Pearl Harbor that day and one often wonders why some die and others live.

I left the seamen's washroom approximately 45 minutes before a 500-lb aerial bomb destroyed the place and set the bow of our ship on the bottom of the harbor. It was the only direct hit our ship sustained and we were very fortunate to have only three men killed.

Our officer, Ensign Crowe, killed in the forward most area, Seaman Warren McCutcheon was killed in the mainmast (above our gun mount) when a bomb hit the number one turret of the USS *Tennessee* which was moored directly astern of our ship. The same bomb shrapnel sprayed out whole quarter deck wounding the first loaders on both sides of me, out of the four of us I alone was not even scratched.

We got news later that day the men that had been wounded on my gun survived although one was severe spinal wound. As the day went on and after the initial attack at 7:55 a.m., we had the sad task of lowering the body of McCutcheon down out of the mainmast to the quarterdeck.

The corpsmen carried the body away and another sailor, who had been working a 50 caliber machine gun with the dead man, just sat on a bucket at the base of the mast for a long time staring into space.

There was another attack by high level bombers about 10:00 a.m., but the smoke from burning ships and oil probably saved us further damage.

That ended the shooting until after dark that night when some of the carrier *Enterprise* planes flew over the harbor. Even though their running lights were on, some gunner on one of the ships opened fire and I think every gun in the harbor opened up and I think you could have read a newspaper from the light of all the tracer bullets in the sky. The firing only lasted a few moments as I guess all the ship controls on all the ships were screaming "cease fire, cease fire."

I think two of the planes were shot down. Seems like we had just got nervously settled down when the word was passed for all hands to search their own parts of the ship to try and locate a Navy yard workman. There had been five workmen come aboard and only four had reported back to the gangway at leaving time.

Word had it the worker had a German name, spoke with a German accent and was believed to be a saboteur.

Now that really put fear into my heart. I'm thinking, "I survived this whole horrible day safely, now some saboteur is going to blow the whole damn ship sky high!"

It was the darkest night, no lights anywhere. I went to search the inside of a clipping room that was totally black. This was the portside which at the time was being used to store some of the flag officers gear. I had picked up a ball peen hammer and was gingerly punching my way around the room. I suddenly touched something with the extended hammer that had just enough give to be a man's stomach.

I was so terrorized I couldn't even scream knowing, if it was the saboteur, I was a dead man.

At this same moment, thank God, Chief "Red" Rutherford came in with a flashlight.

I stuttered, "Shine the flashlight over here Red. I think I've got the SOB."

As it turned out my "saboteur" was a rolled up officer's topcoat setting in a corner on top of a sea bag of other clothing.

So ended my first day/night of the war.

We had heard scuttlebutt the next day that the "saboteur" had been shot near the *California*, but who knows for sure. I do know that he spread a lot of fear and apprehension among our crew.

The following day we were in sort of a shocked daze after looking at all the devastation around us.

The overturned *Oklahoma* next to us, the still smoldering *West Virginia* directly astern of the *Okie*, the battered *Tennessee* astern of us and the *California* off our starboard now sitting on bottom.

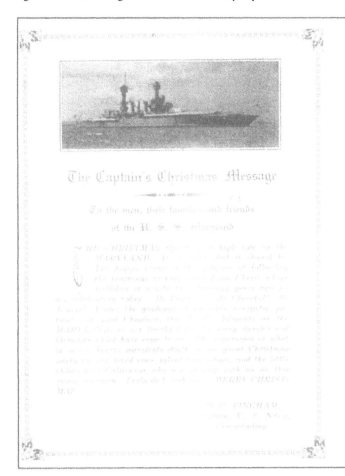

Ford Island on our starboard sat with its burned out hangars and planes. After reading some of the Japanese history of the attack, I'm thankful that Admiral Nagumo didn't listen to Lieutenant Mitsu Fuchida who wanted to launch another air attack on Pearl Harbor as his first attack left lots of targets untouched.

Things aboard until we departed for Bremerton, WA, Navy Yard were uneventful other than cleaning up and having necessary repairs made for sea.

I do know that I never got undressed to sleep until we entered the Straits of Juan De Fuca December 30, always fearful of another air attack, or while at sea, fear of submarines. We didn't really know what to expect after such a dreadful beating December 7.

Preface
The National Archives

Bill O'Dell acquired the copy of the Smooth Deck Log of the USS *Maryland* from the National Archives. It covers the time between 1 November, 1941 and 1 July 1, 1945. It states the position and operation of the *Maryland* with the few exceptions when it was evidently recorded under strict censorship. Also, the dates between 1 August, 1945 and 21 August, 1942 were missing. When the ships location was not listed, it was estimated from the History Book of the USS *Maryland* 1941-1945. Also, this copy has been edited and all pages that had no names or information of interest were eliminated.

The following list is to enable you to make a quick DATE-TIME reference into the Log to find items of interest when you know the approximate time that it happened.

Index to Smooth Log of
The USS *Maryland* (BB-46)
1 November 1941 to 1 July, 1945

(1941)

November 01 at 0744 — Underway for operations off Pearl Harbor, T.H.
" 08 at 1714 — Moored to Pier 5 Pearl Harbor.
" 22 at 0620 — Underway from Pearl Harbor.
" 28 at 1230 — Moored Pier-5 Pearl Harbor.
December 08 at 0658 — 1 man rescued from USS *Oklahoma*.
" 08 at 0642 — Tapping heard from inside the USS *Oklahoma*.
" 08 at 1630 — 7 men rescued from inside USS *Oklahoma*.
" 10 at 1030 — Shifted from Pier-5 to Pier 14 at Pearl Harbor.
" 20 at 1542 — Underway from Pearl Harbor to Bremerton, WA.
" 29 at 1420 — Anchored off Port Orchard, Puget Sound Navy Yard.

(1942)

January 01 — Entered Drydock #4 PHNY.
February 21 at 0833 — Left Drydock #4, Anchored at various Fuel Oil Piers, Ammunition Piers, and then on to Port Townsend, WA. Degaussing Range, ETC.
" 26 at 1426 — Underway from Puget Sound for San Francisco, CA.
March 03 at 1445 — Anchored at San Francisco.
" 27 at 0659 — Underway from San Francisco.
" 31 at 1116 — Moored at San Francisco.
April 14 at 1059 — Underway from San Francisco.
May 10 at 1545 — Anchored at Long Beach, CA.
" 13 at 1100 — Underway from Long Beach.
" 15 at 1148 — Moored at San Francisco.
" 31 at 1013 — Underway from San Francisco. Battle of Midway.
June 19 at 1325 — Anchored at Long Beach.
" 22 at 1145 — Underway from Long Beach.
" 24 at 1127 — Anchored at San Francisco.

July 19 at 1006 — Underway from San Francisco.
" 22 at 1352 — Moored at San Francisco.
August 01 at 1500 — Underway from San Francisco.
" 14 at 1100 — Moored at Pearl Harbor.
September 02 at 0845 — Underway from Pearl Harbor.
USS *Maryland* operated on training exercises off Pearl Harbor until 07 November, 1942
November 08 at 0726 — Underway from Pearl Harbor.
" 12 at xxxx — Crossed the Equator.
" 17 at 1725 — Moored at Fiji Islands. Operated in and out of Fiji Island.
November 27 at 1333 — Moored at Fiji Islands.

(1943)

February—In the middle of the Month—Underway from Fiji Islands to New Hebrides Islands, Havana Harbor, Efate Island.
May, June and July—Remained at Efate Island.
August—Went to Fiji Islands and returned to Aore Harbor Espiritu Santo Island.
" *Maryland* and *Colorado* went to Pearl Harbor and returned six weeks later.
October—Remained at Aore Harbor, Espiritu Santo Island.
November 12—Underway for Tarawa Atoll. First Battle Star.
December 15 at 1410 — Underway from Apamama Island.
" 21 at 0947 — Anchored at San Francisco.
" 29 at 0807 — Underway from San Francisco.
" 30 at 1253 — Anchored at Long Beach.

(1944)

January 01 at 0752 — Underway from Long Beach
" 03 at 1860 — Anchored at Long Beach.
" 13 at 0725 — Underway from Long Beach.
" 21 at 1901 — Anchored at Lahaina Roads, T.H.
" 22 at 1342 — Underway from Lahaina Roads.
" 31 at 0350 — Arrived off Roi Island, Kwajalein Atoll, Marshall Islands. Commenced Bombardment of Roi Island.
February 02 at ???? — Anchored of Roi Island.
" 15 at 1420 — Underway from Roi Island.
" 24 at 0849 — Moored at Pearl Harbor.
" 25 at 1634 — Underway.
March 03 at 1441 — Anchored at Puget Sound Navy Yard, Bremerton, WA.
April 29 at 0834 — Underway.
" 29 at 1535 — Anchored at Port Townsend, WA
" 30 at 2007 — Underway.
May 03 at 1009—Anchored at San Francisco.
" 05 at 1245 — Underway
" 10 at 1934 — Moored at Pearl Harbor.
" 15 at 0811 — Underway.
" 19 at 1732 — Moored at Pearl Harbor.
" 31 at 1636 — Underway.
June 14 at 0545—Commenced Bombardment of Saipan Island.
" 22 at 1334 — Anchored off Saipan Island.
" 22 at 1952 — Torpedoed off Saipan Island.
" 22 at 2007 — Underway.
" 23 at 1650 — TRANS COM BAT DIV FOUR to USS *Saufley* (DD)
" 27 at 1645 — Anchored at Eniwetok Island.
July 01 at 1651—Underway.
" 05 at 1841 — Crossed the International Date Line.
" 10 at 0844 — Moored at Pearl Harbor.
" 11 at 1002 — Entered Drydock #2 at Pearl Harbor.
August 04 at 0910 — Left Drydock #2 and moored at Pearl Harbor.
" 11 at 1900 — Underway for the Degaussing Range.
" 11 at 2014 — Moored at Pearl Harbor.
" 13 at 1258 — Underway.
" 24 at 1540 — Anchored at Purvis Bay, Florida Islands, Solomons Islands.
" 29 at 0523 — Underway.

"	29 at 1500 — Anchored at Purvis Bay.
September 06 at 0842 — Underway.
"	12 at 0535 — D-3 Day, Commenced Bombardment of Pelelieu Islands.
September 12 at 0850 — Plane #2 was hit by Jap firing, Houle, R.C. was wounded. Maintained bombardment all day. Ammunition expended was 170-16", 249-5"/51 and 396-5"/25.
"	13 at 0934 — Commenced bombardment. 1735-Ceased bombardment. Ammunition expended: 148-16", 127-5"/51, and 343-5"/25.
"	14 at 0546 — Commenced bombardment. 1742-Ceased bombardment. Ammunition expended: 165-16", 103-5"/51, and 135-5"/25.
"	15 at 0530 — Commenced bombardment. 1251-Ceased bombardment. Ammunition expended: 331-16", 968-5"/51, and 1070-5"/23.
"	16 at 0704 — Commenced bombardment. 1450-Ceased bombardment. Ammunition expended: 89-5"/51 and 172-5"/25.
"	18——— Spent the day refueling from tanker. Took on a draft of men.
"	19——— Spent the day refueling Destroyers.
"	20——— Lying off Pelelieu Island.
"	21 at 0604— Commenced fire support. 0659 Ceased fire support, Ammunition expended: 24-16". at 1600—Underway for fueling area.
"	22 at 0728— Commenced fueling. 1137-Ceased fueling. Took on 754,000 gals.
"	23 at 0728— Anchored off Palau Island.
"	24——— Loaded ammunition, 649-16", 364-5"/51, and 2700-5"/25.
"	25 at 1514— Underway.
"	28 at 1726— Anchored off Manus Island, Admiralty, Islands.
October	12 at 0741— Underway.
"	17 at 2340— Entered Leyte Gulf, Philippine Islands.
"	19 at 0924— Commenced bombardment. 1556-Ceased bombardment. Ammunition expended: 244-16", 632-5"/51, and 404-5"/25.
"	20 at 0615— Fired on Jap plane, 0701-Commenced bombardment. 0829-Ceased bombardment. Ammo expended: 167-16", 290-5"/51, & 404-5"/25. 2006—Anchored at San Pedro Bay, Leyte Island.
"	21 at 1050— Plane #2 collided with one off the USS *Mississippi*, no injuries.
"	22 at 1845— Shot down a Jap plane.
"	25 at 0359— Opened fire on Jap Task Force in Surigao Straits. 0406—Ceased firing. Jap Ships were sunk or running. 0815—Fired on a Jap plane. 1121-Fired on 3 Jap planes, shot down 1. 1307—USS *Comfort* reported being under attack by Jap planes. 1433—Picked up pilot of F6F from USS *Wasp*—Shot down in Air Raid.
"	28 at 0621— Shot down 1 Jap plane.
"	31——— Underway for Manus Island.
November 03 at 0852 — Anchored at Manus Island.
"	10 at 0610— Underway for Palau Island.
"	13 at 0724—Anchored at Palau Island.
"	14 at 1521— Underway.
"	16 at 0935— Entered Surigao Straits.
"	27 at 1220— Shot down 11 Jap planes, used "wagon wheel" defense. Ammo expended: 365-5"/25, 2215-40mm, and 820-20mm.
"	29 at 1812— Opened fire on Jap plane diving on us. 1813-Plane hit turret #1, Bomb hit between turret #1 and turret #2, Bomb exploded on second deck. Ammo expended: 13-5'/25, 521-40mm, & 818-20mm.
December 02 at 0845 — Underway for Manus Island.
"	06 at 1219— Anchored at Manus Island.
"	09 at 1518— Underway for Pearl Harbor.

"	19 at 0850— Moored at Pearl Harbor.
February 20 at 0757	— Underway on Trial Run, 1829-Anchored at Pearl Harbor.
February —22 to 28	— Operated in and out of Pearl Harbor.
March	04 at 0700— Underway.
"	16 at 1220— Anchored at Ulithi island, West Carolina Islands.
"	21 at 0758— Underway.
"	25 at 1320— Commenced bombardment of Okinawa. 1637—Ceased bombardment. Ammo expended—43-16"
"	26 at 1220— Commenced bombardment. 1600-Ceased firing. Ammo. 116-16".
"	30 ——— All day "Call Fire". Ammo: 36-16", 124-5"/51, 37-5"/25.
"	31 at 1115— Anchored at Kaykio, Kerama Retto fueling and taking on ammo. 1732—Underway—returned to assigned bombardment station.
April	01 at 0652— Commenced bombardment. 1836—Ceased bombardment. Ammo Expended: 148-16", 104-5"/51, and 78-5"/25.
"	02 at 0622— Commenced bombardment. 0805-Plane #2 hit by Jap fire. 1744— Ceased firing. Ammo expended: 74-16" and 338-5"/51.
"	03 at 0243— Shot down 1 Jap plane.
"	05 at 1019— Commenced bombardment. 1825-Ceased bombardment.
"	06 at 0123— Shot down 1 Jap plane. 0859—Commenced bombardment and anti-aircraft firings. 1122—Ceased bombardment. 1643— Shot down 3 Jap planes. 1802—Shot down 1 Jap plane. 1823—Shot down 1 Jap plane. 1825—Ceased firing all batteries.
"	07 at 1207— Anchored at Kerama Rhetto. 1241—Commenced fueling. 1303—Ceased fueling. Took on 194014 gal. 1357—Underway. 1848—Opened fire on 1 Jap plane. 1849-Jap plane crashed on top of turret #3 where bomb went off. 2030—All fires extinguished.
"	08 at 1005— PECR-817 along side to take dead and seriously wounded.
"	09 at 0950— Commenced bombardment. 1019-Plane #2 hit by Jap fire. 1816—Ceased bombardment. Ammo expended: 47-16", & 224-5"/51.
"	10——— All night harassment firing at 5 and 7 minute intervals. Expended 208—5"/25. At 1006—Commenced bombardment. 1259—Ceased firing.
"	12 at 1450— Shot down 1 Jap plane. 1957—Anchored off Okinawa Jima.
"	13 at 0820— Underway. Transferred plane #2 to USS *Biloxi*. 1819—Transferred plane #1 to USS *New Mexico*. 1949—Anchored off Okinawa Jima.
"	14 at 0539— Underway for CONUS.
"	19 at 0709— Anchored at Apra Harbor, Guam.
"	21 at 0652— Underway.
"	27 at 1118— Crossed the International Date Line.
"	30 at 0928— Moored at Pearl Harbor. 1813—Underway.
May 07 at 1332	— Anchored at Puget Sound Navy Yard.
"	08 at 0525— Entered Drydock #2, PSNY.
June 30	——— End of Smooth Deck Log. ———

(Courtesy of Walter J. Mycka)

USS Maryland (BB-46)
Veterans

CLIFFORD P. "CLIFF" ANDERSEN, S1/c, born Sept. 14, 1925, in Salt Lake City, UT. Enlisted in the Navy Feb. 15, 1944.

Attended boot camp in Farragut, ID. Assigned USS *Maryland* April 1944; USS *Lewis* (DE-35) October 1945.

Participated in battles in: Saipan, Tinian, Peleliu, Anguar, Leyte, PI; Surigao Strait, Okinawa. Memorable experiences: torpedoes at Saipan; sea battle at Surigao Strait; hit by kamikaze Nov. 24, 1944, Leyte Gulf; Sea and air battles Okinawa; hit by suicide plane.

Discharged at Okinawa "6B" Div. as S1/c, May 1946. He is authorized to wear six Battle Stars.

Married and has three children, eight grandchildren and five great-grandchildren.

Andersen worked for the railway mail service for 10 years. He resigned and moved to Arizona for his daughters health. He then went to work for G.E. computer department and worked his way up the management team to supervise advanced process engineering. He retired from there after 23 years, the company had been merged with Honeywell before his retirement.

JOHN H. ASHBY, S1/c, born March 16, 1925, in Centertown, KY. Enlisted in the USNR July 16, 1943. Stationed in Great Lakes, USS *Maryland*, 3rd Div. Participated in battles in Tarawa, Kwajalein, Saipan, Palau, Leyte and Okinawa.

Memorable experiences: He was in the gun room when the plane hit on top of turret #3. He was not hurt, only shook up a little. Clean up the next day was bad; lots of body parts.

He was awarded eight stars. Discharged Feb. 26, 1946, as S1/c.

Returned to Kentucky and went to Ohio to work for GM as toolmaker for 35 years. Retired to lake in Kentucky. He has one daughter and two grandchildren. Presently doing very little, fishing, traveling, and doing church work in missions.

FIRMAN J. "JOE GUNS" BALZA, GM1/c, born Sept. 25, 1923, in Humboldt, WI. Enlisted in the Navy January 1941. Served aboard USS *Maryland* April 1941.

April 1944 served on four other ships, a net tender and two APAs and an LST.

Participated in Pearl Harbor Dec. 7, 1941. Midway June 1942; Tarawa September 1943; Kwajalein February 1944.

Memorable experiences was in Bikini for operation "Cross Roads" in 1946.

Awarded American Defense, American Theater, South Pacific Theater and Good Conduct.

Discharged February 1947 as GM1c.

Married to Nathalie and has two daughters and two granddaughters. Worked for 38 years for a utility company. Retired and now involved with EAA.

FRANCIS V. BANKES, SF3/c, born March 17, 1911, in Independence, KS. Enlisted in the USN Dec. 23, 1931. He went through boot camp at San Diego, CA, boarded USS *Maryland* June 9, 1932.

Memorable experiences: when Pacific fleet went the east coast in May 1934 and going through the Panama Canal.

Honorably discharged Dec. 16, 1937, as SF3/c. Married Elizabeth Hulse Sept. 28, 1935. He had a family of five. Employed at Puget Sound Naval Shipyard. He has been retired for the past 30 years.

CARL V. BARNES, Carpenter Mater 3/c, born May 11, 1925, in a rural community of Simms, TX. His parents were share croppers in Simms. He joined the Navy in February 1943 in Amarillo, TX. Was sent to San Diego, CA, for boot camp. After boot camp, he was sent to Treasure Island, CA. From there he was sent to New Caledonia. He was on work details until he was assigned to the USS *Maryland* (BB-46). He came aboard July 1943. Assigned to the 6-"B" Div. After the battle of Tarawa he was transferred to the "R" Div. where he spent the rest of his Navy time. He was assigned to Report Party #2 from Tarawa, to Kwajalein, to Saipan, to Palau, to Leyte, to Leyte Gulf, to Okinawa. He was assigned to Magic Carpet Duty.

Was discharged Nov. 8, 1945, as *carpenter mate 3/c. Returned to Amarillo, TX. Returned to the Santa Fe Railroad and retired after 44 years of service to the Santa Fe Railroad. Barnes has two children.

JAMES H. "PETE" BATCHELLER, Commander, born July 2, 1918, in Mattapoisett, MA. Grad USNA February 1941. Served USS *Maryland* March 1941 to September 1943 "B" Div. J.O.

He served on various ships, stations and staff; CINC PAC Flt and Standing Guard NATO. Participated in battles in Pearl Harbor Dec. 7, 1941.

Memorable experiences include: being commanding officer USS *Huse* (DE-145) in Hunter Killer Group North Atlantic; participation in sinking five German subs.

Batcheller was awarded two Bronze Stars. Retired June 30, 1961, as commander USN. Married and has three children and seven grandchildren.

Employed 27 years as a strock broker and V.P. Retired and traveling all over the world with his wife.

RICHARD W. "DICK" BEAMAN, Y3/c, born Dec. 28, 1923, in Lincoln, NE. Joined the USN March 1943. Went to boot camp at Farragut, ID. Was assigned to the USS *Maryland* September 1943, where he spent the rest of his Navy time working in the Engineering Department Log room.

While on board the USS *Maryland,* was involved in seven major combat operations. He was one of the remaining crew to stay on board for the "Magic Carpet" duty bringing troops home after Japan surrendered. He

was discharged from the Navy in April 1946 and returned to his home in Lincoln, NE and worked with his father in the heating and air conditioning business for 15 years.

He moved to Watsonville, CA in 1961 and retired from GTE Sylvania in 1982. He is an officer of the USS *Maryland* (BB-46) National Veteran's Association. He has been very active in Lions Club International, having served as a District Governor in 1982-1983. He married Annie Jeanette Sims in Berkeley, CA in April 1946. They have two sons and four grandchildren.

ROBERT G. "BECKY" BECKSTRAND, RM3/c, born Jan. 12, 1925, in Rockford, IL. Drafted July 1943, chose Navy, and was sent to Farragut, ID for boot camp and radio school. Was assigned to USS *Maryland* in July 1944, spent "watch" time in Radio Central copying Morse Code, battle station in Main Battery Firing Room (spotter's circuit).

During his time aboard ship, the *Maryland* was involved in the invasions of Palau, Leyte and Okinawa, and in the naval battle of Surigao Strait. Remained crewmember until April 1946, when he was discharged.

In 1950 he graduated from Oberlin College in OH and in 1953 from Luther Theological Seminary. Married in 1950 Dorothy Wade (of Elmira, NY). They have four children and eight grandchildren and now live in Stoughton, WI.

He has served as pastor of Lutheran congregations in Iowa, Minnesota and Wisconsin (ELCA). He is retired now but helping a nearby congregation two days a week.

ROBERT E. BELLOWS, S2/c, born Sept. 2, 1927, in South Milwaukee, WI, May 1945. Served in the Navy as S2/c, 4th Div. Attended boot camp in Great Lakes, USS *Maryland*.

Stationed in Pearl Harbor, Magic Carpet, service between Hawaii and U.S. Mainland.

Discharged July 19, 1946. Married Sept. 3, 1949. He has four children including oldest son a present, 23 year Navy veteran. Employed 25 years as city of Milwaukee policeman. Retired and enjoying his three grandsons and his R.V. with his wife.

ANGELO "TONY" HENRICO BELOTTI, born Nov. 7, 1919, Bigelow, AR. From November

1938-February 1939, in recruit training, rate AS, USN Training Station, Norfolk, VA; February 1939-July 1943, aboard USS *Maryland* (BB-46), rates from AS to shipfitter 1/c; Battle Station: Repair Four. Belotti is a Pearl Harbor survivor.

From July-September 1943, Treasure Island, CA, for new assignment; September 1943-December 1944, aboard USS *Carter Hall* (LSD-3), rates shipfitter 1/c to chief shipfitter, starboard repair party; December 1944-February 1945, in transit to USS *Titania* (AKA-13) and served aboard from February-July 1945, chief shipfitter after repair party; July 1945-January 1946 in transit to FLTSERVSCOLS, USN Repair Base, San Diego, CA, rate chief shipfitter to warrant carpenter, Welding School.

From January 1946-July 1946, aboard USS *Iowa* (BB-61), rank warrant carpenter, ship's carpenter; July-August 1946, in transit to New Orleans, LA, for discharge. His awards include the Good Conduct Medal, American Defense Service Medal w/Fleet East, American Campaign Medal, Asiatic-Pacific Campaign Medal, WWII Victory Medal, Navy Occupation Medal, Europe Asia Clasp, Philippine Liberation Ribbon and Pearl Harbor Commemorative Medal. He was discharged Aug. 18, 1946.

Married in 1945 and died March 26, 1989. Belotti is buried in National Cemetery, Little Rock, AR. He is survived by one son and one granddaughter.

DONALD H. "BLIMP" BLIMLING, 1/2/c,
was born Jan. 13, 1925, in Woodson, IL. He went to boot camp at Farragut, IN, Camp Walden, Co. 183, and assigned to the USS *Maryland*, May 22, 1944, in executive office. He started out preparing and distributing morning orders throughout the ship by order of Commander Goldman. He was moved to liberty cards, then to records, captain's mast and other office duties. During battle he was assigned to fire control and helping to batten down the hatches.

At Okinawa he clearly remembers, being with another shipmate closing the hatch when a Japanese plane hit turret #3. He could see the Kamakazi pilot's smiling face before the hit. He managed to get back to the base of #3 turret when the plane and bomb exploded. The Lord was surely looking out for him because he was not hit. Only one shipmate came down off the #3 turret alive. A suicide plane also hit the USS *Maryland* in the Philippines, where Voyles, a buddy was killed. He was also at Marianas Islands, Peleliu and Surigao Strait.

He was married May 20, 1945, while home on 30-day leave. He has two sons, two daughters and nine grandchildren. Discharged March 1945.

Blimling has been employed by the State of Illinois, Anderson Clayton Foods and was elected county commissioner for eight years. He is now engaged in farming.

JOHN W. BOSSERT JR., lieutenant commander,
born July 30, 1918, Baltimore, MD. Enlisted Baltimore Oct. 7, 1937. After boot camp and Woodworking Service School at Norfolk was assigned to USS *Maryland's* R Div. and reported aboard Sept. 28, 1938. Was at Pearl Harbor. After attack assisted in removal of trapped sailors from capsized USS *Oklahoma*. He was promoted to warrant carpenter and was transferred from USS *Maryland* Sept. 30, 1943. Last sea duty was chief engineer of USS *Neosho* (AO-143). He retired March 1, 1958, as a lieutenant commander.

During his naval career he served aboard nine ships and held various short duty positions including Bureau of Ships where he worked on ammunition loading and fuel transfer problems.

His awarded campaign ribbons were American Defense, Pacific Theater w/5 stars (Pearl Harbor, Palau, Saipan/Tinian, Iwo Jima and Okinawa); American Theatre; Navy Occupation; World War II Victory; Good Conduct.

He and his wife, Teresa, now reside in Cape Leonard, MD, in a house he built himself. He has three children, four grandchildren and two great-grandchildren.

ARTHUR R. BOWDON, OD, lieutenant (S.G.),
born March 23, 1917, in Margaret, AL. Enlisted USN March 15, 1942 (V7 Program). On active duty June 1943. Went to Midshipman School at Columbia University and Optical Maintenance School at Mare Island, CA. Commissioned ensign in October 1943 and assigned to USS *Maryland* January 1944 as optical maintenance officer anti-aircraft gunnery officer on 40mm and 5" guns. Participated in seven major combat operations.

Awarded Philippine Liberation Ribbon, two stars, Asiatic-Pacific Theater Ribbon, six Stars, American Theater Ribbon, World War II Victory Ribbon.

Discharged March 1946 as lieutenant (S.G) and returned to University of California. Graduated as Doctor of Optometry. Was in private practice in Santa Rosa, CA until retirement in 1982. Now living in San Rafael, CA enjoying retirement, travel and woodturning. Married, four daughters, four grandchildren.

DALLAS JEFFERSON "JEFF" BRACKIN, MM1/c,
born July 30, 1919, in Merryville, LA. Enlisted March 20, 1940, in Beallmont, TX.

Served in USN, USS *Maryland* as seaman to MM1/c, A Div.; San Diego Training Station, Maryland 1940 to October 1943; GMC ADV Diesel School, Ohio-SCTC Miami - ATA-187, November 1944 to January 1946.

Participated in Pearl Harbor battle Dec. 7, 1941, and Midway (Temp. to USS *Solace* for surgery); USS *Maryland*; Okinawa; ATA-187.

Memorable experiences: USS *Maryland* December 7 Pearl Harbor; learning diesel engines, which was

his lifetime career; Kamikazes of Okinawa; end of the war and realizing it was over.

Awarded American Freedom, Asia, PAC, Good Conduct, Pearl Harbor December 7.

Discharged March 21, 1946 as chief MM and C. MO, MM.

Brackin is married and has one daughter, three grandchildren and one great-grandchild. He was employed with Sun Oil Company and retired after 36 years. He now enjoys playing golf.

RICHARD M. BRAEUTIGAM,
born April 27, 1920, Fredericksburg, TX. Joined the Navy July 9, 1937. Reported aboard USS *Maryland*, navy yard, Bremerton, WA. Served his first enlistment on *Maryland* 1937-1941.

After 1937, six more classmates from Fredericksburg, TX reported aboard the *Maryland*, 1938-1940: Lou Wahrmund, Rudy Kiehne, John Land, Bill Bierschwale, Francis Walch and George Grobe.

Received seven medals plus many battle stars, WWII and Korean Conflict.

Served on six ships: USS *Lassen* (AE-5), *Guadalupe* (AO-32), *Shipley Bay* (CVE-85); *Kleinsmith* (APD-134), *Okahogen Appazo*, *Boxer* (CVA-21), NTC, MSTS WESTPAC.

Retired from the Navy 1937-1958 after 21 years. Retired aircraft supervisor, 1959-1982.

Married 50 years plus to Jennie B. from South Boston, MA. They have three children, seven grandchildren and 12 great-grandchildren.

RALPH W. BRIGHT, EM1/c,
born Nov. 26, 1922, at Glennbrook, OR. He enlisted in the Navy at 6 p.m. on Dec. 7, 1941, was sworn-in on Dec. 10, 1941, and shipped out to San Diego, CA, where he was issued uniforms and trained before boarding the *Maryland* in Bremerton, WA, 27 days later.

He participated in seven battle campaigns across the Pacific to Okinawa. He was discharged an electrician's mate first class on Oct. 9, 1945, and graduated in journalism from the University of Oregon in 1948. He married Genevieve Caughren, of Havre, MT, the same year.

In addition to the newspapers and printing, he worked in marketing and personnel relations. His last tour of duty was specializing in healthcare and pensions of employees before retiring in 1986.

WILLARD A. "WILLIE" BRUCE, RM3/c,
born Nov. 20, 1925, in Glasgow, MT. Joined Navy September 1943. Went to boot camp, Farragut, ID. Went to NTS (Radio) School Farragut, ID. He was then assigned to USS *Maryland*. Duty aboard ship was CR Div. (Communications-Radio). While on board the USS *Maryland* was involved in five major combat operations. He was one of the remaining crew on board for the "Magic Carpet" duty bringing troops and Air Force personnel home after Japan surrendered. He

was discharged from the Navy April 5, 1946, at PSC USNB-Bremerton, WA. He went home to Glasgow, MT, where he owned and operated a dry cleaning and laundry business. He also managed an aviation research center for Boeing Commercial Aircraft Company. He

also was a consultant for Boeing when he retired in June of 1994.

He is active in several civic organizations, American Legion Veterans of Foreign Wars. Past commander VFW.

Bruce is married and has three daughters and four sons and 12 grandchildren. One son is a commissioned officer in USN.

THOMAS EUGENE BUNTING, F1/c, born
March 22, 1922, in Niles, CA. Enlisted USNR March 30, 1942.

Attended boot camp, San Diego, CA. Outside repair shop. Military locations include Treasure Island, SF, California, USS *Maryland* (BB-46). Participated in Okinawan Campaign. Discharged Treasure Island, CA.

Memorable experiences: during heavy smoke periods while off Naha they rigged paper cup and string telephone in lower after space. Now enjoying the good life.

Awarded American Theater Medal, Asiatic-Pacific and Good Conduct.

Discharged Oct. 5, 1945, as F1/c. Married March 7, 1947, (49 years) and has three sons, seven grandchildren and two great-grandchildren.

Employed as Alameda County Sheriff's Deputy, California, 1948-1973. Retired and resides on five acre farm and commercial fishing.

EDWARD LYLE CARNEY, SKD3/c, born
Nov. 7, 1907, in Washing, IA (Washington). Enlisted October 1943 in Navy, SKD3, Supply Div.

Stationed in San Diego, CA; Pier 91, Seattle, WA.

Participated in battles after he went aboard December 1943 until hit in Leyte Gulf and they returned to Bremerton.

Memorable experience: Left *Maryland* in Bremerton, 30 days leave. Assigned to destroyer tender, and on it until war ended. SKD frozen so sent to Pier 91 disb. office. Discharged because of age.

Discharged December 1945.

Married. Retired (88 years old). Sold insurance and real estate.

GLENN H. CONNER, SMC, born April 27,
1921, in Ionia Co., MI. Graduated from Lowell High School in 1938. Enlisted in the USN on Sept. 24, 1940. Boot training in Great Lakes, IL, Co. #79. Assigned to the USS *West Virginia* (BB-38) at Bremerton Naval Shipyards, Bremerton, WA. From Bremerton to Hunter's Point, CA, taking on ammunition and proceeding to Long Beach, Home Port, and Pearl Harbor, HI.

First assignment was Deck Force, learning the fundamentals of seamanship and all phases of communication. Assigned as signal striker, was transferred to combat ships as a flag signalman under Adm. Anderson and Capt. Carter, Chief of Staff. Prior to Dec. 7, 1941, combat ships and flag complement was transferred to the USS Mary*land* (BB-46). After reaching Pearl Harbor, the USS *Maryland* joined the fleet and participated in annual fleet maneuvers off Pearl Harbor. Saturday, December 6, was the annual ship and personnel inspection by the Pacific Fleet Commander.

Sunday morning, December 7, he awoke to reveille and planned to attend Church services on the USS *Oklahoma* (BB-37), tied up alongside his ship, the USS *Maryland*. He heard gunfire, 5" 25 caliber, going off thinking it was part of the inspection. It was interrupted by GQ: Man your battle stations! We are being attacked by foreign aircraft (they didn't say "Japs") with a Red Sun on them!

His General Quarters Station was on the Signal Bridge. He had to work his way up to the Bridge, through all the hatches which had been dogged down, and then closed from behind him as he went. Arriving on the Signal Bridge, Capt. Carter (Chief of Staff combat ships flag) gave him a message to send to the USS Ca*lifornia* (BB-44) regardless of the dangers. The message was sent by semaphore as the halyards to flag hoist were shot away! His 12" signal search light burned out, he called on the 24" carbon light, gave semaphore and sent the message. As they were being strafed by enemy aircraft, Capt. Carter issued order to SEEK COVER! Conner can still remember, even to this day, Capt. Carter's exact words as he shook his fist at the enemy, "You have won the first round, but there will be many more round to come!" This has never left his mind and how right he was in his prediction.

The USS Okla*homa* (BB-37) had capsized, several sailors could hear S.O.S. being tapped out on the bottom of the ship. Officer of Deck was notified and that started the procedure for rescue. They started to cut through with torches but to no avail due to the flammable material. The concern was for the men they were trying to rescue those within. The decision was made to use a pneumatic hammer to cut through the double hulled bottom to rescue those within. They watched from the Signal Bridge of the USS *Maryland* as approximately 32 survivors were taken aboard. The first thing most of them asked for "Give me a cigarette", and a breath of fresh air after being confined in their tomb for more than 28 hours. They were rescued on December 8 at 11:00 a.m.

Connor remained in Pearl Harbor until repairs had been made to damage from two bomb hits. He left Pearl Harbor with three destroyers for escort and proceeded to Bremerton, WA, for a complete modification and new armament.

Combat ships were transferred at San Francisco to new ship USS *North Carolina* (BB-55) until he was transferred to the new USS *Oglala* (CM-4). The USS *Oglala* (CM-4) was sunk at Pearl Harbor, raised and made into the small craft repair ship at Long Beach Shipyards. He proceeded to Hollandia, New Guinea, where he was transferred to the USS *Wasatch* (AGC-8) Communication ship as a flag signal of the 7th Fleet Flag under Adm. Kinkaid. After the capture of the Philippines, he was transferred to Seattle Naval Hospital, then to Great Lakes Hospital and, after treatment, was transferred to USS Sab*le* Aircraft Carrier on Lake Michigan at Chicago Outer Harbor.

When the USS *Wolverine* and USS *Sable* were decommissioned, he was assigned to NROTC, Purdue University, Lafayette, IN, teaching communications to NROTC trainees.

Enlistment completed, he was separated from naval service on Nov. 18, 1946. He joined USNR and was recalled to active duty on Aug. 12, 1950. He assigned as chief-in-charge USNR and MCRTC Grand Rapids, MI, until 1953. He was transferred to USS *J.C. Owens* (DD-776) and then discharged to inactive duty until recalled to NROTC recruiting at Lansing, MI for

three tours of active duty. Discharged from USNR in November 1967.

Awarded received on active duty include: World War II Victory Ribbon, American Defense w/Fleet Clasp, American Area Ribbon w/Star, Asiatic-Pacific Area Ribbon w/3 Stars, Philippine Liberation Ribbon w/2 stars, Good Conduct Ribbon w/star and the Congressional Pearl Harbor Medal.

Married on Oct. 16, 1943, he was blessed with two sons and one daughter who gave him seven grandchildren and 11 great-grandchildren. His post naval service included employment by the Michigan State Police in Lansing from which he retired in 1980. He currently resides in Chestertown, MD, in the summer and Spring Hill, FL, in the winter. What is he doing today? Taking it easy and staying around as long as the good Lord will let him.

M.J. "MIKE" COTTER, born June 14, 1923, in
Big Spring, TX. Enlisted in USN at Clovis, NM, March 1941. Trained at NTS, San Diego. Boarded the *Maryland* in May 1941 and served on *Maryland* until discharged in July 1946. Was involved in all major combat operations the *Maryland* was involved in during WWII.

He moved to Littlefield, TX, in 1946 and worked for GTE 31 years and a rural telephone company for eight years, most of this time as a C.O. equipment technician. He retired in 1986 after serving at various locations in Texas and New Mexico.

He was active for about 20 years as a volunteer in scouting and youth baseball and 15 years as a volunteer fireman.

Cotter is married and has one son, one daughter and four grandchildren. He and his wife, Nell, spend time as available in their R.V. He is a member of PHSA, VFW and Maryland Vets Association.

CARL E. CURREY, FC1/c, born Sept. 15, 1918,
in Claudell, KS. Enlisted in the Navy Jan. 17, 1939, serving as firecontrolman "F" Div.

Stationed USNTC Great Lakes, IL, USS *Maryland*, USS *Colorado*, USS *Aucilla* (AO-56).

Participated in battles in Pearl Harbor, Philippine Liberation, Okinawa and Iwo Jima.

Memorable experiences include good ship and crew.

Awarded the American Defense, American Campaign, Asiatic-Pacific, European Theater. Discharged Sept. 26, 1945 as FC1/c.

His wife is deceased and he has two daughters. Employed as salesman and now retired in Greeley, CO.

OWEN DANLEY, born Aug. 19, 1923, in Washita,
AR. Enlisted in Navy May 7, 1943, serving as laundryman third class, S Div.

Stationed in San Diego, CA; USS *Maryland*. Participated in battles in: Tarawa, Kwajalein, Roi

Islands, Saipan, Peleliu, and Anguar Island, Leyte, Sea Battle Surigao Strait, Okinawa.

Memorable experience: surgery for service connected injury at Bremerton Navy Hospital on V-J Day. Recuperated at Sun Valley, ID and mustered out at New Orleans.

Married to Laylene May 24, 1953. Employed with Amoco Oil Co. P.P.L. for 34 years. He is now retired.

JUSTIN J. DAVID, S1/c, born April 28, 1925, Lakeland, LA. Volunteered in Navy Feb. 7, 1943, at Jackson, MS. Boot camp training was in Company 43-52 at San Diego, CA. He was assigned to the Mar*yland* on July 21, 1943, and served in the 6AL division during his entire time on board.

He served on the *Maryland* during all of her major battles. He was wounded at Okinawa when a kamikaze plane struck the *Maryland* on April 7, 1945. His battle station was as a gunner on one of four 20mm guns on top of main battery turret #3. There were a total of 18 men on this turret top, and when the plane struck the turret its bomb exploded and he was the only one left alive.

After being treated in various Navy hospitals he was discharged at USN hospital, New Orleans, LA, on Nov. 14, 1945. He attended Ole Miss and graduated from its law school in June 1952. Most of his working years were as an attorney with the Veterans Administration, from which he was retired in September 1983. He and his wife Annette have five children and live in Shreveport, LA.

MARK ELDRIDE DE LONG, CWO3, born Aug. 26, 1912, in Jeffers, MN. USN CHCARP 8-46. Enlisted Dec. 21, 1934, as S2/c, San Francisco, CA. Honorably discharged Aug. 10, 1940, San Francisco, CA.

Enlisted Jan. 15, 1942, Bremerton, WA. Retired June 3, 1952, San Francisco, CA, medical retirement, CWO3.

Participated in Asiatic-Pacific battles. Memorable experience includes being a Pearl Harbor Survivor. Division officer USS Maryland, USS Manchester and others.

Awarded Good Conduct w/3 stars, Area Medal, WWII Victory Medal, Occupation Service Ribbon, American Defense Medal w/Fleet Clasp, American Area Medal, Asiatic-Pacific.

Married to Erika V. De Long MD April 12, 1952. They have daughter Joanne, Tacoma, WA, who has two children, three grandchildren; daughter, Ruth, Boulder, CO, two children, stockbroker.

De Long attended San Francisco College, 1952-1953. Employed in real estate and insurance broker 1952-1955. Traveled in Europe 1955-1957; NASA 1959 to 1969, retired. Bred and raced horses, 1969 to 1996. He died May 15, 1996 and is buried in Sunset Memorial Park - No. Olmsted, OH.

EUGENE L. DESSERT, Captain, USNR, (Ret.), born May 18, 1914, in Tekoa, WN. Enlisted in the USN April 10, 1940. Served in the Boiler Div. as apprentice seaman without pay.

Attended First Class 1940 Midshipmen's School, Northwestern University, Chicago. Reported December 1040, USS *Maryland* as ensign; engineer, Boiler Div. Left USS *Maryland* April 1943.

The *Maryland* went to Bremerton for repairs and then to South Pacific, Efate, Fiji. It participated in no battles.

Memorable experiences include witnessing the frightful devastation of Pearl Harbor, being below decks and not knowing exactly what was going on.

Awarded the World War II Victory Medal, Asiatic-Pacific w/2 stars, American Theater, American Defense w/star.

Discharged January 1946 as lieutenant commander. Married and has two stepchildren, one granddaughter. Employed with Standard Oil, Kaiser Aluminum; 29 years Lockheed Space Division, Sunnyvale, CO, managerial positions in personnel/finance. He died Oct. 15, 1996.

LAWRENCE "LARRY" EUGENE DIBB, CM1/c, born Dec. 5, 1923, in San Diego, CA. Joined USNR September 1941. He was called to boot camp, San Diego Naval Training Station, CA Dec. 8, 1941. Assigned to USS *Maryland* January 1942, R Div. His battle station was damage control, fire & rescue and diving repair. He left the *Maryland* after seven major engagements May 1945. Discharged October 1945 at Camp Elliott, San Diego, CA.

Received Commendation w/Combat Distinguishing Device, Good Conduct, American Campaign, Asiatic-Pacific w/7 stars, World War II Victory Medal, Philippine Liberation w/2 stars and Philippine Presidential Unit Citation.

Married in August 1945. He has two sons, one daughter and six grandchildren. Retired from automotive business after 45 years and professional dog handler and kennel owner after 30 years.

FREDERICK "FRED" W. EGGER, F1/c, born Oct. 11, 1926, at Amazonia, MO. Joined the USNR Nov. 1944 at Portland, OR. Went to boot camp in Farragut, ID and to BE School at Great Lakes, IL. He was assigned to "M" Div. of the USS *Maryland* June 1945 while she was in drydock in Bremerton, WA. Stood watches in main drive engine room after the USS *Maryland* returned to sea duty and took part in the "Magic Carpet" runs.

Was discharged in Bremerton, WA, in July 1946 and returned to Oregon where he worked in sawmills and construction for several years. After graduating from Oregon State in 1959 he and wife Elaine moved to Hawaii in 1960 where he worked as a civilian engineer at Pearl Harbor until returning to Oregon in 1975.

He retired from Bonneville Power Administration's engineering staff in 1987 and now lives on a small acreage near Canby, OR, and along with his wife enjoys traveling in their fifth wheel trailer.

ARTHUR ERESMAN, MUS1/c, born Feb. 22, 1922, in Cleveland, OH. Enlisted November 1942. Served with the USNR. Attended boot camp at Great Lakes, IL; Bremerton Navy Yard band; USS *Maryland.*

Participated in battles in Marianas, Palau, Leyte invasion, Battle of Surigao Straits, Okinawa.

Memorable experience includes composing a march honoring Capt. J.D. Wilson and making a presentation on the quarter deck late 1945.

Awarded Asiatic-Pacific w/4 stars, Good Conduct Medal.

Discharged January 1946 as Mus1/c. He has one son and one daughter. Retired school band director; symphony orchestra member (clarinet). Hobbies include, cycling, darkroom photography and astronomy.

LLOYD V. ERION, born in Hillsboro, OR, May 11, 1919. He enlisted in the USMC in February 1940 and went to boot camp in San Diego. He was assigned to the 7th Div. of Marines on the USS *Maryland* in May 1940.

He participated in the defense of Pearl Harbor on Dec. 7, 1941. He was transferred to the 3rd Marine Div. in October 1943 and landed in Empress Augusta Bay, Bougainville in November 1943, and also participated in the initial landing and capture of Guam on July 21, 1944.

Erion was discharged with the rank of sergeant in January 1945 at San Diego. His most memorable time in the Corps was at Pearl Harbor. Retired frm Merck, Sharp and Dohme in 1984 after 29 years of employment.

He is married, has two sons and six grandchildren. He serves as a volunteer for the National Park Service. His hobbies include ice skating and painting. He lives in South San Francisco, CA.

CHARLES LINDBERGH FLORIDA, S1/c, born June 26, 1927, in Praco, AL. Enlisted Sept. 27, 1945, USN, S1c, SS. NTS San Diego, CA. He served on the USS *Maryland* (BB-46).

Memorable experiences: just the honor of having served on the USS *Maryland.*

Discharged July 20, 1946 as S1c. Married Pearl Dennis June 1, 1956. He has four children (three boys and one girl), seven grandchildren.

Employed as teacher, junior high English; elementary school principal; high school principal; CEO Regional Education Service Agency, NW Georgia. Retired (AB/BS Jacksonville St. U; MA and EdD University of Alabama.

ANTHONY FONTECCHIO, born Nov. 9, 1919, Iron Mountain, MI. Enlisted Dec. 13, 1939, USN as

CMM. Stationed on USS *Maryland*, USS *Arcadia*, Korean War.

Stationed at Pearl Harbor Dec. 7, 1941, Pacific Fleet. Participated in eight major combats (Marshall Islands, Tarawa, Okinawa.

Memorable experiences: stationed on USS *Maryland* when Japan bombed Pearl Harbor.

Awarded Asiatic-Pacific Ribbon w/8 stars, Philippine Liberation w/2 stars, American Defense w/star, American Theater and Pearl Harbor Commemorative.

Returned to Iron Mountain, MI. Worked at veterans hospital for 27 years as assistant engineer. Married and has one son and one daughter and four granddaughters. Fontechhio died Sept. 9, 1991.

HOWARD J. "FRENCHY" FREYOU SR., S1/c,
born Jan. 23, 1925, in New Iberia, LA. Enlisted USN July 1943 as S1/c, 5th Div. Stationed in San Diego, CA and Okinawa.

Participated in six invasions and two sea battles: Kwajalein, Tarawa, Okinawa, Leyte, Saipan, Palau, Guam, and Philippine Islands.

Memorable experiences: Transferred off of the BB-46 stationed in Okinawa for the occupation of Japan where he spent 5 1/2 months. Went through a typhoon that pushed liberty ships on the beach. Three days later five tons of dynamite blew up on the island. Hit by two suicide planes on the Philippine Islands and Okinawa and one torpedo in Saipan.

Awarded eight battle stars. Discharged Dec. 20, 1945.

Married to Beatrice Boutte Freyou, four children: Howard Jr., Maryland, Donna and Dean; six grandchildren and one great-grandchild. Farmer and school bus driver. Retired and enjoys spending time with wife, family and friends.

HARRY "GABE" GABRIELSON, Radioman 3/c CR,
born in Milwaukee, WI, enlisted in the USN Dec. 27, 1941, and reported to boot camp in San Diego, CA. Participated in seven major battles before being discharged Dec. 6, 1945.

Married and has two sons, one daughter and two step-daughters. On Dec. 16, 1992, his wife was hit 200 feet from their home by a speeding car driven by a youth under the influence. Gabe is confined to a

wheelchair as a result of a car accident that broke his back 20 years ago but is still able to drive a car.

Army ATS crew member for the Bureau of Narcotics and Western Electric Telephone Company employee before retiring in Ventura, CA.

PAUL F. GALLAGHER,
born Sept. 13, 1918, in San Francisco, CA. Joined the USN, August 1939. Went to boot camp in San Diego, CA. Reported aboard the USS *Maryland* in October 1939. He is a survivor of the Japanese attack on Pearl Harbor and was a radioman third class at that time. Also served at the USN operating base in Londonderry, Northern Ireland and at the USN Command Headquarters, European Theater of Operations in London, England. Discharged as a chief radioman in August 1945. Entered civil service with the city and county of San Francisco.

Retired in June 1978. He is very active with the Pearl Harbor Survivors Association. He is a widower with three daughters and six grandchildren. His most memorable experience was meeting the King and Queen of England during their war time visit to Leith docks, Edinborough, Scotland, where they inspected the first group of USN personnel to arrive in Scotland in 1942.

CARLUS HENRY GIBSON, S2/c,
6 AL Div., born June 23, 1924, Flippin, AR. He was drafted in October 1943 and went to boot camp in San Diego, CA. He awaited orders at Shoemaker, CA, and boarded the USS *Maryland* on Dec. 24, 1943, serving as sky lookout in Main Mast.

He was aboard the *Maryland* during seven invasions and one sea battle when Jap fleet was met and defeated in the Surigao Strait. He made many friends in Tacoma, Bremerton, San Francisco and Pearl Harbor when ship was in for repairs. He was in "Magic Carpet" crew that brought troops home from South Pacific after Japan's surrender.

Discharged Dec. 11, 1945, he held various jobs, including tugboat captain before becoming machinist. He retired from Cameron Iron Works in 1984 and lives near Houston at Conroe, TX in the country home he built himself. Married since 1953, he has two sons, two daughters and six grandchildren. He organized neighborhood watch and served as its president for 10 years. Member of Baptist Church, Masonic Lodge, VFW.

RAYMOND G. GLUMACK SR., Captain,
born in Marble, MN on Jan. 24, 1918. He was accepted into the Naval Aviation AVCAD program in April 1940 and assigned to NAS Pensacola for flight training. He graduated in May of 1941 as a naval aviator and was commissioned ensign USNR in May of 1941. He was assigned to Observation Sqdn. 4, USS *Maryland*.

After the Pearl Harbor damage to the ship was repaired, *Maryland* returned to the Pacific fleet to assume aggressive wartime actions against the Japa-

nese. The combat operations took place throughout a vast area of South Pacific, and it's many islands. The flight operations became very demanding, and the operational hazards were of greater concern to the aviators than the Japanese. Those were difficult, but, very exciting days, month after month.

In March of 1943, Lt. Glumack (now promoted) was detached from M*aryland* at Habana Harbor, Villa, New Hebrides, and ordered to shore duty at NAS Alameda as commanding officer, Scout Observation Service Unit 3. He retired from the Navy in April 1963 with the rank of captain.

Glumack says that "operating seaplanes from battleships and cruisers is the most difficult and demanding flying the Navy had to offer. I loved the M*aryland*. It was a great ship, and I am proud to have served on her decks."

J.C. GORDON, S1/c,
born in Wayne Co., TN, July 14, 1920. Enlisted in the USNR July 14, 1943. Served as seaman first class Div. 6B. Stationed on USS *Maryland* South Pacific. Received basic training in San Diego, CA.

Participated in battles in Okinawa, Tarawa, Kwajalein, Saipan, Palau and Leyte.

Discharged Nov. 11, 1945, as seaman first class. He has two daughters, three sons, 10 grandchildren and one great-grandchild.

Employed as fire fighter with Milan Army Ammunition Plant. Retired and member of masonic lodge.

RAYMOND L. GORDON, Y3/c,
born July 28, 1925, Inglewood, CA. Joined the Navy July 27, 1943. Received his boot camp training at the SDNTC, CA. He went aboard the USS *Maryland* (BB-46) Oct. 18, 1943. He was first assigned to the 5th Div. and about a year later transferred to the captain office obtained the rank of Y3c. On May 13, 1946, he was transferred to the commander Columbia Sup Group 19th Fleet Portland, OR. He was there until he was discharged from the Navy in Long Beach, CA on July 23, 1946.

When he returned home he worked for the Chevron Oil for five years, farmed for two years, with Xerox for 27 years and with Phillip Morris for ten years and then retired. My retirement years main project is tracing family history.

Married for 45 years, had six children and seven grandchildren.

WILLIAM "BILL" JAMES HALIGAS, born May 2, 1926, in Elgin, IL. Joined the Navy at Denver, CO December 1943. Assigned to naval training station at Farragut, ID. He was assigned to the 4th Div. His battle station was in the lower powder handling room of turret #4.

Major battles included Saipan, in the Marianas Islands; Peleliu, in the Palau Islands; the Battle of Leyte Gulf in the Philippines; the sea battle with the Japanese fleet in Surigao Strait and the Battle of Okinawa. The ship was damaged by a torpedo, two bombs and two kamikaze suicide planes while he was aboard.

Immediately after the Japanese surrender he was assigned occupational duty on Okinawa where he spent six months. He was discharged on April Fools Day 1946 and returned to Denver where he met and married his wife Betty. They have two daughters, one son, seven grandsons and one granddaughter.

At this writing he is still involved in the dry wall distribution business along with his son and son-in-law. He started the first exclusive dry wall distribution business in America in 1959.

ROBERT T. HALLEY, EM2/c, born May 10, 1925. Enlisted Feb. 13, 1942, in USN. Served in E Div., USS *Maryland.* Attended boot camp, Great Lakes, MM School.

Participated in seven major combat operations. Memorable experiences: after the war, attended Gyro School, had duty after in China, Pago Pago, including ships company on LST-219 - Tugs and dry docks. Took part in A-Bomb Test.

Discharged Dec. 7, 1947 as EM2/c. He lived in Ohio and had five daughters, one son and four grandchildren. Moved to Shreveport 1976. Employed in sales for Honeywell Inc. Retired in 1993.

JOHN HALVIS, PhM2/c, born July 17, 1925 in Greece. Enlisted September 1943, USNR as PhM2/c with H Div.

Attended boot camp at Great Lakes, New Orleans Naval Hospital; Whiting Field, NAS; Base #8 Naval Hospital Pearl Harbor; USS *Maryland*. Participated in battle of Okinawa.

Memorable experiences: becoming member of crew of USS *Maryland* and meeting many fine people during his time on board. Being involved in "Magic Carpet" duty.

Discharged April 1946. Married and has three children and two grandchildren. Retired as lab technician from Copperweld Steel Co. Now enjoying retirement and traveling. Resides in Warren, OH.

H.R. "BUD" HANLY, COX, born March 22, 1918. Enlisted in the service Dec. 15, 1941. Served with 6B Div. Stationed at San Diego, Treasure Island.

Participated in battles in Gilbert Island, Marshall Island, Okinawa, Marianas, Caroline Island and Leyte.

Discharged Oct. 20, 1945 as cox. Married and has three daughters and four grandchildren. Hanly was self-employed. Retired and resides in Calistoga, CA.

THOMAS EARL HANNON, MM2/c, born Dec. 29, 1909, in Tacoma, WA. Enlisted July 7, 1930 in Navy as machinist mate II-C, A Div.

Stationed in San Diego, CA. Attended Machinist School, Hampton Roads, VA. Assigned USS *Maryland* July 1931. Left ship June 26, 1936 (discharged date).

Awarded Good Conduct Medal. Discharged June 26, 1936. Married March 18, 1933, and has two sons. Widowed Aug. 8, 1988. Employed as tool and die worker at Boeing. During war, grocery store/restaurant owner. Retired for 25 years and is now blind but still lives on his own.

BOB H. HANSEN, GM2/c, born Oct. 29, 1923, in Denver, CO. Enlisted March 27, 1941. Served as gunner's mate third class, 3rd Div.

Stationed on the USS *Maryland,* USS *Antigua* ammo ship, USS *Samuel Chase.*

Discharged March 1946 as gunners mate second class.

When he came home in December of 1946, he married the girlfriend he's had from first grade. They have three daughters. Hansen worked in construction for many years. About 23 years ago he dabbled in antiques as a hobby. He now has an antique store in Elizabeth, CO which still keeps him busy and active.

GEORGE HOBART HARTLE, lieutenant, born Feb. 13, 1911, Hickory, NC. Enlisted July 5, 1928. Served on board USS *Maryland,* from 1928 to 1942, in the B Div.

On board for the Hoover Cruise (1928), with then president-elect, Herbert Hoover. On board *Maryland* on Dec. 7, 1941, when Japanese attacked. Served aboard USS *Kingfisher,* USS *Antares,* transferred to Sub Chasing Training Center, Miami, FL, to train for new destroyer escort for anti-submarine warfare. Transferred to USS *Wm. C. Cole* (plank owner) in 1943. Spent remainder of war in South Pacific, and was involved in both Okinawa and Iwo Jima invasions. Hit by kamikaze off Okinawa. Served under Superinsmat, NY until transferring to Fleet Reserve in 1949. Retired in 1959 at highest rank held, lieutenant. Spent 26 years as branch chief of facilities operations for NASA, Brook Park, OH. Married for 47 years to wife Ethel, one daughter, one son and one granddaughter.

RALPH WILLIAM HETTINGER, firecontrolman 1/c, born Jan. 29, 1921, in Windsor, CO. Enlisted January 1942 in USN as firecontrolman first class, F Div. Attended boot training, San Diego, CA. Boarded USS *Maryland* August 1942, San Francisco, CA. Participated in battles in Pacific Theater. Discharged September 1945 in California.

Married March 1944. He has two sons and two grandchildren. Farmed with his father until October 1946 at Windsor, CO. Employed with Great Western Sugar Co. 1946-1986 in Colorado, Nebraska, Montana.

Hettinger died April 20, 1993, in Longmont, CO.

KENNETH E. HILL, SC1/c, born Jan. 12, 1919, in Phillipsburg, KS. Enlisted in USN July 21, 1936. Attended boot camp, Great Lakes, IL. He was assigned to USS *Maryland* November 1936. Spent a year on deck force, 1st Div., then to Supply Div. as a ships cook striker. On Dec. 7, 1941 he was a SC1/c, remained aboard until promoted to chief commissary steward, April 1943. June 1943 reported aboard USS *Weber* (DE-675). Made 14 round trips to Europe within 18 1/2 months. During Korean War he served on the USS *Consolation* (AH-15) and the USS *Chuckawan* (AO-100).

Retired as a chief warrant in the Supply Corps September 1959. Awarded American Defense w/Fleet Clasp, Asiatic-Pacific w/2 Stars, European-African Campaign and Star, Good Conduct w/5 stars, Occupation w/European Clasp, World War II Victory Medal, Korean Defense and Pearl Harbor Medal.

He will never forget engagements he participated in, and making chief aboard the USS *Maryland.*

Married Lois M. Shehi in 1938 and they have three children, six grandchildren and nine great-grandchildren. Hill is completely retired and moved to the desert in 1990.

VAUGHN HILL, Captain, 1/c, turret, born Feb. 27, 1915, in Norris City, IL. Enlisted in the USN Nov. 23, 1939. Stations include: Great Lakes, USS

Maryland (BB-46) 3rd Div., Turret 3, US destroyer base, San Diego, CA.

Awarded American Defense w/star, Philippine Liberation w/2 stars, Asiatic-Pacific Ribbon w/8 stars, American Theater Ribbon and Victory Ribbon.

Discharged Dec. 14, 1945. Married and has son and daughter. Employed at dry cleaning shop. Now retired, residing in Norris City, IL, and resting.

LESLIE EVERETT HINTON JR., S1/c, was born Sept. 5, 1924, in Birmingham, AL. He joined the USNR in 1943 and went to boot camp in San Diego, CA. Assigned to the *Maryland's* 6AH Div. ws Oct. 18, 1943. He was involved in seven major combat operations and transferred off in the Magic Carpet Diminish. He was assigned to Brown Beach, Okinawa as a security guard until his discharge in 1946.

Upon his return to Birmingham he married and later retired from a cast iron company after 35 years. He was active in the Boy Scouts for 25 years and received the Silver Beaver Award. His marriage of 45 years recently ended with the death of his wife, Katherine. He has two daughters living in Houston and Birmingham.

Hinton is a member of the National Veteran's Association, (USS *Maryland*).

HERSHEL "HERSH" L. HUFFMAN, RT2/c, born Aug. 4, 1922, in Blackwell, OK. Moved to Wichita, KS, in 1928. Joined the Navy Reserve September 1939. Called to active duty September 1940. Attended training and Radio School at San Diego, CA. Assigned to the USS *Maryland* October 1940 where he spent the rest of his Navy time assigned to CR Div. He made RT2/c. Served as radio technician until discharged September 1945.

Huffman received seven stars, Pearl Harbor, Tarawa, Kwajalein, Saipan, Palau, Leyte and Okinawa. Also received American Defense, American Theater, Asiatic-Pacific and World War II Victory Medal.

Married to his wife Janie in 1947 and has two sons, David and Dan and six grandchildren. Retired from Hughes Aircraft Company as senior associate engineer August 1987, Torrance, CA. Member USS Maryland Association and Pearl Harbor Association.

EDWARD J. JAEGER, PhM1/c, born Sept. 11, 1924, in Garfield, NJ. Enlisted USN Oct. 27, 1942. Attended boot camp at Great Lakes NTC, IL; Hospital Corps School at San Diego, CA.

Stationed: USN Hospital, Pensacola, FL; USN Mobile Hospital #5, Noumea New Caledonia; USS *Maryland* (H Div.) July 20, 1943, through June 12, 1945; USN Air Facility, Roosevelt Field, Mineola, NY; USN Air Station, NY, NY. Discharged Jan. 10, 1946.

Re-enlisted USNR, Peoria, IL, March 24, 1947. Discharged March 23, 1952.

Saw action aboard USS *Maryland* at Tarawa,

Kwajalein, Saipan, Peleliu, Leyte, Surigao Straits and Okinawa.

Earned BS in chemical engineering, June 1950; Washington University, St. Louis, MO.

Married to Charlotte Hoitsma Sept. 10, 1955, and has three daughters and three grandchildren. Employed as a chemical engineer 1950 until retirement in 1993. Active as high school and college sports official. Now residing in Bridgewater, NJ.

HARRY D. JOHNSON, born at Port Angele, WA, on Oct. 10, 1924. He became interested in the Navy when he visited the fleet when they came to Port Angeles almost every year.

Adm. Beardslee, fleet admiral in the late 1800s, helped found the naval Elks Lodge, the only naval lodge in the country.

On turning 17 he told his folks and he would like to join the Navy. His mother said, "Son, you know we will be in this war soon." He replied with 17 year old wisdom, "Oh maw, what do you know?" He joined Co. 41-139 in San Diego in October 1941. At that time a person could enlist anytime before their 18th birthday and get out on their 21st birthday. They called it a kids course. After six weeks training he was on his way home on a nine day boot leave. As the train was going through Northern California a stewart ran through the cars saying "Pearl Harbor has been bombed."

Everyone looked at their seat partner, and asked, "Where is Pearl Harbor?" He went back to San Diego and was assigned to a draft to Bremerton where the Maryland was being repaired after the attack. He went aboard on Jan. 4, 1942, and joined the Victor Div. which was a gunnery division in charge of ammunition, small arms and the airplane catapult.

His most memorable time aboard was the year he was the catapult captain and got to launch the aircraft. He participated in every operation until the war's end which happened about the time his enlistment expired. He received his discharge in Seattle in December 1945 that same month he went to work in a pulp mill and retired 40 years later as journeyman electrician.

He has been married for 35 years and has two children. He spends his leisure time golfing and some traveling.

DARRELL V. KAMERY, was born July 25, 1921, in Taft, CA. He joined the Navy Oct. 10, 1939, in Long Beach, CA. After boot camp at NTC San Diego, served aboard USS *Maryland* (BB-46), in the "F" and "RA" Divs. from Dec. 15, 1939-Aug. 1, 1945. He attended Fire Control School in Washington, DC until assigned in April 1946 to staff, commander JTF-1, Operation Crossroads, Bikini Atoll. January 1947 returned to FC School and instructed until August 1951. Transferred to Naval Mission to Rio de Janiero, Brazil, until May 1954. Returned to FC School and in November 1955 assigned to USS Canberra (CAG-2). May 1957 sent to NTC San Diego as instructor, FT-A

School until transfer to Fleet Reserve as FTC July 2, 1959.

After naval service he remained in the San Diego area working for Control Data Corporation for 14 years followed by 12 years accounting work in the floral industry in Encinitas, CA.

Since retirement, in August 1985, he is self-employed for his family of three sons, three daughters, 10 grandchildren, and one great-granddaughter.

WILLIAM R. KEMP, S2/c, born Feb. 7, 1926, in Pleasant Plains, IL. Enlisted April 14, 1944. Served with USNR Div. 2.

Military locations: Turret #2 16 in powder mag.

Participated in battles in: Palau, Philippines, Leyte Gulf, Okinawa, Leyte Gulf Sea Battle.

Memorable experiences include the kamikaze attack in Okinawa and the Leyte invasion. He worked in the Chiefs mess for a long time. He liked it because it was easy work.

Awarded the Victory Medal, Asiatic-Pacific Campaign Medal w/3 stars, Philippine Liberation Ribbon w/2 stars.

Discharged May 26, 1946, as S2c.

Employed at Allis Chalmers for 35 years. Now retired and enjoys hunting, fishing, and camping.

FREDERICK R. KOERNER, born Feb. 11, 1919, in Sidney, IL. Enlisted in the USN Oct. 12, 1946, serving in E Div., firecontrol shop. Attended boot camp, Great Lakes Naval Training Center. Ford Motor Co., at Detroit, MI; for electrical school. Aboard *USS Maryland* June 1941.

Participated in the Pearl Harbor attack, Tarawa, Kwajalein, Saipan, Palau, Leyte Gulf, Surigao Strait, and Okinawa.

Memorable experience: 07:55 Dec. 7, 1941, standing topside and watched the first wave of Jap bombers come over Ford Island and drop bombs. He then watched torpedo bombers run on the yard docks. Koerner then realized what was going one and went below deck to battle station.

Awarded seven campaign ribbons. Discharged May 1946 as temporary warrant, permanent chief elect. mate.

Married and has two sons and two daughters. Operated electric motor repair facility. Retired, residing in Terre Haute, IN, tending lawn and flowerbeds.

DONALD F. KRYSAN, CCM (PA), born June 22, 1918, in Calmar, IA. Joined the USN Dec. 7, 1936. Went to boot camp at San Diego.

He was assigned to USS *Maryland* in April 1937 in the 3rd Div. and a few months later to the carpenter shop (R-Div.) On board *Maryland* during Pearl Harbor attack. Worked on bottom of USS *Oklahoma* after attack, rescuing personnel from the ship. Transferred from *Maryland* late in 1943 and reported to USS *Oglala* (ARG-1) being outfitted as an internal combustion repair ship. (Yes, the one sunk in Pearl Harbor and later raised.)

He was promoted to ensign in 1944 and later selected for permanent commission as limited duty officer. During next 14 years, he served in the following ships and stations: USS *Little Rock* (CL-92); Naval Damage Control Training Center, Philadelphia; Fleet Training Group, Guantanamo Bay, Cuba; USS *Pittsburgh* (CA-72); inspector Naval Materials Office, New York and Garden City, Long Island; USS *Independence* (CA-62).

On retiring from the Navy in 1959 as a lieutenant commander he worked for the Maryland Casualty as manager loss control department, retiring from there in 1984. He is married, has one son and two grandchildren.

J. ROBERT "BOB" LAIZURE, Rm3/c, born
July 5, 1924, in Columbus, KS. Joined the USN Aug. 7, 1943. Went through boot camp and radio material school at Farragut, ID. Assigned to the USS *Maryland* in July 1944.

Although trained as a radioman, his station was a loader on a 20mm AA gun; was involved in four major combat operations. Most memorable action was the direct Japanese Zero Kamikaze hit on his battle station at Leyte. After a second kamikaze hit at Okinawa, he transferred to CR Div. and received the rate of RM3c. Received numerous decorations, including the Purple Heart and Bronze Star.

He moved to Los Angeles, CA, after the war and went to work as a television technician. Later worked in the instrumentation lab of Rockedyne that tested rocket motors; subsequently worked for Packard Bell Computers. Now owns a janitorial supply company. He has been very active in his local church, having served numerous leadership positions. He is married and has three daughters and five grandchildren and resides in Huntington Beach, CA.

WERNER JOHN LAND, GM1/c, born Nov. 3,
1920, in Fredericksburg, TX. Enlisted July 12, 1938. Assigned USS *Maryland* Oct. 15, 1938. Attended Gunner's Mate School, Gun Factory, Washington, DC.

On board USS *Maryland* on Dec. 7, 1941. Transferred to USS *Petrof Bay* (CVE-80) Oct. 12, 1943.

Memorable experiences includes being on board

durinb peace time and wartime. Went through Panama Canal in 1939.

Awarded Good Conduct Medal and South Pacific Campaign bars and medals.

Discharged Sept. 24, 1945, as chief gunners mate. Married Anita and has two daughters, Teresa Taylor and Marlis Weatherly and three grandchildren.

Employed 32 years wholesale building materials salesman. Presently doing volunteer work at St. David's Hospital in Austin, TX.

HAROLD DEE LANSDALE, S1/c, born April
4, 1924, in Tyler, TX. Moved three weeks later to Fordyce, AR. Joined USN Feb. 19, 1943. Completed boot camp at San Diego, CA. Assigned to the *Maryland* in August 1943 where he spent the remainder of the war. While on the *Maryland* was involved in seven major combat operations, serving in the 2nd Div. battle station upper powder turret #2. Discharged Jan. 26, 1946.

After returning home he worked in construction for Arkansas Power and Light Company and in 1956 he was self employed as owner of Lansdale Electric Company where he retired in 1990.

He spent 23 years in the Arkansas National Guard and retired from that service in 1984 with the rank of E7.

Now he works at home keeping a big yard and garden. He is married and has two daughters and three grandchildren.

WILLOUGHBY A. LEE JR., PFC, born Sept.
20, 1924, in Fredricksburg, VA. Enlisted at Des Moines, IA December 1943. Served in the USMC.

Stationed Recruit Depot, San Diego and Sea School, Bremerton Navy Yard, Marine Guard. Transferred to USS *Maryland* April 1944 at Bremerton, WA.

Participated in battles in: Marianas, Saipan, Peleliu, Palau, Leyte and Okinawa.

Memorable experiences: When they were in Pearl Harbor, July, August, September 1944 having one bow replaced. He was guard on the forward gangway with orders for only yard repair. Crew only to pass. When Adm. Nimitz and ten of his party came aboard unchallenged for they were repair crew inspectors.

Discharged December 1945. Married and has three sons, two daughters and 11 grandchildren. Employed as carpenter and building contractor. Retired, but still building cabinets.

WARREN P. LOWERRE, Commander, born
Oct. 9, 1918, in New York City. Graduated from US Naval Academy in June 1940. Ordered to duty in USS *Maryland* where he continued throughout WWII and the later transfer of the *Maryland* to the Reserve Fleet in Bremerton in 1946.

During his tour in *Maryland,* he served as assis-

tant navigator and secondary battery officer, was plotting room officer during all operations from Tarawa to Leyte Gulf, and was air defense officer during the Okinawa invasion. Was later assigned briefly as navigator and became gunnery officer two months prior to V-J Day. Awarded Navy Commendation Ribbon and Bronze Star. Is now a retired commander, USNR.

After leaving active duty in February 1947, Warren settled in Dallas, TX. He was employed by Texas Instruments for 20 years in marketing and then as manager of Governments Contract Administration. He later owned and operated Plastex of Dallas, a sign and plastic fabrication business.

He was married in San Francisco on May 18, 1942, to the former Yvonne Belt, of Maryland. They have two sons, one daughter and five grandchildren.

THOMAS EUGENE MANN, born May 31,
1926, in Whitney, TX. Enlisted June 9, 1944, in USN, CR Radio Div.

Stationed in San Diego, CA; Camp Catlin, T.H; USS *Maryland.*

Participated in battles in Okinawa and Shima.

Memories of the USS *Maryland:* They invaded Okinawa on Easter Sunday April 1, 1945, on or about April 4 Franklin Delano Roosevelt died and there were many tears in sailors eyes. On April 7 a kamikaze suicide plane dove into their number four 16" gun turret. There were 37 men killed. The 500 pound bomb concussion stripped the soles off of sailors shoes that were located topside or on the mast. On about April 10 the Japanese ordered out the biggest battleship afloat named the Yamota. Our ship (among others) was ordered to intercept the *Yamota* in the China Sea. They went full steam (diesel) for a day and a half. When over the P.A. system came "Bull Halsey and his gruman dive bombers have the *Yamota* stilled in the water!" Mann was top deck aft and immediately sailors danced with sailors. Then many sailors sailed their caps into the sea. Tears of happiness were in everyone's eyes. (They had been plenty scared for the *Yamota* had 19" guns and they knew they would lose many ships before they were in range of the *Yamota.* (The largest battleship ever built).

Afterwards, Ensign H.L. Cravens and Mann walked near the hatch to enter the ship when Capt. J.D. Wilson emerged through the hatch. (Apparently, he had seen the sailors throw their caps overboard from the bridge). They all saluted and the Captain addressed Ensign Cravens saying, "Ensign Cravens did you see any men throw their caps overboard?" Ensign Cravens hesitated a few seconds, then responded, "No I didn't sir." The captain walked by them on the port side smiling and saying, "I didn't see any of them either!" He proceeded aft to many bare-headed sailors. (It was a general court martial to throw your cap over the side, because your name was stenciled inside the cap.

Awarded Asiatic-Pacific and one Battle Star. Discharged May 17, 1946. He has daughter Dawn Lashelle born Nov. 6, 1973, son Guy Bradley, born July 14, 1955.

Employed at railroad telegraph, car sales and insurance sales. Retired and resides in Hillsboro, TX.

VIRGIL EUGENE MARTIN, CWO, born
May 9, 1909, in Aline, OK. Enlisted February 1928 in USN. Went aboard the USS *Maryland* in 1932. Served as apprentice seaman. Worked in the mailroom. Stationed at Pearl Harbor before the war, San Pedro, CA.

Participated in battle at Pearl Harbor. His memorable experience includes seeing the Hawaiian Islands before the war and before they were deployed.

Knighted by Queen Willamia of the Neithlands while on the USS *Renville.*

Discharged March 1948 as chief warrant officer. Married and had one daughter and three grandchildren.

Built a mobile home part and then went into the backhoe excavating business. Now retired. Enjoys golfing and woodworking crafts. He now resides in Mt. Shasta, CA.

ROBERT MASSEY JR., SM2/c, USN, born
April 16, 1924. Enlisted October 1941. Boots in San Diego and aboard the *Maryland* in January 1942 until August 1945. Discharged September 1945.

Reenlisted January 1951. Assigned to the *George A. Johnson* (DE-583). Stationed at Treasure Island, CA. Discharged November 1954 as QM2/c. Awarded medals and bars for Asiatic-Pacific w/7 stars, American Defense, Philippine Presidential Unit Citation, plus Philippine Liberation Medal w/2 stars, Korean Service Medal, American Theatre and Navy Good Conduct.

Aircraft instrument mechanic for United Air Lines in San Francisco for eight years. Retired from Hewlett Packard Labs in Palo Alto, CA in July 1985.

Married Vada in 1944 and has two daughters, Gail, Carole and four grandchildren.

Enjoys bowling with VFW, golf and traveling. Also getting together with ex-signalmen E.J. Swenson, F.A. Moore and wives from Salem, OR to celebrate their very close wedding anniversaries of 1944.

JAMES ADDAMS MCALLISTER, Captain,
born Dec. 16, 1915, in Covington, VA. Served aboard USS *Maryland* June 1939-1943, USS *Hornet*, USS *Washington*, SURASDEVDET (Key West, FL; San Francisco Naval Shipyard; Navy Electronics Laboratory, San Diego, CA; UNDERSEAS RESEARCH Center, La Spezia, Italy; Bureau of Ships, Washington, DC.

Where US Naval Academy, Annapolis, MD (B.S.); Navy Postgraduate School and UCLA (MS).

Participated in Pearl Harbor, Iwo Jima, Saipan, Philippine Sea, Okinawa, Kwajalein.

Memorable experience: was officer-of-deck for the 4-8 watch on *Maryland* on Dec. 7, 1941. Was relieved 15 minutes early and was having a "leisurely" breakfast when the Japanese attacked (at 0755).

Awarded Commendation by fleet commander for design of star shell computer, American Defense Service Ribbon w/Bronze Star, American Area Service Ribbon, EAME Service Ribbon, Asiatic-Pacific Area Service Ribbon w/3 Bronze Stars, Philippine Liberation Campaign Ribbon w/2 Bronze Stars, Victory Ribbon.

Dischargded Sept. 1, 1962. Achieved the rank of captain, USN (four years).

Professor Emeritus (engineering), California State Polytechnic University, Pomona, CA.

Married June 26, 1942, to Dr. Bernice Jacklyn Lyons at Stanford University Chapel. Two sons: Bruce Hugh (University Professor and author); John Milton (teacher, artist, musician).

JAMES P. "MAC" MCANULTY, GM3/c,
born Sept. 24, 1919, in Russellville, AR, Pope County.

He served the *Maryland* from 1941 to 1945, volunteering the day after Pearl Harbor. Some locations were Nav. Tra. Station, San Diego, CA/ Rec. Sta., S.D.; USS *Maryland* Rec. Sta., Terminal Island, CA and the great Pacific Ocean. He once said, "You've not seen anything, until you've seen the ocean turn "blood red". Returning from WWII, he became a farmer raising cattle, chickens and turkeys. In their home, one would naturally learn about and feel a part of the *Maryland*, as her picture hung proudly there always. He was married, had a daughter, son-in-law and one grandson.

He passed away Nov. 19, 1990. His wife passed away Oct. 8, 1991. They were the best father and mother anyone could ever have. They are remembered daily, for their family misses them with all their hearts. In carrying on, the *Maryland* proudly hangs in their home today.

RICHARD B. MCBRATNEY, Water Tender
1/c, born Feb. 12, 1916, Kansas City, KS. Enlisted May 12, 1934, 41st Div., 8th Bn., USNR, Kansas City, MO. Served USNR, fireman first class, B Div.

Military locations, stations: USS *Barney*, USS *Jacob Jones*, destroyers of East Coast Command; USS *Maryland* at Pearl Harbor. Reported aboard on Oct. 22, 1941.

Battles participated in: Pearl Harbor Dec. 7, 1941; Tarawa, Gilbert Island Oct. 20, 1941; Kwajalein Jan. 31, 1943; Saipan June 14, 1944; Palau, Sept. 12, 1944; Leyte Oct. 19, 1944; Okinawa, March 25, 1945. Night surface action, against the enemy in Surigao Strait on night of Oct. 24-25, 1944.

Awarded Good Conduct Medal Navy, American Defense Service Medal w/Fleet Clasp, American Campaign Medal, Asiatic-Pacific Campaign Medal w/7 Bronze Stars, World War II Victory Medal, Navy Occupation Medal Asia Clasp, National Defense Medal, Korean Service Medal w/Bronze Star, United Nations Service Medal, Philippine Liberation Medal w/2 Bronze Stars.

Discharged Sept. 9, 1945. Married Mildred A. McBraley. He has a daughter, Patricia Ann Deatherage. Both are living in Kansas City, MO, and two grandchildren, both grown.

Retired as of Feb. 12, 1981, at the age of 65. He is the secretary of the USS Ward Chapter 2 of the Pearl Harbor Survivors in Kansas City, MO, and has been for the last 15 years.

LLOYD C. "MAC" MCCORD, S2/c, V-6,
USNR, born Feb. 23, 1921, in Autauga County, AL. Joined the Navy, Aug. 25, 1942. After four weeks basic training at San Diego, CA, he was sent to the Navy Receiving Station, Pearl Harbor.

He was assigned to the USS *Maryland* (BB-46) on Oct. 18, 1942. He spent all his Navy time aboard battleship *Maryland*.

Assigned to the 3rd Div. This division, along with the 1st, 2nd, and 4th Divs. were responsible for manning the battleshps' main batteries consisting of four turrets, two forward, two aft with 16" guns in each turret, 45 caliber.

He participated in the following major combat operations: Tarawa, Kwajalein, Saipan, Palau, Leyte and Okinawa.

At Saipan, when the Japanese Aerial Torpedo exploded into their bow on June 22, 1944, general quarters sounded immediately, and it was a dash to battle stations. It was the first physical damage inflicted on the *Maryland* by the Japanese since Pearl Harbor.

At Leyte, a kamikaze hit them on Nov. 29, 1944, and again, at Okinawa, they were hit by a kamikaze on April 7, 1945.

He received the following awards and medals: Good Conduct Medal, World War II Victory Medal, American Campaign Medal, Asiatic-Pacific Campaign Medal w/9 stars, Philippine Liberation Medal w/2 stars, Philippine Republic Presidential Unit Citation Badge.

Discharged Dec. 11, 1945, from the Naval Air Station, Nola. He returned to his hometown, Prattville, AL, where he still resides. McCord worked for Moss Gordon Continental Gin, as a machinist until medical retirement in 1973. He is married, has a stepson and four grandsons.

L. ROBERT MCWILLIAMS, F1/c, born
Sept. 11, 1925, in Los Angeles, CA. Enlisted Aug. 18, 1943, in the USN, oil gang, B Div.

Attended boot camp San Diego; basic engineering school, San Diego. Stationed USS *Maryland*. Participated in battles: Marshall Islands, Marianas, Western Caroline Islands, Leyte Operation, Okinawa Gunto.

Memorable experiences: left MOB D. Hospital New Caledonia, December 1944. Put on SS *Lurline* with 500 Army WACS. Wonderful Christmas.

Awarded Philippine Liberation, two Bronze Stars, Asiatic-Pacific w/5 stars, World War II Victory Medal, American Area, Purple Heart.

Discharged Dec. 16, 1945 as F1/c. He has four sons, two daughters. Remarried and has four stepdaughters, 22 grandchildren. Employed as public school teacher and administrator. Presently involved with the operation of his cattle ranch and resides in Montague, CA.

JOHN PAUL MICHAEL, PFC, USMC, born
Oct. 2, 1925, in Rogersville, AL. He was 18 years old when he enlisted in the USMC on Dec. 22, 1943. After enlisting he was sent to Marine base at San Diego for boot camp and advanced training. He was assigned to the USS *Maryland* as part of the Marine Detachment on April 25, 1944. He boarded the *Maryland* at Bremerton,

WA, and remained on board until Oct. 31, 1945. They participated in action against the enemy at Saipan, Palau, Leyte, Surigao Strait, and Okinawa. He received the Pacific Theater Ribbon w/5 stars, Philippine Liberation Ribbon w/2 stars, American Theater Ribbon and Victory Ribbon.

He was discharged on Nov. 20, 1945, at Camp Lejeune, NC. He returned to Athens, AL, started and operated a business until he retired in 1990. He and his wife Peggy, have been married for 50 years and have three sons: David, Robert and John and a grandson, John Dylan.

As he reflects back to the time that he spent in Leyte Gulf, there are many things that come to mind. The hours spent on those 40mm guns, and nights without sleep. He spent many anxious moments when they were under kamikaze attack, knowing that if the plane was not destroyed in the air his future was in doubt. The hot humid days, made worse by the extra gear that was worn during general quarters. The awesome and unforgettable show of firepower at Surigao Strait that was made more spectacular by the darkness that it broke. Remembering these things that occurred at Leyte and others that happened throughout the course of the war, he considers himself fortunate to have come through it all with only a ruptured eardrum.

LELAND A. MICHELSEN, SF1/c, born in Los Angeles, CA. Enlisted October 1941 in USN. Attended boot camp in San Diego.

Military locations: Cub Button, 7 ships and Able/Baker bomb test at Bikini Atoll. Participated in numerous battles.

Memorable experience: on "shake down" of Maryland in 1942 he fell out of a hammock and broke three ribs. After landing in hammock netting he passed out. He was found at reveille and taken to sickbay; 30 seas; Aleutian Islands.

Discharged in 1947 as SF1/c. Married and has six children and four grandchildren. Employed with police department for 27 years. Now at Glendova Country Club as maintenance supervisor.

GAIL R. MILLER, Electrician 3/c, born in Marion, OH July 22, 1925. Enlisted in the USN, Feb. 11, 1943, USNRV-6, E Div.

Stationed NTS Great Lakes, NT School, Great Lakes, USS Maryland (Sept. 1943).

Participated in all battles from 1943 to 1945. Discharged Feb. 23, 1946, as electrician 3/c. Married and has two sons, one stepson, three grandchildren and three great- grandchildren. Employed as GTE technician 1947-1985. Retired and enjoying hobby of growing orchids.

HAROLD L. MILLER, S1/c, born Jan. 29, 1924, in Glendale, AZ. Enlisted Aug. 29, 1942. Served 6 AL and ship service division (laundry). Attended boot camp San Diego, CA.

Stationed aboard USS Maryland Oct. 2, 1942, at Pearl Harbor (only six weeks from being sworn in Phoenix. Participated in all battles to end of war.

Memorable experiences: sea battle in Philippines, being gunner on 20mm watched from deck.

Discharged Dec. 16, 1945, as S1/c. Self-employed as electrician and refrigerator company in Ajo, AZ, since 1960. Retired and travels US, Japan, China, and Russia.

RUSSELL F. MILLER, CBM, shown with his wife. I received the photo during the 1945 Holiday Season, and subsequently they lost touch with each other. In a phone conversation I had with Jack "Pappy" Roberts CWO just before the Denver reunion; I learned Russ had passed away some years before. It is only fitting and proper, that his name should be remembered, and be included in the USS Maryland 75th Anniversary history book.

Our initial meeting came about, on my first night aboard the "Mary" Dec. 10, 1940, while hanging up our hammocks alongside each other in the 1st Div. compartment. Their relationship grew, and being from neighboring states, helped in the beginning.

He became very skilled in firing the 30 caliber 1903 Springfield on the 200 yard rifle range in the "islands". He captured for himself an almost perfect score winning the coveted honor as "expert."

Russ along with "Pappy" as pointer and trainer respectively, complimented by an excellent crew of Gunner's Mates in #1 turret, scored 12 hits for a perfect score.

Russ, as a coxswain, handled the (50-foot) motor launch with professionalism. Making landing starboard side to, with only a single screw (propeller) was not an easy task - but he seemed to master it very quickly.

Russell's name is also listed as a contributor on page 229 of the book Day of Infamy by author Walter Lord.

As a BM2/c on March 15, 1943 our ship was anchored off the northern Fiji Islands when he was assigned for duty to the Yorktown, VA Mine Warfare School. But the suddenness of the transfer, caught me unaware, and low on funds. However, both Russ and "Pappy", stepped in, and loaned me twenty dollars each for additional expenses that might arise and especially to purchase a new peacoat to ward off the frigid cold at home.

On arriving home I immediately wrote letters to their mothers in Wisconsin and Texas. Along with two money orders, I expressed my gratefulness for the kindness their sons had shown me. *Submitted by Ed Swanson*

HENRY G. "HANK" MILLETTE, EM2/c, born June 10, 1926, in Minnesota. Enlisted June 1943. Boot camp, Camp Hill Farragut, ID. Assigned to the USS Maryland's electrician I.C. shop, September 1943. Reassigned April 1946 to the USS Seidor (CVE-117) for two atomic bomb tests on Bikini Atoll. Completed testing and reassigned to NAS Orote Guam MI. Discharged, San Francisco June 17, 1947.

Returned to St. Paul and engaged in heavy industrial electrical construction for 40+ years. Active in Electrical Workers Union for 35 years and occasionally flew commercial sea planes. Retired in 1988. Active in law enforcement for 35+ years as a licensed part-time sheriff. Retired in 1995 as captain of an 85 man unit of the Sheriff's Lake and Trail Patrol.

He has been married for 50 years, has four children and ten grandchildren. His retirement is spent fishing and hunting in Minnesota with winters in Florida and Arizona.

ROLAND A. "PAPPY" MILLS, PhM2/c, born Dec. 15, 1914, in Montague, TX. Joined USN August 1941. Went to Corpus Christi, TX, Naval Air Station, then sent to San Diego, CA, Naval Training Station to boot camp. Sent to Bremerton, Washington, Naval Hospital for duty. Assigned to the USS Maryland February 1942. While on board USS Maryland was involved in all major combat operations through the Battle of Leyte Gulf.

Ship was hit by a Jap suicide plane. Mills was knocked out. When he came to, remembers giving shots to two wounded sailors. Memory very dim and sketchy after that. He remembers being sent off ship to an island hospital. Memory began to return while aboard transport ship to San Francisco. He was sent to naval hospital in Charleston, SC. Received medical discharge February 1945. Returned to Wichita Falls, TX. Had five jobs in next few months. Went to work for White Home and Auto Stores December 1945. Retired in 1975. He is married (52 years), has two children, a son and daughter.

FOSTER A. MOORE, Y1/c, born Aug. 8, 1924, in Los Angeles, CA. Enlisted Nov. 27, 1941, in LA. Went to boot camp in San Diego, CA. Boarded the USS Maryland in January 1942, in Bremerton, WA, and assigned to the gunnery division. Later assigned to the CS Div., then subsequently to the captain's office. Was the captain's talker of the bridge during general quarters. In early 1944 was transferred to new construction in Bremerton, WA, and then to the USS Roi (CVE) an escort carrier, then to Admiral McCain's Flag Allowance until discharged on Oct. 24, 1945.

Married April 1944 during leave to present wife, Alice. He has one son, one daughter and five grandchildren, one great-grandson. Joined the Los Angeles Police Department in February 1948. Served 20 years and retired April 1968. After retiring from LAPD traveled full-time throughout the US and Canada by motorhome for close to four years with Alice. Now living in Salem, OR.

HOMER LEE MOORE, S1/c, born Paoli, OK April 26, 1923. Enlisted July 1942 USN, S1c, 6AL.

Stationed for four weeks, boot camp, San Diego, CA. Went aboard USS Liberty transport ship to Pearl

Harbor, boarded USS *Maryland,* first of September 1942.

Participated in Tarawa, Gilbert Islands, Marshall Islands, Marianas Islands, Guadalcanal, Kwajalein, Saipan, Leyte and Okinawa.

Memorable experiences: he remembers when he got some new officers aboard ship. This one officer in his first battle told Moore when he shook his fist, start firing. Moore had a suicide plane in his sights and when he looked at the officer, he ran. Moore emptied his magazine at the plane. Everybody ran except Capt. Ray, L.B. Schyler and Moore.

Discharged December 1945 as S1/c. Married for 50 years to Nyla and they have three children. One son, Jerry and two daughters, Betty and Linda. They also have seven grandchildren. He was employed as a truck driver for 25 years. Owned his own business since 1974. Now retired and resides in Dolan Springs, AZ.

LEO R. MORGAN, SMC, QMC, born June 2, 1920, in Lenexa, KS. Enlisted Aug. 7, 1939, USN, CS. Attended boot camp Co. 21-1939 San Diego.

Stationed USS *Maryland* (BB-46) August 1939-August 1943); USS *Raymond* (DE-341) September 1943-September 1945.

Participated in Pearl Harbor and second battle Philippines.

He was on following ships after Pearl Harbor: USS *Shoshone* (1946); USS *Huntington* (CL-167) (1947); Admiral's Flag Carrier Division 5; USS *Valley Forge* (CV-45) (1950-1951); USS *Kearsarge* (CV-33) (1951-1952); USS *Ariskany* (CV-34) (1953); USS *Rendova* (CVE-114) (1954-1955); USS *Halsey Powell* (DD-686) (1956); USS *Tingey* (DD-539) (1956); USS *GRRKE* (DD-783) (1956-1957).

He returned from the European Theater in 1948 and served in recruit training at Newport, RI, for three years.

He taught at the Sonar School at the 28th Street Naval Station, San Diego, CA, teaching in the Signal School for two years 1958-1959.

Awarded China Service Medal, United Nations Service Medal, Navy Occupation Ribbon, American Defense Service Medal, American Theatre Campaign Medal, World War II Victory Medal, Korean Service Medal (with K-7-8-9 stars), National Defense Service Medal, Presidential Unit Citation (one blue enameled star), Philippine Liberation Campaign Ribbon (w/B Star), Navy Occupation Service Medal (Europe), Good Conduct Medal (6th award), Navy Unit Commendation (secretary), Asiatic-Pacific Theatre Campaign Medal (w/4B Stars).

Memorable experiences: He was on watch on bridge during the attack. He worked three days getting 35 men out of the bottom of the Oklahoma Dec. 7-9, 1941.

Discharged Aug. 17, 1959 as SMC, QMC. Married to Bonnie Long Dec. 9, 1945 and has six children,

20 grandchildren and two great-grandchildren. Now retired barber.

WARNER S. MORGAN, PhM2/c, born Jan. 25, 1926, in Oklahoma. Enlisted Jan. 14, 1944, USNR, H Div.

Attended boot camp, Farragut, ID. Stationed on USS *Edwards* (DD-663). Participated in battles in Peleliu, Philippines, Okinawa, Magic Carpet.

Memorable experiences: After Okinawa sailing home, especially through the Straits of Juan DeFuca into Seattle, WA. Home at last. Back in the good old USA. Awarded the usual medals.

Discharged May 1946 as PhM2/c. Married and has four children. Employed as investment banker, now retired. Resides in Prescott, AZ.

NORMAN E. MORTON, ADRC, born Sept. 7, 1915, in White Cloud, MO. Joined the USN March 26, 1934. After recruit training at Norfolk, VA, was assigned to the USS *Maryland's* Firecontrol Div. In 1936 he was assigned to VP-6 and flew the first squadron of PBYs the Navy ever had from California to Pearl Harbor, TH. In 1940 Morton entered Machinist Mate School at Norfolk, VA. His next assignment NAS Miami, FL, where he met and married Alice Cox. They have one daughter.

In 1941 he was assigned to VN-15 at Jacksonville, FL. In 1943 he was assigned to VP-72 and deployed to the Central Pacific (Ellis, Gilbert, and Marshal Islands). He retired in 1959, did commercial fishing for 13 years. He now owns and operates the "Bar Nothing Ranch" on Whidbey Island, WA.

GARLAND L. "SALTY" MOUNTZ, SKD2/c, born July 3, 1920, Wellington, KS. Entered USN, enlisted Oklahoma City, OK, August 1942. Stationed USNTS, San Diego, CA. Boarded USS *Maryland* (BB-46), September 1942. Assigned to Arrowhead Springs Naval Hospital San Bernardino, CA, February 1945.

Fought battles: Tarawa, Gilbert Islands, Nov. 20, 1943; Kwajalein, Marshall Islands, Jan. 31, 1944; Saipan, Marianas, June 14, 1944; Peleliu, Palau Islands, Sept. 12, 1944; Leyte Gulf, Philippine Islands, Oct. 19, 1944.

Aerial torpedo at Saipan, thought they were going back to the States. Upon going into dry dock, they found

out they were already building their new bow for the *Maryland* in Pearl Harbor.

November 24, 1944, they took a suicide plane, he dove on them in Leyte Gulf, hit them on the port side of turret #2, a 500 pound bomb went down three decks and exploded. Thirty-one enlisted men were killed, one officer and 29 enlisted men were injured.

Awarded US Navy Good Conduct, American Defense, American Campaign, Asia-Pacific w/4 stars, World War II Victory. Discharged January 1946 SKD2c.

Married Jan. 27, 1945, Wellington, KS and has one son, two daughters, four grandchildren.

Employed at Chevrolet-Olds dealership, parts department, Wellington, KS, for three years. Milk and ice cream business Wellington/Wichita, KS, 34 years. Now employed at the Southwest Kansas Area Agency on Aging, Dodge City, KS.

VINCENT U. MUIRHEAD, CDR, USN (Ret.), born Feb. 6, 1919, Dresden, KS. After graduation from USNA in February 1941, he joined the *Maryland* as Rangefinder and optical officer and received a jump start from the Japs on December 7. In 1942 he became 3rd Div. officer. He departed for flight training in March 1943, joined Air Group 16 and ended the war as XO, VBF16, leading a flight of Hellcats on the last fighter dawn patrol over Tokyo.

Duty tours following the war: navigator/exec., CVE-66; grad student, USNPGS and CIT; maintenance officer, ATU-12; Staff, COMFAIRJAX; CO, FASRON 795; BUAER Rep, Ft. Worth; HU-1; Chief Staff Officer, COMFAIRPHIL; XO, NATTC, Memphis.

After retiring in 1961, he was a professor of aerospace engineering at the University of Kansas for 28 years, 12 as chairman of the department. He is the author or co-author of two books and numerous technical papers. His research included tornadoes/vortices; Venus probes; shock waves and nuclear blasts; drag reduction.

In 1943, he married Bobby Thompson of Dallas, TX. They have three daughters. He served as an elder at the Southside Church of Christ in Lawrence, KS, for 24 years. He is an Associate Fellow in the American Institute of Aeronautics and Astronautics, member of the American Academy of Mechanics and the American Society of Engineering Education. He was elected to Tau Beta Pi and Sigma Gamma Tau honor societies and received the Air Medal.

WALTER J. "WALT" MYCKA, GM1/c, born Aug. 5, 1919, Braddock, PA. Enlisted Oct. 23, 1940, Pittsburgh, PA, USN. Served on USS *Maryland* (BB-46) (1940-1941); USS *Randolph* (CV-15) (1944-1946). Assigned to USS *Maryland* (BB-46) Dec. 17, 1940. Went to boot camp in Newport, RI. Transferred to Advance Gunnery School, Washington, DC, June 1944. Reassigned to the USS *Randolph* (CV-15), September 1944. While aboard the *Maryland* and *Randolph* he was

involved in all the naval Pacific combat operations except Saipan.

Memorable experiences: (copy of acknowledgment of suggestion), inventing a cocking device for a 20mm automatic weapon achieving a firing position from 30 seconds to five seconds.

Medals include all authorized Pacific Naval Combat Operations (1941-1945) except Saipan.

Discharged Dec. 4, 1946. Married in 1944 and has one son, two daughters, five grandchildren. Entered prison service 1948 at Mill Point, WV. Transferred to Denver area in 1955, where he presently lives.

Employed US Department of Justice (Bureau of Prisons) (1948-1971) Denver Parks and Recreation (1972-1981).

Presently retired completely. Pursuing hobbies, officer of the Maryland National Vets Association and Pearl Harbor Survivors Mile Hi Colorado Chapter #1.

JAMES L. NICHOLS, YNC, born Sept. 12, 1920, in Oklahoma. Enlisted in USN, Sept. 24, 1940, captain's officer. Stationed USS *Maryland* (BB-46), Nov. 15, 1940, Commander 5th Fleet Staff 1943.

Participate in Pearl Harbor, Gilbert Island, Marshall Island, Marianas Island.

Memorable experiences: Pearl Harbor attack: It took 20 to 30 minutes to get permission from damage control to open a hatch so he could get on top side. Received awards for six major battles in the Pacific.

Discharged July 7, 1960. Married for 51 years and has one son, one daughter and two grandchildren. Employed FAA, Oklahoma City, OK. Retired in 1972. Resides in Mesa, AZ during the winter months. Travels in motor home in the summer.

MICHAEL P. OAKLAND, MUS3/c, born June 17, 1925, in Martins Ferry, OH. Enlisted Sept. 21, 1943, in the USN.

Stationed Great Lakes, IL; San Diego Destroyer Base, USS *Maryland,* Sampson, NY.

Participated in battles in Saipan, Peleliu, Leyte Gulf, Philippines, Japanese Fleet confrontation at Leyte.

Memorable experience includes being torpedoed at Saipan. Hit by Japanese suicide plane at Leyte. Met uncle in seabees stationed at island of Tulagi. Spent 1 1/2 years at Naval Hospital in Sampson with T.B.

Awarded four Battle Stars. Discharged July 26, 1946.

Married to Beverly and has daughters Karen, Kathleen, son Tom, and five grandchildren. Employed at Bank of Akron, Akron, OH; Wells Fargo Bank, CA. Retired and active with CBML, Orange, CA.

WALTER T. OBERMEIER, born Aug. 30, 1921, Crocker, SD, enlisted USN, Omaha, NE, September 1940, Great Lakes IL, boot camp.

Boarded *Maryland* November 1940, apprentice seaman, advanced to chief firecontrolman during continuous duty aboard from Pearl Harbor through Okinawa. Transferred from Maryland August 1945.

Served in commissioning detail, USS *Sicily* (CVE-118) and aboard until late 1946.

Student and instructor at Firecontrol School, Washington, DC until 1952. Married Mary Lou Balles there February 1950 and has three children.

Loaned to the Brazilian Navy 1952-1953, advisory capacity, firecontrol equipment, on the former US cruisers *Philadelphia* (CL-41) and *St. Louis* (CL-49).

Firecontrol Technician School, Washington, DC, 1954, then to pre-commissioning detail USS *Canberra* (CAG-2) (formerly CA-70), the second guided missile cruiser in the USN.

Transferred to Fleet Gunnery School, San Diego, CA, instructor 1957. While there, promoted to master chief firecontrol technician November 1958 as part of the first promotional increment of the newly established rates of senior and master CPO.

In 1959 assigned to inspector, Naval Material, to study the new Anti-Submarine Warfare System ASROC at Librascope Company, Glendale, CA, then proceeded to Fleet Sonar School, Key West, FL, to help set up a course of instruction or ASROC.

Transferred to Fleet Reserve July 1960. Worked at Navy Calibration Laboratory, NAS, North Island. At 75 years of age, now continue in good health in retirement.

WILLIAM H. O'DELL, SSML3/c, USS *Maryland* (BB-46), born July 17, 1926, Kansas City, MO. Enlisted USN July 28, 1943, boot camp San Diego, CA, in Co. 302. Went aboard USS *Maryland* (BB-46) October 1943.

Saw action at Tarawa, Gilbert Islands, Kwajalein, Marshall Islands, Saipan, Marianas Islands, Palau, Caroline Islands, Leyte and Philippine Islands.

Entitled to wear Asiatic-Pacific, American Area, Philippine Liberation and World War II Victory Medals.

Left the *Maryland* August 1945 for shore duty at USNRS Pearl Harbor for about 15 months, came Stateside November-December 1946 and aboard USS *Prairie* (AD-15) (Com-Des-Pac) until May 1947 and was sent home for discharge July 15, 1947.

After discharge, went to work for Los Angeles Co., CA, and then took up printing (GI Bill), learned and worked at printing Los Angeles, CA, until October 1965 when he went to work for the Office of State Printing in Sacramento, CA, from which he retired February 1987. Married Jan. 25, 1947, to Sue Donna Shirley and they have one son.

RODERICK "ROD" OLIVER, GM1/c, born in Groesbeck, TX, March 26, 1921. Joined the USN Sept. 12, 1939. Went to boot camp San Diego, CA. After boot camp, worked at fire station on base until next group

completed training. Assigned to the USS *Maryland* January 1940. After a time in Deck Force in 4th Div., was assigned to Turret 4 to strike for gunners mate. He was sent to Electrical Hydraulic School at destroyer base, San Diego, arriving two days before attack on Pearl Harbor. Returned to USS *Maryland* upon completion of school.

Transferred, GM2/c, in early 1943 to new construction, going to Gunnery School, Washington, DC. Spent the rest of the war on the USS *Stockham* (DD-683) in the South Pacific. Discharged Oct. 22, 1945, at Camp Wallace, TX, as chief gunners mate.

Spent next 40 years in oil exploration. Retired in 1985 after the death of his wife, Jacqueline, in 1984. Returned to his hometown of Groesbeck. Married Madeline Stevens Shelton. He has been active in civic affairs, serving on the city council six years. Belongs to the Lions Club, American Legion and is a Mason. He has two sons, two daughters, nine grandchildren, and one great-granddaughter. He and his wife enjoy traveling in their travel trailer.

ROLAND LEROY PAGE, S2/c, born Sept. 14, 1922, in Franklin Co., AR. Served in the USN. Training USNTS, San Diego, Co-43-85. Served in USS *Maryland* (BB-46).

Participated in battles in: Tarawa, Gilbert Islands, Nov. 20, 1943; Kwajalein, Marshall Islands Jan. 31, 1944; Saipan, Caroline Islands June 14, 1944; Palau, Marianas Sept. 12, 1944; Leyte Invasion, Philippine Oct. 19, 1944; Sea Battle Surigao Straits Oct. 25, 1945, Okinawa, Marianas March 25, 1945.

Awarded Victory Medal, Philippine Liberation, Asiatic-Pacific, American Theatre, Asiatic-Theatre w/ 7 Bronze Stars. Discharged Oct. 7, 1945 Memphis, TN, as S2/c.

Married to Ruby Lee Page (nee Nichols) June 25, 1945. Corporal in US Army. Remained in the Navy Reserve or 15 years as chief CCM. Married 51 years, celebrated 50th anniversary (1995). He has one child, two grandchildren and one great-grandchild.

Employed 31 years in Civil Service in Arkansas and California (Army, Navy, Marine Corps).

CHARLES R. "CHARLIE" PEAY, BM1/c, born Sept. 4, 1920, in Collinsville, OK. Enlisted Nov. 4, 1940, in the USN, bosn'mate first class, 6AL Div.

Attended boot camp in San Diego. Stationed on USS *Enterprise* (before WWII), USS *Maryland* March 3-41-46. Decommission of *Maryland, West Virginia, Lexington, Indiana,* NAVSTA, Seattle, WA.

Participated in seven engagements the *Maryland* was in.

Memorable experiences: being blown up and losing a shoe at Saipan; first leave in five years at the end of WWII; his division men lost at Okinawa; all the camaraderie of shipmates and friends and pride of USA Navy and family.

Awarded Asiatic-Pacific w/5 stars, Victory Medal, Philippine Liberation w/2 stars. Honorably discharged Feb. 18, 1946, BM1/c.

Married for 49 years, has four children (three boys and one girl) two of boys deceased. Employed at Tulsar Beechcraft, 25 years line service manager. Retired. Enjoying his wife and family. Traveling and antiquing.

EDWIN PETERSON, Y3/c, F Div., born March 21, 1914, in Webster, SD. Joined the USN in April 1933. Trained at San Diego Naval Training Center. Assigned to the gunnery office on the *Maryland* in August 1933, based in San Pedro.

Traveled to Hawaii, the Midway Islands, through the Panama Canal to Cuba, El Salvador, Haiti, the East Coast, and numerous trips up and down the West Coast, from San Diego to San Pedro, San Francisco, and Bremerton, WA. He took part in a daring rescue of the USS *Macon,* a dirible that went down 130 miles south of Big Sur in May 1945.

Ed was discharged in April 1937, and settled in San Diego, CA. He reenlisted in 1942, as yeoman second class assigned to amphibious training command, Pacific in San Diego, and was on his way to the Philippines and Japan when the war ended. Discharged in November 1945 as chief yeoman. He married Ramona in 1936; four children, eight grandchildren and seven great-grandchildren. Ed worked as a manager for Safeway Stores until 1968, then worked for the 4th District Court of Appeals until his retirement in 1978. He remains active with various court functions.

CLARENCE R. PFUNDHELLER, CBM(T), born June 17, 1920, in Bridgewater, IA. Enlisted Jan. 11, 1939, in USN, deck force, 4th and 6-B Div. Stationed GL NTC; USS *Maryland* 1939-1944; LCS (L) 120. Gun captain 5" anti-aircraft gun at Pearl Harbor and until he left ship.

Participated in battles in Pearl Harbor, Tarawa, Kwajalein, Okinawa.

Memorable experiences include catcher on USS *Maryland* baseball team, Pearl Harbor.

Awarded Good Conduct Medal, Asiatic-Pacific w/4 stars, Philippine Liberation, American Theater, American Defense w/star.

Discharged Oct. 5, 1945. Married 1944 to Leatha. She died 1992. They have three daughters, seven

grandchildren, and two great-grandchildren. Married in 1993 to Mable, three children nine grandchildren and 10 great-grandchildren.

Employed county road maintenance; hardware store employee, general store owner; feed distributor sales; custodian school. Retired and does volunteer work. Go to schools with Pearl Harbor video.

Member USS Maryland (BB-46), National Veteran Association, charter member Iowa PHSA, life member PHSA, life member American Legion, life member Veteran of Foreign Wars.

WILLIAM ROBERT PINKSTON, AM2/c, born in Henryetta, OK. Enlisted Dec. 14, 1942 in the USN. Served as AM2/c, aviation. Stationed USNTS, San Diego, USS *Maryland.*

Participated in battles at Gilbert Islands, Marshall Islands, Marianas Islands, Western Caroline, Leyte and Okinawa. Received nine Battle Stars.

Awards include American Theatre, Asiatic-Pacific Area w/7 stars, Philippine Liberation w/2 stars, Good Conduct Medal, Combat Air Crew Wings.

Discharged Oct. 20, 1945. Married to Mary Louise Pinkston. Three months after discharge hired for Angeles PD. Retired 1967 as detective sergeant. Now employed as rancher.

JOSEPH P. "JAY" QUINN, CEM, he was born Jan. 10, 1922, in Monroe City, MO. Joined USN September 1940. Attended boot camp at Great Lakes, IL. He was assigned to the M-Div. electricians on the USS *Maryland* in December 1940. After two years as a main drive electrician, he transferred to the fire control electricians shop in the E-Div. on the *Maryland.*

He was on the *Maryland* when the Japanese attacked Pearl Harbor on Dec. 7, 1941, and stayed on the *Maryland* until it was decommissioned. He was discharged in September 1946.

He joined the medical equipment division of the General Electric Company after discharge from the Navy and retired from GE in 1984. He started a medical equipment business in 1984 and retired from this business in 1992.

Married and has three sons, four daughters and 11 grandchildren.

ROBERT JAMES RELL, EM2/c, born July 6, 1918, in Philadelphia, PA. Enlisted Oct. 28, 1943, in the USN, serving as EM2/c, E Div.

Stationed Sampson, NY, Great Lakes, IL, USS *Maryland.*

Participated in battles in Saipan, Tinian, Guam, Palau, Leyte, Samar and the Philippine Sea Battle.

Memorable experiences include loading ammunition and working in the boiler rooms when they first came around.

Awarded Philippine Liberation, Victory, Pacific w/4 stars.

Discharged April 12, 1946. Married for 50 years and has one son, one daughter and two grandchildren. Received BS degree, E.S.B. Storage Batteries. Now retired.

CLARENCE E. RENNER, born Feb. 11, 1920, in Tampico, IL. Entered USN, Sept. 10, 1940, serving as ship's cook.

Stationed USNTS, Great Lakes, IL; USS *Maryland;* USS *J. Franklin Bell;* AATB Beni Saf, Algeria; USS *LST* 176, 209, 524, USN AAB, Falmouth, England, USS *YMS* 228, NAS Edenton, NC, USNAS Norfolk, VA.

Participated in battles in Pearl Harbor, European African Area, Asian Area, D-Day invasion.

Memorable experiences include the day Pearl Harbor was bombed, he was in the supply room issuing supplies when chaos was heard. He then went to his battle station to handle ammunition during the bombing.

Awarded American Medal, Victory Medal, Good Conduct and EAME. Discharged Nov. 15, 1946, as ships cook first class (Aug. 1, 1943).

Renner has 15 children (10 living), 31 grandchildren, 14 great-grandchildren.

Carpenter for two years in Walnut, IL. Moved to Rock Falls, IL, and worked for the Plumbers and Pipefitters until retirement in 1985. Retired, member of PHSA Chapter #1 in Illinois.

ROBERT E. RINEHOLT, EM1/c, born in White Pigeon, MI. Joined the USN Sept. 16, 1940. Went to boot camp at Great Lakes, IL and was assigned to the USS *Maryland* November 1940 as an electrician in E Div.

He was on board the USS *Maryland* at Pearl Harbor on Dec. 7, 1941, when the Japanese attacked. Received the Purple Heart for wounds received. He was involved in the six major battles. His unforgettable memory of WWII is that Sunday morning of December 7 when he had planned to go ashore with two Navy buddies from home, but they were both killed. He was discharged November 1946.

He is now living in Harrison, MI, after retiring in 1987 as maintenance supervisor at the United Methodist Children's Home in Worthington, OH. He is married, has two daughters, one son, three grandchildren and two great-grandchildren.

STEPHEN EARL ROSS, born June 2, 1921, in Kansas City, KS. Joined the USN Sept. 10, 1940. Boot camp at USNTC Great Lakes, IL. He was assigned to the USS *Maryland* with Walter T. Obermeier (Obie) who became his life long friend, they joined the ship at Bremerton, WA November 1940. While aboard from November 1940-June 1945 he was to survive the attack on Pearl Harbor, and participate in six major battles (Midway, Tarawa, Kwajalein, Saipan, Palau, Leyte and Okinawa, Gunto).

In June 1945 he left the USS *Maryland* for F.C. "B" School in Washington, DC. Thereafter he was assigned to the USS *Manchester* February 1946 to October 1948. He then attended FC Advanced Mark 56 School in Washington, DC. At this time he was married. His next assignment December 1948 to June 1950 was to the USS *Roanoke,* a cruiser - for outfitting, commissioning, and shake down to the Caribbean and later to the Mediterranean. During this time he attended school at General Electric in Pittsfield, MA and Damage Control School His next assignment June 1950-June 1951 were to the USS *Ludlow* (DD-438) and the USS *McCelland* (DE-750) where he made C.P.O. and another transfer to USN Instructor training school, Norfolk, VA. From there he was assigned to the NROTC unit as Illinois Institute of Technology, Chicago, IL. August 1951 to June 1954 as assistant to the Professor of Naval Science. His son Stephen was born during this assignment. Then he was assigned to F.T. "B" School, Washington, DC June 1954-August 1955, where he was again with his former USS *Maryland* shipmates (Obermeier, Kammery, Diet, Shupp and Ring). At this time his second son David was born. Following this school he was assigned to the US Naval Guided Missile School at CONVAIR, Pomona, CA October 1955-April 1956 and then to U.S. Guided Missiles School at FADTC, Dam Neck, Virginia Beach, VA, as enlisted instructed May 1956 to September 1960. While there he attended Radar School at U.S. Naval Avionics Facility, Indianapolis, IN.

He retired after 20 years, 12 days on Sept. 22, 1960, as Guided Missiles technician chief (GMTC), and later returned to FTMC by the USN.

He moved to Acton, MA in September 1960 employed by Raytheon as technical writer, systems instructor and field engineer for 19 1/2 years until his sudden death May 17, 1980.

He is survived by the his wife Florence, two sons, Stephen E. (Jr.) and David E., and one granddaughter, Rebecca.

RAYMOND A. RUSSELL, ENG2/c, born in Bellmore, Long Island, NY, Dec. 17, 1904. Enlisted Nov. 27, 1922. Served as engineer, M Div.

Stationed Naval Training Station, Newport, RI, USS *Maryland.*

Memorable experiences include Hawaiian, Australia, New Zealand cruise July 1925.

Discharged Nov. 26, 1926. Widower and has two children.

Employed as fruit and dary farmer in Red Hook, NY. He is now 91 years old and retired.

HOWARD A. SAUER, Lt Cmdr, born Dec. 24, 1918, Los Angeles. Reported aboard as a reserve ensign May 1942, from Reserve Officers Training Corps, University of California, Berkeley. He was assigned as port gun control officer in five-inch 51-caliber secondary battery. Lt. J.N. McNaughton was secondary battery officer and Lt. Springer was fifth division officer. Battle station was secondary forward in the foretop.

After a few months Mr. Springer went to submarine school, and Howard became fifth division officer. (Mr. Springer received the Navy Cross and was lost when the USS Tang sank in October 1944.)

The Secondary Battery delivered many bombardments from Tarawa to Okinawa, and the port battery had one counterbattery action at Saipan. The port battery, using proximity fuse equipped five" 38-caliber shells - later shot down an attacking Japanese torpedo plane.

The most memorable sight for the foretop crew was Japanese battleship Yama*shiro* receiving gunfire hits from battleships, cruisers, and destroyers during the Battle of Surigao Strait, Oct. 25, 1944. At the war's end was assigned as main battery plotting room officer. In a bombardment qualification just two 16-inch rounds were fired. It was a *Maryland's* last big-gun shoot.

He remained in the peacetime Navy and was honorably discharged in January 1953.

RUDOLPH L. "RUDY" SCHAEFFER, EM3c, born July 27, 1921, Fairview Park, OH. Moved to North Olmsted, OH, and graduated from North Olmsted High in 1939. Joined the USN (USNR-V6) in Aug. 24, 1942. He attended boot camp at Great Lakes Naval Training base and was assigned to the USS *Maryland* in October 1942.

He went aboard ship as a yeoman for about six months in the captain's office, standing watch in pilots house and battle station on five inch broadsides guns. Later he was transferred to Electrician's Div. in power shop, with mess cooking duties. Standing watch in steering aft and main distribution boards.

His experience, kamikaze aircraft suicide bomb explosion, battery locker room explosion, Leyte Gulf invasion, Okinawa battle and liberty at Fuji Islands.

In 1944 he was transferred to Williamsburg, VA, for further electrical schooling.

War ended and he was discharged from Great Lakes, IL on Dec. 3, 1945, returning home to attend business college in Cleveland, OH. Later he married and has three children, (one son, two girls) and 10 grandchildren.

He retired from Conrail RR, 33 years. Activities include mail handling, union work BRAC and data processing department. Total service 33 years and now resides in Middleburg Heights, OH.

KARL A. SCHWARTZ, Sgt, born March 22, 1916, in Menominee, MI. Entered USMC April 21, 1941. Stationed USS *Maryland* Earl, NJ.

Participated in Pearl Harbor, Gilbert Islands, Marshall Islands, Saipan, Peleliu, Leyte and sea battle of Surigao Strait.

Memorable experiences include: helping sailors man 5" 25 gun Dec. 7, 1941; standing guard on forecastle with loaded rifle when President Roosevelt and General McArthur came to see their ship in drydock with out bow; The Surigao Sea Battle; Gallon of gasoline with farmer matches for a cork under a box car full of ammunition, can to swing, farmer matches never light when wet.

Awarded Expert Rifleman Fleet Marine Discharge Medal, American Defense, American Campaign, Asiatic-Pacific, Pearl Harbor and Philippine Medal and World War II. Discharged as sergeant Oct. 20, 1945.

Married 47 years to Arlene. Employed four and a half years building new railroad cars. Self-employed, mink and beef cattle. Now 80 years old and retired.

DENZIL G. "SCOTTY" SCOTT, born Oct. 28, 1920, Campbell, MO with basic training in Great Lakes, IL. His first duty station was USS *Maryland* (BB-46) from November 1940 until May 1943. During the Japanese attack on Pearl Harbor he was at General Quarters in a powder magazine. He was transferred from *Maryland* to a new construction and assigned to USS *La Vallette* (DD-448) until end of war. Other duty stations included a carrier, two light and one heavy cruiser, an ice breaker, a transport and a cargo ship.

His most memorable duty was in the Ceremonial Guard, Anacostia, Washington, DC.

His medals include Good Conduct w/2nd and 3rd Awards, American Campaign, American Defense w/ Fleet Clasp, Asiatic-Pacific w/8 stars, Philippine Liberation w/2 stars, World War II Victory, Occupation Service, Korean Service, China and United Nations Service.

He was transferred to Fleet Reserve and released to inactive duty April 1960 as a gunner's mate chief senior (E8). He retired from Federal Civil Service in 1980. Married to Mary Carey for 54 years. They have three daughters, four sons and nine grandchildren. His youngest son was a Naval Academy graduate class 1977. Hunting and fishing continue to be his favorite hobbies.

JOHN D. SCOTT, QM3c, born June 25, 1919, Mt. Vernon, IL. Enlisted USN Sept. 10, 1940. Enlisted

and served in Illinois National Guard, September 1936 to September 1940.

Stationed USNTS, Great Lake, IL. He served aboard USS *Maryland* (BB-46) from Nov. 15, 1940-Aug. 28, 1943. He served aboard the USS *Diver* (ARS-5), November 1943 to September 1945. Served in operations, Flag 16th Fleet, New York City, November 1945 to September 1946.

Memorable experiences: (without permission) He ordered "open fire on the Japanese airplanes" over the *Maryland's* intercom system before 0800 when the Japanese first started their attack on Pearl Harbor, Dec. 7, 1941. North and South Pacific operations aboard the *Maryland*. North Atlantic, pre-invasion in English Channel winter and spring 1944. Normandy invasion June 1944. First allied ship to enter Cherbourg Harbor, France 1944; occupation of Bremerhaven area, Germany December 1944 to September 1945; aboard the USS *Diver* ARS-5.

Awarded American Defense, American Area, Asiatic-Pacific, EAME, Occupation Germany, Victory, Good Conduct, Pearl Harbor Commemorative.

Discharged USN Nov. 15, 1946. Married for 44 years to Ermaline and has three children, nine grandchildren and four great-grandchildren.

Member USS Maryland Vets and life member Pearl Harbor Survivors Association.

Retired from McDonnel Douglas after 21 years in aerospace industry. Helped to build America's first space craft and jet fighter planes.

WALTER T. "WALT" SELBY, Turret Captain1/c, born March 9, 1922, in Cambridge, OH. Entered USN Sept. 11, 1940. Went to boot camp at Great Lakes. Stationed USS *Maryland* December 1940 to 1944; USS *Topeka* 1944-1946; USS *Salem* 1951 to 1952.

Participated in battles in Pearl Harbor, Tarawa, Kwajalein, Okinawa, various surface engagement.

Memorable experiences include being a member of turret one maintenance crew on USS *Maryland* (BB-46); three months public speaking tour with Incentive Div., USN; duty with 6th Fleet in the Mediterranean.

Awarded Pre-Pearl Harbor Ribbon, Pearl Harbor Dec. 7, Ribbon, Asiatic-Pacific Area Campaign Medal w/5 stars, US Navy Occupation Medal (Europe), Good Conduct Ribbon.

Discharged Aug. 16, 1946 as turret captain first class.

Married and has two sons, daughter, six grandchildren and one great-grandchild. Employed as machinist for seven years; inspector for Department of Defense for 25 years. Enjoying retirement in Colorado and Arizona.

EARL SHACKELFORD, 2nd Lt., born in Dallas, TX, Jan. 17, 1924. He went aboard the *Maryland* on July 1, 1942, in San Francisco and left her in December 1943, in Long Beach. He served in the CR (Flag) Div.

He received the Naval Commendation Medal for

services as radioman while on the flag staff. Besides Tarawa, after leaving the *Maryland*, he was involved in the Eniwetok, Saipan/Tinian, Iwo Jima and Okinawa invasions.

He was discharged in November 1945 and enlisted in the US Army in July 1948. In November 1949, he was commissioned a second lieutenant. During the Korean War he served for 18 months with the 68th AAA Gun Bn. He was awarded the Bronze Star w/7 Battle Stars during these hostilities.

He has been married for 50 years, has three children and four grandchildren. Most of his working years were spent in the auto parts business.

WILLIAM HAROLD (RED) SHAPPLEY, MM3/c, born June 1, 1924, in Memphis, TN. Joined the USN Jan. 29, 1943, and went to boot camp at San Diego, CA. Went aboard the USS *Maryland* on July 20, 1943, and made the rate of MM3/c. While on board received eight stars from the Asiatic-Pacific Area and two stars from the Philippine Liberation and a Victory Medal World War II. In September 1945 transferred to Terminal Island. Made one more trip overseas after the war aboard the USS *Comet* to pick up soldiers in New Guinea.

Married Genevieve Welle in Bellflower, CA in December 1945 and discharged from the Navy on March 16, 1946.

Lived in Memphis for ten years and back to California for 35 years. Retired in 1985 from McCullagh Leasing Div., of Control Data. In 1991 moved to Fountain Hills, AZ.

LESLIE VERNON SHORT, Chief Mineman E7, born Dec. 14, 1921, in Plains, KS. Enlisted Sept. 25, 1940, in USN, seaman 6A Div.

Stationed Great Lakes NTS; USS *Maryland* (BB-46); Mine Warfare School; two years instructor, worked in the mine force until 1962 and retired E7 CMN.

Participated in the Pearl Harbor battle Dec. 7, 1941. Awarded citation by C.W. Nimitz. Discharged July 25, 1962.

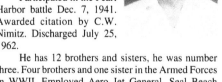

He has 12 brothers and sisters, he was number three. Four brothers and one sister in the Armed Forces in WWII. Employed Aero Jet General, Seal Beach Ammo Depot, Boeing Aircraft Co. Lives in Derby, KS, doing as little as possible. His health is so so.

LEO M. SHUMARD, Chief Fire Controlman, born March 29, 1916, in Madison, IL. Entered the USN July 5, 1938. Went through boot camp in San Diego. Transferred to USS *Maryland* Dec. 12, 1938, in F Div. and made FC1/c on Aug. 1, 1942. Sent to Advanced Fire Control School, Washington, DC on May 1, 1943. Upon completion, Sept. 30, 1943, he was assigned to

new construction, USS *Willoughby* (AGP-9), made CFC on this Pt tender and was aboard in Brunei Bay, Borneo at end of the war. Was involved in actions at Pearl Harbor, Midway, and Leyte Gulf plus invasion at Biak, Mindoro, PI. Palawan, PI and Borneo.

Awarded American Defense w/star, American Theater, Asiatic-Pacific w/ 3stars, Philippine Liberation w/2 stars, Good Conduct. Honorably discharged Oct. 25, 1945.

Married Gilma M. Johnson June 12, 1941, who died Nov. 10, 1976. He had one daughter, Sally Kristin of Arcata, CA. He worked as a brick and stone mason until retirement on April 1, 1978, and now lives in Ocean Shores, WA with his present wife, Betty. His brother, **Gene D. Shumard,** enlisted in the USMC August 1938 and went through boot camp at San Diego, CA. Then was assigned to the USS Maryland September 1938. He served in teh Marine Detachment aboard until March 1941 then transferred Wake Island and became a POW. When the island fell on Jan. 21, 1942. Spent the war years in various POW camps in Woosung, China, Manchuria and was liberted in Tokyo. After his release and discharge from the service, he worked as an electrician in California.

He married Irene Brands in 1947 and had three children: Patsy, Jeanie, and David. He moved to Atlanta, GA where he retired and passed away March 20, 1986.

ROLAND W. SIEH, Lt., born Nov. 9, 1919, in Henry Township, Brown County, SD.

Enlisted in the USN Dec. 10, 1941, at Aberdeen, SD. Sent to boot camp at Navy Station San Diego, CA. January 11, 1942, transferred to US battle ship *Maryland* at Bremerton, WA when the Pacific Fleet was being repaired as the result of Japans bombing of Pearl Harbor. August 3, 1942, received commission as ensign MSNR aboard USS *Maryland*.

With orders to report to US Maritime Service as training officer on TV Avalon, Avalon, CA. Transferred to Maritime Service as training officer 1944. Then transferred to Port Director School at Port Hume, CA. Assigned to Communications for merchant ships taking part in invasion of Japan.

Also attended Armed Guard School and transferred to SS *Mauna Kea* as commander of Navy gun crew. President Truman authorized the atomic bomb drop on Japan which ended the war.

Released from active duty Dec. 30, 1945, and sent on inactive duty. Remained in Naval Reserve until Sept. 12, 1956. Released from naval service with honorable service, with rank of lieutenant.

Awarded American Campaign Medal, Asiatic-Pacific Campaign Medal, World War II Victory Medal.

Married to Lavohn Herron Feb. 15, 1943. Married for 53 years and have five children. In civilian life they farmed and ranched in South Dakota. They camped in the Black Hills of South Dakota in 1996.

RICHARD P. SIMONIS, BMCS, born Aug. 9, 1916, at Rosholt, WI. Wondered around the country for

years and joined the USN Sept. 10, 1940, and did his boot training at Great Lakes, IL, and then reported aboard the *Maryland* in November 1940. In 1943 as BM2c was transferred back to the States for new construction. Assigned to USS *PCS 1451* and after commission they went to San Pedro and San Diego for shakedown and then was assigned to Com. 17 at Adak for duty. They never reached Adak as when they reached Dutch Harbor they were assigned to operate from there. They did many things, such as hauling the P*adre* from island to island; hauled whiskey to the Russians at Cove Bay where they were transferring many ships to them. Back to the States when it was over and assigned to recruiting and sent to Albany, NY; Quonset Point, RI NAS. Made CBM (A) in 1945 and CBM while at Syracuse in 1946. Discharged in 1948 and joined the Naval Ready Reserve. Made BMCS in 1973 and was discharged in 1975 and then moved to his present home in Pennsylvania.

Married at NAS Quonset Point on Aug. 22, 1946 and will celebrate 50 years of happiness soon. They had 11 children of which 10 are living and nine married. They also have 29 grandchildren and seven step-grand-children, 12 great-great children and two more on the way.

JAMES EUGENE SINOR, GM3/c, born June 18, 1925, in Cleveland, TN. Enlisted in the USN Feb. 26, 1943. Attended boot camp in San Diego, CA. Stationed Nuemea New Caledonia, USS *Maryland* (BB-46). Discharged Jacksonville, FL.

Participated in battles in Tarawa, Nov. 20, 1943; Kwajalein Jan. 31, 1944; Saipan June 14, 1944; Palau Sept. 12, 1944; Leyte Oct. 19, 1944; Okinawa March 23, 1945.

Memorable experience: took fish at Saipan; took suicide plane at Leyte and another at Okinawa on May 7, 1945; on top of turret #3 at which he was inside, standing on landing platform of right gun.

Awarded seven battle stars, American Defense, Philippine Liberation, SW Pacific, Presidential Unit Citation and Victory Medal.

Discharged Jan. 22, 1946. He has three sons and five grandchildren and one great-grandchild. Employed at Good Year Tire and Rubber Co. for 38 years. Now retired and resides in Akron, OH.

BRADFORD A. SMITH, CPO, born July 25, 1918, in Los Angeles, CA. Enlisted May 1938 in USN, F Div.

Participated in all the battles in which the *Maryland* was involved.

Memorable experiences include Pearl Harbor; an officer was killed alongside of Smith after he had told Smith to move over.

Awarded usual medals on *Maryland.* Discharged December 1945 as CPO.

Employed with National Cash Register Company. He now enjoys traveling in his RV.

JULIAN J. "SMITTY" SMITH , BM3c, born Jan. 9, 1926, in Golden Meadow, LA. Joined the USN March 1944. Went to boot camp in Great Lakes, IL, and to Camp Perry, VA.

Assigned to the USS *Maryland,* firing boilers, on November 1944 until March 1946. After a month at the ammunition dump in Belle Chase, LA, he was discharged from the Lake Front Receiving Station in New Orleans on April 6, 1946.

He returned to Golden Meadow and began work

in the oil fields until he entered the electrical business as an independent contractor. He is active in the American Legion and has served three terms as commander. He also held several offices in the Knights of Columbus and is a member of the Board of the Lafourche Parish Fire District #3. He is married, has three daughters and three grandchildren.

HOWARD P. "SWEDE" SORENSON, SF1/c, born May 24, 1916, Marne, IA. Enlisted USNR Denver, CO, Dec. 13, 1941, and after boot camp at San Diego went aboard the *Maryland* where he served in the R Div. shipfitter shop. He was involved in seven major combat operations and received a citation for his part in shoring bulkheads after their torpedo hit at Saipan. He was transferred for release from the USN August 1945.

He returned to Denver, CO, where he had served an apprenticeship becoming a journeyman steamfitter in 1941. He worked at this trade until retiring in 1981.

Sorenson has a daughter, son and three grandchildren. Widowed in 1987. He married Jacqueline (Jackie) Feb. 6, 1995, and both are doing everything possible to enjoy life. They couldn't be happier.

CHARLES EDWARD STAGGS, MOM1/c, born Sept. 8, 1919, in Keo, AR. Joined the Navy Dec. 10, 1941. Went to boot camp in San Diego. Was assigned to the USS *Maryland* while it was being repaired at Bremerton, WA from damage at Pearl Harbor. It sailed to the South Pacific to Guadalcanal, Espirito Santos and the Fijis as back up for the fleet. In 1943, he was sent to Kwajalein on a freighter which was chased by a Jap sub after it left San Pedro. At Kwajalein, he was on a detail to bury bloated dead Japs covered with flies. Then assigned to a crash boat where he got sea sick and was put in the boat pool. He returned to San Francisco May 10, 1945, as he had enough points to return to the states and sent to Tanfaran in San Bruno, CA, and discharged on Sept. 20, 1945.

He returned to his former job with Arkansas Ice and Storage Co. After a year, he moved to Los Angeles and worked for Eastside Beer and Pabst Blue Ribbon as a draft beer serviceman. In 1963, he moved to Santa Rosa, CA, where he retired from Sonoma County Community Hospital where he had worked as a maintenance man.

He was active in the American Legion Post 21 which gave him a fitting funeral and also honored him

by flying his casket flag on Memorial Day 1995 at Post 21s Ave of Flags. He had succumbed to pancreatic cancer on Oct. 21, 1994. He left his wife, son, daughter and three grandchildren.

RHEA STARR JR., EM1/c, born Feb. 14, 1924, in Imboden, AR. Joined Navy Oct. 2, 1942, at Phoenix, AZ. Went to boot camp in San Diego, CA, for three weeks then assigned to electrician school in San Diego. After completing school in February 1943, was assigned to the USS *Maryland* and boarded her in New Caledonia in South Pacific in March where he spent remainder of his Navy time in E Div., working on telephones and engine room.

While on board the USS *Maryland* he was involved in all operations from Tarawa, (where they took two prisoners), to Okinawa. Also, he made several trips on "Magic Carpet" duty after Japan surrendered.

He was honorably discharged Dec. 31, 1945, and returned to his home in Imboden, AR.

He retired in 1985 and lives in Jonesboro, AR where he enjoys spending time with his five daughters, six grandchildren and two great-grandchildren.

KENNETH A. "CASEY" STENGEL, CSK, born Jan. 29, 1917, Mauston, WI. Enlisted Sept. 26, 1940, USN, storekeeper, S Div.

Stationed NTS Great Lakes, IL; USS *Maryland* (BB-46); SCTC Term. Island, CA; USS *Edgecomb* (APA-164), USS *Xanthus* AR.

Participated in battles in Pearl Harbor, three South Pacific combat missions. Attack on Japan at the time of her surrender to US.

Memorable experiences: after being at Pearl Harbor and other So. Pacific Island missions, it was good to see Japan on her knees surrendering.

Awarded American Defense, one star, American Area, Asiatic-Pacific Area, Good Conduct and one star, World War II, Victory Communication Ribbon. Discharged Nov. 30, 1946, as CSK. Married Lois Schermerhorn July 1, 1942. He has two sons, one daughter, four grandchildren and three great-grand-children.

Employed with Civil Service as contract specialist. Started A.F. Academy as chief of buying division.

Retired 22 years ago on 12 acres. Spend the winters in the South, either Florida, Texas or Arizona.

WILLIAM ARTHUR STEPHENS, E7 HTC, born in Gordon, TX. Enlisted Nov. 1, 1929, in USN as 5th, 6th S&R Divs.

Stationed USNTS, San Diego, CA; USS *Maryland;* USS *Denebola,* USS *Delta,* US Sub base, Groton, CT; USS *Orion,* USS *Proteus,* USS *Fulton.*

Participated in four air battles in North Africa. Awarded American Defense, Good Conduct, National

Defense, American Campaign, EAME Campaign, Victory Medal.

Discharged March 23, 1956 as E7 HTC. Married twice and has no children. Employed with Texas Lubricant Corp. Now employed as salesman.

PAUL W. STEWART, Chief Machinist's Mate, born June 21, 1920, at Custer, OK. Moved to Louisville, KY, in 1925. He enlisted in the USN June 25, 1940. Went to Great Lakes, IL and was discharged April 1947. He was at Pearl Harbor on the day of the attack on the USS *Maryland* (BB-46). At that time he was on watch in the forward engine room.

He has the American Defense Medal, American Area Medal, Asiatic-Pacific Area Medal, eight stars, Philippine Liberation Medal, World War II Victory Medal. Joined the Naval Reserve at Pasco, WA and retired Nov. 25, 1980, chief machinist's mate. He was married in Louisville, KY, Sept. 27, 1947, moved to Richland, WA, November 1947 for his job at Hanford, WA. He has four daughters. He passed away Sept. 3, 1992.

EUSTACE E. "GENE" STOREY, BM2/c, born May 31, 1922. Enlisted Sept. 4, 1940, USN BM2/c, 6B. Stationed USS *Maryland,* USS *Winged Arrow,* USS *Brazos.*

Participated in Pearl Harbor, Gilbert Island, Marshall Island, Leyte, Marianas, Western Caroline Island, Okinawa Operation.

Memorable experience includes six years serving with wonderful people. His fondest memory is the first reunion in Milwaukee, WI, where he was reunited with those he served with 30 years ago.

Awarded seven Battle Stars and Good Conduct Medals. Married when discharged and has one son. Employed with Gates Rubber Co. as supervisor. He is a laryngectomee (no vocal cords). Retired.

He was the sole founder of the USS Maryland Veterans Association holding the first reunion in Milwaukee, WI in 1974. He has been active every since he was discharged in 1946. One of 11 who organized the Pearl Harbor Survivors Association, Long Beach, CA 1958.

EDMUND S. "ED" SWANSON, born Nov. 8, 1918, in Minneapolis, MN. Enlisted in the USN June 7, 1939. Discharged Sept. 10, 1945, as CBM. Basic training at Great Lakes, IL. Assigned to Torpedo Station Keyport, WA Oct. 1, 1939, for 14 months. Transferred to the USS *Maryland* Dec. 10, 1940 to March 15, 1943. Attended Mine Warfare School, Yorktown, VA. Assigned to YMS-198 for 10 months, operating out of Newport, RI. Assigned to YMS-381 for overseas duty - 14 months.

Operating with 10 other wooden hull YMSs, they shared in sweeping of moored but mainly for magnetic mines off invasion beaches at Normandy. Exploding or detonating their first torpedo shaped, bottom hugging, magnetic mine was a great thrill for all of them. But sadly they lost two ships one from a new pressure type, dropped by parachutes at night, the other a tentacled moored mine in the entrance to Cherbourg's harbor.

He would like to revert to his first love the USS *Maryland.* Especially to some of his former shipmates whose names may be missing from this book and the deep impressions they left within him.

BM1/c Reeves set the tone throughout the 1st Div. with measured discipline and southern drawl - a very able leader. Henry Caley BM2/c from Ishpeming, MI. Very knowledgeable in seamanship and respected by all. He completed his four year hitch in early 1941, got married, and he remembers seeing him later as a foreman rigger in the Bremerton Shipyard. "Pappy" Roberts BM2/c, later CWO, was something special for he showed by his actions that he cared for his men. His deep voice seemingly gruff at times permeated throughout the 1st Div. Compartment. In charge of a working party especially in the double bottoms made sure everyone was accounted for after the last dog was secured or working over the side in dry dock, painting or chipping paint kept a watchful eye on all secured life lines. Chief Charles "Buck" Evans, Gunners Mate in #1 Turret, a likeable person and respected by all and very thorough in what he does. Who later lost his life, from the kamikaze armor piercing bomb that penetrated the deck between #1 and #2 turret.

HAROLD O. SWANSON, SKD1/c, born April 4, 1922, in Omaha, NE, joined the USN April 1943. Went to boot camp at Farragut, ID. Assigned to service school NTSch (storekeeper) at Farragut, ID August 1943. Graduated December 1943 number eight in class of 153 qualified for duty as SK3/c. Reported for duty aboard USS *Maryland* Dec. 28, 1943. Participated creditably in operations for capture and occupation of Marshall Islands, the Marianas (Saipan), Palau, the Philippine Islands (Leyte), night surface engagement and wipe-out of enemy fleet in Surigao Straits and then to Okinawa. Advanced SKD2/c Dec. 17, 1944, SKD1/c May 19, 1945.

Participated in "Magic Carpet" duty bringing troops home following the Japanese surrenders. The *Maryland* caught an aerial torpedo at Saipan, "kamikaze" in Leyte Gulf, and another "kamikaze" at Okinawa. Discharged on Jan. 12, 1946. Returned to Omaha to same job held when life interrupted for war time service. In 1947 became involved in petroleum distribution business until retirement. He has been married 54 years, with three sons and two daughters, plus 13 grandchildren and one great-grandchild. It's been a good life!

PAUL F. SWEET, FC3/c, born Feb. 2, 1924, in Ketchum, OK. Enlisted Dec. 11, 1941, Seattle, WA, trained at San Diego and Balboa Park Station, CA, assigned to USS *Maryland* , Bremerton, WA, Jan. 5, 1942, with the 6B Div. January 1943 transferred to F Div.

Served in AA Btry. directors through all major combat operation of the *Maryland.* His most vivid memories of the war are the suicide air attacks at Leyte and the surface battle at Surigao Strait.

After three years and eight months, in September 1945 he was transferred to Fire Control School, Washington, DC. While enroute, the atomic bomb was dropped on Hiroshima. He declined school and was discharged on Oct. 8, 1945.

He returned home to Longview, WA, worked a year in Alaska as cook and second mate on a 120 foot steel tug boat. He graduated from Washington State University in 1954. Retired in 1985 having worked 29 years in Public Health as Environmental Health Director of four counties in Washington and Oregon. He was instrumental in organizing the Chehalis, WA. Lions Club in 1964 and served as charter secretary. Other membership are National and Washington State Environmental Health Associations and the USS Maryland (BB-46) National Veterans Association. He and his wife Bette, have two daughters and one son, nine grandchildren and two great-grandchildren. He resides in Chehalis, WA, plays a lot of golf, likes to travel and enjoys spending time with his grandchildren.

EDWARD J. SWENSON, S1/c, born Nov. 11, 1924. Enlisted USN Dec. 6, 1941, USS *Maryland* 1942-1945; Flag, commander Battleship Div. 6 on USS *North Carolina* and USS *Washington* April 1945 until discharged November 1945. USNR to 1947. Enlisted USCG November 1947. Served in several Coast Guard Cutters West Coast and Alaska as quartermaster second class to chief warrant boatswain. Graduated US Treasury Law Enforcement Officers Training School, special investigator, Coast Guard Intelligence, subsequently Chief Intelligence and Law Enforcement, 17th Coast Guard District. Retired as lieutenant (JG) December 1963.

Awarded following medals: Asiatic-Pacific w/7 Battle Stars, Philippine Liberation Medal w/2 stars, Philippine Presidential Unit Citation, Japanese Occupation, Korean Service, National Defense Service, United Nations Service and others.

Retired as legal operations manager, Oregon State Accident Insurance Fund December 1980. Retirement activities include collection and restoration of antique clocks and travel with Libbie, his wife since 1944.

LEO W. "SYLL" SYLLIAASEN, EM1/c, born Aug. 29, 1922, in Mission Hill, SD. Enlisted June 10, 1941 in USN and USNR March 3, 1963-August 29, 1982. Retired as chief electricians mate.

Stations Great Lakes, IL, Diesel School Ford Motor Co., Dearborn, MI; USS Ma*ryland,* USS *Pittsburg.*

Participated in battles in Tarawa, Kwajalein, Saipan, Leyte, Okinawa, Palau, Turrets 2 and 3 (16" guns).

Memorable experiences: At Tarawa, his curiosity aroused, he left the turret went top side to see the action. His curiosity quickly satisfied he retreated to the turret never to go top side again during battle.

Awarded American Defense, Asiatic-Pacific, American Campaign, World War II, Philippine Liberation, Good Conduct, USNR Meritorious Service, Armed Force Reserve.

Discharged June 7, 1947. Married Betty Dec. 23, 1943, and has two daughters, one son, six grandsons, two great-granddaughters, one great grandson.

Employed as chief electrician VA Hospital, owner 3/D Electric Inc. Electrician Ford Research and Engineering, (all in Dearborn, MI) Electrician GAF and Barkley Dam, in Kentucky. Retired assistant chief electrical inspector, city of Sacramento 1979. Sacramento Bee newspaper, resident electrical inspector C.S.U.S. (he was a workaholic) (theBee and C.S.U.S. were after he retired). Leo died Jan. 7, 1993, and is buried in the National Cemetery, Santa Nella, CA.

FRANK CALVIN THOMAS JR., ADC, born Dec. 16, 1919, in Oak Hill, WV. Served in USN, seaman first class, 3rd Div., Aviation Div.

Stationed USS *Maryland,* NAS Ford Island, NAS Alameda, USS *Torpedo* VR-22, Fasron 102, VF-173, Pearl Harbor, NAS Cecil Field.

Memorable experiences: being in the tops of USS *Maryland* on December 7 and looking down on the gun crews standing by for ammo.

Awarded six Good Conduct, Asiatic-Pacific, Navy Occupation Service Medal (Asia) same for European, China Service Medal, Philippine Liberation, American Area Campaign Medal.

Discharged July 1, 1960. Married to Ann Margurite and has onedaughter, Beverly Ann. Employed 14 years, NAS Jacksonville. Now retired.

CARLOS THOMASON, CWO-4, born Feb. 12, 1912, in Texas. Enlisted Aug. 7, 1930, in USN. Stationed USS *Maryland* 1931-1934, E Div.; USS *Ramapo,* USS *Maryland* Fleet Air Wing II.

Memorable experiences: He was assistant supply and disbursing officer FAW-II on Admiral Prices staff.

He retired with permanent rank of CWO-4. Married to Jean and has two daughters and three grandchildren. Employed in banking. Resides in Phoenix, AZ, where he is now retired and traveling.

WALTER TODD TUCKER JR., born July 2, 1921, in St. Petersburg, FL. Enlisted Aug. 6, 1940, in USN. Served 1st Div., 2nd Div., 5th Div., F Div., M Div. on the *Maryland.* Recruit training Platoon 100

Norfolk, VA. Reported aboard *Maryland* November 1940.

Participated in Pearl Harbor battle. Transferred to new construction September 1942.

Memorable experiences include: looking out the port side of the *Maryland* the morning of Dec. 7, 1941, and saw Japanese planes bombing and straffing the *Maryland* and Oklahoma.

Married to Rosa for 52 years. He has three children: Albert, Susan and Leslie. Retired customer services manager.

STAN J. VAN HOOSE, born Nov. 11, 1920. Enlisted Aug. 20, 1940, in USN. Stationed Norfolk, VA, basic training; USS *Maryland;* Pathfinder, USN Navy Yard Mare Island #4 AO42 1946-1948 as navigator; *Prince George* APA-160.

Participated in battles in Pearl Harbor, Midway, Solomon Island, Tarawa, Kwajalein, Saipan, Palau.

Memorable experience includes: Solomons; sneaking into Japanese Islands before invasion for info and navigation material for invasion chart making.

Discharged Aug. 21, 1948. Married Veronica (Vernie) Borzick in San Francisco, CA, Nov. 6, 1943. Moved to Beloit, WI, in 1950. Open own paint, wall paper, picture frames, distributor of Kirby and Hoover vacuum cleaners. Retired. Enjoys country music; guitar, banjo, fiddle. Hunting and fishing.

HOLLICE LLOYD VOYLES, Y2/c, Ex Div., born March 29, 1925, in Atlanta, GA. He was the fifth of seven sons born to Conner and Ola Voyles. Prior to duty in the Navy he was employed by Western Union and the Corps of Engineers, South Atlantic Div.

His father signed a consent for him to enter the Navy on Jan. 26, 1943. He arrived in San Diego, CA, on Feb. 10, 1943, for boot camp. He reported aboard the USS *Maryland* on July 20, 1943.

After the battle at Roi Islands of the Marshall Islands, near the end of January 1944 the *Maryland* was sent to the Navy Yard at Bremerton, WA, for overhaul. He learned his brother just two years older than him had also been in the same battle and died on a hospital ship on Feb. 2, 1944. He was given a 30 day leave to visit his family.

He was killed in a kamikaze attack on Nov. 29, 1944, off Leyte Island, Philippine.

Voyles was buried on the Island of Leyte, Philippine. His body was returned home to the United States where he was buried in DeKalb County, GA, on Sept. 5, 1948.

BOB LEE WALKER, SK2/c, born March 1, 1911, in Estelline, TX. Joined USN on Feb. 25, 1943. Remembering how he felt when he first saw "his" ship as she lay at anchor in Efate Harbor, New Hebrides, he was awestruck by her sheer size and thrilled to be assigned to her. He served as storekeeper second class for the duration of WWII.

While stationed on USS *Maryland* he was involved in six major combat operations: Tarawa, Kwajalein, Saipan, Palau Group, Leyte Gulf and Okinawa. After his discharge Oct. 5, 1945, he moved to Fort Worth driving 18-wheelers for Mashburn's, Miller Trucking Company and Container Corp., before becoming manager of a White's Auto Store. In 1955 he moved to Corpus Christi to manage the auto center, and later manager Shaffer's Muffler Shop until his retirement. Happily married for 62 years to the light of his life, Kitty (Barnett), they have a son, daughter, and three grown grandchildren who bring him joy.

Like many others who served during WWII, he recalls the senseless tragedies of war, but remembers why they fought. As he hoists the Stars and Stripes each day, the memory of his old shipmates is honored with dignity, respect, gratitude and pride in having served his country alongside them on such a fine old battleship.

WILSON WEEKS, MM1/c, born Oct. 16, 1921, in Benson, NC. Joined the USN May 1940. Went to boot camp at Norfolk, VA, and was assigned to USS *Maryland* November 1940 where he spent the rest of his Navy time working in the engine room (machinist mate) six years.

He was involved in seven combat operations and received seven Battle Stars. He was one of the remaining crew to stay on board doing duty bringing troops home after Japan surrendered. Discharged from the Navy May 1946, he returned to his home in Benson, NC. Farmed with his father for four years. Weeks moved to Newton Grove, NC in 1950. Retired from Carolina Power and Light Co. in 1985 after 31 years. He was a Pearl Harbor Survivor. He was married to Leola for 52 years, had one son Allan and two granddaughters. He passed away March 29, 1996.

LEONARD ARTHUR WILDER, MM2/c, born July 24, 1924, in Tulsa, OK. Enlisted USN Aug. 22, 1941, MM2/c, B Div.

Stationed USS *Maryland* (BB-46). Attended boot camp and machinist school in San Diego, CA. Boarded *Maryland* in San Francisco, January 1942.

Participated in all battles after Pearl Harbor. Discharged September 1945.

Memorable experiences: His battle station was on brass valve wheel under a vent on seaman's third deck. When ordered to change stations, was upset, but two weeks later the man who took his place was killed when suicide plane hit and flame from explosion came down vent.

Later while in sick bay for minor surgery, he decided to go to battle station during Philippine battle. A suicide plane hit the ship, killing nearly everyone in sick bay.

Discharged September 1945. Moved to Baytown, TX, October 1945. Married in May 1945. He has one son and two granddaughters. Worked for Exxon for 37 years. Retired as section supervisor in October 1982. Enjoying traveling, hunting and fishing.

VERNON RAY WILLIAMS, PhM3/c, born July 16, 1925, in Milford, TX. Enlisted Oct. 2, 1943, USN, HA1/c.

Attended boot camp, San Diego, CA; Shoemake, CA; USS *Maryland* May 4, 1944.

Participated in battles: Marianas Island Campaign, Saipan, Philippine Seas, battle of Palaus, Peleliu. October 7 arrived in Leyte Gulf. His ship involved in Surigao Strait battle.

November 17, 1944, spent time in Pearl Harbor for repair. Returned to Leyte Gulf. November 29, 1944, was killed by a Japanese suicide plane diving into ship, somewhere in Leyte Gulf.

He received medals for American Campaign, Asiatic-Pacific Campaign, World War II and the Purple Heart. Achieved the rank of H1/c. Effective Dec. 1, 1944, rank of petty officer third class, PhM3/c.

Buried in US Armed Forces Cemetery Tacloban #1 Leyte Grave 535. Later returned to Hillsboro, TX, for burial in Ridge Park Cemetery August 1948. He was survived by M/M Charlie Williams of Malone, TX. He had six brothers, three sisters and nieces and nephews.

EDD W. WILLOUGHBY, born Oct. 14, 1915, in Eldorado, AR. Enlisted USN Jan. 13, 1941. Attended boot camp, Norfolk, VA. Served USS *Boreas* April 14, 1941-June 12, 1941. December 7, 1941, Pearl Harbor attack; June 1941-March 1948 USS Maryland (BB-46) Boiler Div.

Made chief water tender March 1945; senior chief boilerman 1958. Involved in eight combat operations. Helped decomission. Reenlisted on board Jan. 12, 1947. Pac.Res. Fleet Bremerton, WA, April 1948-September 1949; USS Ca*valier* (APA-37) September 1949-November 1951; Receiving Station San Diego, CA, December 1951-June 1952; USS Cheva*lier* (DDR-805)

June 1952-September 1954; Recruiting duty Eldorado, AR, October 1954-April 1957; USS Cook (APD-130) April 1957-August 1960.

Retired August 1960. Moved to Eldorado, AR. October 1960-October 1964 operated garage and service station.

Moved to Ledyart, CT, October 1964 and worked at General Dynamics, elect boat Groton, CT. 1970 started to work at Connecticut College as service engineer. Retired

Married Ann Miller August 1947. They have three sons, John, Michael and Pat. Ann died June 1988. He remarried in 1990 to Virginia Smith. They live in Augusta, SC.

JOHN J. "JACK" WOLF, MM3/c, born Nov. 16, 1926, in Omaha, NE. Joined the USN in Omaha, NE, on Nov. 27, 1943. Went to boot camp at Farragut, ID. Attended basic engineering school in Great Lakes and school in Philadelphia. Assigned to the USS *Maryland* in Hawaii where he spent the rest of his Navy time working in A Div.

While on board the USS *Maryland,* was involved in six major combat operations. He was one of the remaining crew to stay on board for the "Magic Carpet" duty bringing troops home after Japan surrendered. He was discharged from the Navy in February of 1946. He returned to Omaha and worked in the printing business until he retired.

He is very active in his church, the Knights of Columbus, and the VFW where he served in the Honor Guard. He is married and has four children and seven grandchildren.

OREN W. WRIGHT, born July 30, 1919, at Leavenworth, WA. He joined the USMC in Yakima, WA, September 1940 went through boot camp and sea school in San Diego, CA. Transferred to Bremerton aboard the USS *Enterprise,* then joined the 7th Div., USS *Maryland* Dec. 6, 1940.

He was a member of the Marines color guard when the Japs attacked Pearl Harbor Dec. 7, 1941. Combat station was on the 5.51 broadsides, as they were useless for anti-aircraft, he was ammo passer on one of the 1.1 anti-aircraft guns until it jammed, then ammo passer on a 5.25 gun.

He fought fire on the fantail, burning oil from USS *West Virginia* was main hazard, with a sailor he can't identify.

Later transferred to Pearl Harbor hospital for knee operation, then guard duty at the Pearl Harbor Marine station. 1944, transferred to North Carolina for scout sniper and training, then to Camp Elliott, San Diego where joined Co. F, 29th 2nd Bn. Marines to Guadalcanal where the 6th Marine Div. was formed and trained.

The 6th Marine Div. attacked Okinawa, Easter Sunday 1945. Company F was in the second wave. He was radio man after the regular man was injured.

The 2nd Bn., F Co. was almost wiped out on Sugar Loaf Hill on June 19, 1945. Wright received grenade and rifle wounds.

Transferred to Bremerton aboard the USS *Atlanta.* Discharged November 1945. He became land and construction surveyor, street and sewer superintendent, QC inspector, construction engineer, and inspector nuclear plants, copper projects in Iran, Algeria, Saudi Arabia and Bolivia.

Also Palo Verde nuclear plant was head of QC inspection all nine cooling towers. South Vietnam was superintendent at Phan Thiet Air Base.

He married twice, losing both wonderful wives to heart attack and stroke, presently living in Aroville, WA, and Sun City, AZ, and is a busy rock hound.

Courtesy of Capt. R.G. Glumack

USS Maryland Roster

This roster was provided by the USS Maryland Association and was the most current one available at the time we received it.

- A -

ABRAMS, MAXWELL
ADAIR, HENRY
ADKINS, JR., ALLEN M.
AIELLO, JOSEPH
ALBECK, HAROLD
ALCOSER, JOE
ALLEN, ROBERT
ALVARADO, VALENTINE
AMBROSIA, CLARENCE
AMOS, ARVIL E.
AMY, ALVIN E.
AMY, HUBERT R.
ANDERSEN, CLIFF P.
ANDERSON, LEIGHTON
ANDRETTA, COSMO L.
APPLEBURY, CARL W.
ARMSTRONG, WAYNE F.
ARNAUD, JACK J.
ARNOLD, GAYLORD
ASHBY, JOHN H.
ATCHLEY, GEORGE
AUSTIN, GEORGE E.
AUTRY, WILFORD A.

- B -

BAGGETT, ALVIN
BAILS, ROBERT L.
BAKER, BURDELL
BAKER, HUGH R.
BALL, DWAYNE R.
BALLARD, GEORGE H.
BALOK, JOHN B.
BALTZER, RICHARD P.
BALZA, FIRMAN J.
BANGS, ROBERT R.
BANKES, FRANCIS
BARKER, HUGH R.
BARNES, CARL V.
BARNETT, CLIFFORD W
BARRY, GEORGE J.
BATCHA, JOHN
BATCHELLER, J.H. "PETE"
BAUER, HERMAN
BEAMAN, RICHARD W.
BECKSTRAND, ROBERT G.
BEHM, MELVIN
BELISLE, FRANK E.
BELL, DAVID W.
BELLOWS, ROBERT E.
BENTON, RALPH
BERDIKOSKI, RALPH E.
BERKHEIMER, H. ALLEN
BERLIER, JOHN
BERMAN, BOB
BETHEL, GEORGE L.
BICKEL, ARNOLD
BILSEND, DUANE K.
BIPPERT, ALVIN A.
BIPPERT, LEROY H.
BIPPERT, REINHART L.
BLACK, DELBERT D.
BLACKFORD, A. VINCENT
BLAND, JAMES P.
BLIMLING, DONALD H.
BODEMAN, DONALD W.
BOEHLERT, BILL
BOLANDER, ALFRED M.
BOLE, WAYNE R.
BOLIN, AARON

BOND, L.S.
BOOHER, LARUE
BOSSERT, JOHN W.
BOWDEN, ARTHUR
BOWMAN, WALTON A.
BOYINGTON, JOHN W.
BOYS, ROBERT P.
BOYSEN, NORMAN
BRACKEN, D.J.
BRAEUTIGAM, RICHARD
BRANHAM, PAUL L.
BRAUER, ROBERT W.
BREWER, JAMES C.
BRIGHT, RALPH W.
BROCK, A.V.
BROMWELL, FRANK H.
BROWN, LEONARD
BROWN, ROBERT E.
BRUCE, WILLARD
BRUTON, W.E. "JACK"
BUCHANNAN, ANDREW
BUCHER, W.W.
BUCK, GEORGE
BUENNINGER, FRED
BUGGINS, ALBERT E.
BUNJES, JOHN V.
BUNTING, THOMAS E.
BUREK, VALERIAN P.
BURKHART, TYSON
BURLEY, CAPT. THOMAS
BURROW, HERBERT
BURTON, WILLIAM J.

- C -

CADE, CLINTON L.
CALLAWAY, BILLY U.
CAMPBELL, ALAN J.
CARNEY, EDWARD L.
CARR, ROBERT
CARRON, NORVAL A.
CARRUTH, EDWARD N.
CARTER, DONALD E.
CARTER, KENNETH C.
CATLIN, ERLING V.
CAYCE, CLARENCE P.
CHAMBERS, DAN T.
CHAMPEAU, HAROLD
CHAPIN, M.E.
CHAPMAN, DAVID E.
CHAPMAN, DOUG
CHAPPELL, EDMOND R.
CHAPPELL, FRED H.
CHASE, WILLIAM H.
CHRISTENSEN, KENNETH W.
CHRISTIANSEN, ARNOLD W.
CLAUSEN, GAIL L.
CLAWSON, KERMIT J.
CLAYTON, RAYMOND W.
CLEVELAND, RALPH E.
CODY, ROBERT E.
COE, MELVIN E.
COFFEY, G.A.
COFFMAN, WAYNE W.
CONNER, GLENN H.
CONSALARO, CORTEO
COOLEY, HAROLD M.
COOLEY, VENTON J.
COOPER, JACK
COPENHAVER, HOWARD
CORN, JAMES H.

COTTER, M.J.
COTTINGHAM, JACK
COWIN, ZANE G.
CRAFT, HORACE D.
CRAMER, DELMAR W.
CRANE, RAYMOND
CRAWFORD, FELDER
CRENSHAW, HOWARD
CROOM, JAMES W.
CROSARIOL, RICHARD
CUNNINGHAM, HAROLD L.
CUNY, F.A.
CURRY, CARL E.
CUTLER, LEO

- D -

DAKE, HERBERT L.
DANLEY, OWEN
DAUGHTERY, JAMES P.
DAVID, DUDLEY
DAVID, JUSTIN J.
DAVIS, C.M.
DAVIS, EDWARD A.
DAVIS, HALE H.
DAVIS, S.A.
DAVIS, WALTER F.
DAVIS, WALTER W.
DE BUSK, ELMER C.
DE MIN, JAMES
DEAHN, WILLIAM H.
DEEG, HAROLD
DELAY, JACK T.
DELONG, MARK E.
DELUHERY, FRANCIS J.
DENNIS, FRANKLIN
DERKOWSKI, MAX
DI MARTINO, EMANUEL
DI MARTINO, ANTHONY D.
DI MENNA, E.A.
DIBB, LARRY E.
DIETRICH, WILLIAM H.
DIETZ, ARDEN M.
DIETZ, FRED
DIMOND, Jr., CLARK W.
DIVIN, STEVE
DONEY, CLARENCE
DONOVAN, RAY P.
DORSEY, J.E.
DOWING, BERL
DOWNS, R.A.
DREWRY, JAMES A.
DUCKWORTH, CARL R.
DUKE, HUGH R.
DUNCAN, ROBERT S.
DUNN, CHARLES H.
DUNNING, GORDON

- E -

EBERHARDT, C.W.
EDQUIST, HERBERT E.
EDWARDS, RICHARD
EDWARDS, W.G.
EGGER, FRED W.
ELLIS, WILLIAM A.
ENGLISH, THOMAS T.
EPPS, HOWELL R.
ERESMAN, ARTHUR
ERION, LLOYD V.
ESPOSITO, ERNEST
ETCHISON, D.T.

EVERETT, ALLEN L.
EVERETT, BILLY E.

- F -

FALKNER, JOHN D.
FARMER, JOHN R.
FERCH, MAX L.
FETZER, RAY
FINCH, CHARLES E.
FINDLEY, GERRY
FINKENBINDER, P.H.
FIRMES, W.J.
FISCHER, FRED E.
FISCHER, JAMES J.
FLEENER, CECIL M.
FLORIDA, CHARLES
FLYNN, FREEMAN
FOLTZ, THURSTON
FORD, JUSTIN A.
FORSELLES, CHARLES G.
FORSTER, ALFRED
FOSTER, MALCOM L.
FOX, JAMES E.
FRANCIS, CAPT. JACK
FRAZIER, EUGENE F.
FREDERICKS, JACK J.
FREEMAN, JAMES R.
FREYOU, HOWARD J.
FRONCZAK, LEO. J.
FROST, DAYTON
FRYDENLUND, MARVIN W.
FRYE, KEITH E.
FRYE, MARION W.
FULKERSON, CHARLES
FULSTONE, LAWRENCE
FUNK, LLOYD C.

- G -

GABRIELSON, HARRY
GAFFORD, WALTER A.
GALLAGHER, PAUL F.
GAMMONS, DONALD E.
GARDNER, GEORGE W.
GARRISON, WILLIAM E.
GARVEY, LAWRENCE A.
GASBARRO, ANTHONY S.
GEISSLER, ALBERT P.
GHOLSEN, C.F.
GIBSON, C.H.
GILES, WILBERT A.
GILMORE, GIL
GLUMACK, RAY
GLYNN, C.J. "CLIFF"
GODDARD, L. JACK
GOLDEN, WILLIAM A.
GOLDSMITH, NORMAN J.
GOODMAN, CLYDE H.
GOODMAN, WILBERT E.
GORDON, J.C.
GORDON, RAYMOND L.
GRAY, GLENN
GRAY, JOHN E.
GREEN, FRANK J.
GREENWALD, JOE
GRINDSTAFF, ART
GROBE, GEORGE H.
GROH, WILLIAM H.
GROVE, CHESTER L.
GRUBER, STANLEY
GUARINO, EDWARD N.

GUEY, JOHN A.
GUFFY, BILL
GURULE, ABEL F.
GUYNN, HARLEY B.

- H -
HABERMAN, THEODORE H.
HAKLITCH, F.A.
HALE, V.R.
HALIGAS, ROBERT
HALIGAS, WILLIAM J.
HALL, FRED
HALLEY, ROBERT T.
HALPERN, BERNARD
HALSTEAD, DAVID M.
HALVIS, JOHN
HAMBY, FLEET A.
HANCHETT, ALBERT L.
HANER, ALVA L.
HANES, CLYDE E.
HANLY, H.R. "BUD"
HANNAH, ROBERT L.
HANNON, THOMAS E.
HANSBERRY, DEAN R.
HANSEN, BOB H.
HANSEN, GORDON W.
HANSON, RUSSEL K.
HANSON, WILBER
HARDING, JACK
HARLAN, LESCAR
HARMON, JAMES W.
HARRIS, ORVILLE M.
HARRIS, ROBERT C.
HARTLE, GEORGE H.
HAST, BERNARD
HAY, GEORGE P.
HEADY, DARWIN R.
HEIN, MAX
HENRY, PAUL G.
HENSEL, ROGER F.
HERMANSON, D.L.
HESTON, TOM.
HICKS, CHARLES E.
HIGGINS, J.A.
HILL, KENNETH E.
HILL, OCIE
HILL, VAUGHN W.
HILLMAN, LESTER R.
HILLYER, JAMES J.
HINTON,Jr., LESLIE E.
HIRSCH, L.E.
HOBERT, C. EDWARD
HOLLIS, STEPHEN
HOLM, RALPH R.
HOLMS, EPHRAM P.
HOLP, ROBERT R.
HOLSTEIN, J. FRED
HOPE, CHARLES H.
HOPE, WILLARD O.
HOUGHLAND, HERBERT
HOULE, ROBERT C.
HOUSER, GALEN D.
HOWARD, CHAS. W.
HOWARD, SAM
HUBER, WILLIAM H.
HUFFMAN, HERSHEL
HUGH A., FRANK
HULL, HAROLD
HURON, LEO
HUTCHIN, EDWARD L.
HUTTERMAN, LLOYD G.

- I -
IRBY, DON A.
ISELI, JOHN F.

- J -
JACKSON, ALBERT C.
JACKSON, GEORGE D.
JACKSON, JESSE R.
JACKSON, WILLIAM S.
JAEGER, EDWARD J.
JAGODITSCH, HAROLD L.
JAMES, HENRY
JEFFREY, RICHARD P.
JENSEN, ROBERT H.
JOHNSON, CLARENCE
JOHNSON, HARRY D.
JOHNSON, JAMES A.
JOHNSON, JEROME
JOHNSON, JOHN W.
JOHNSON, MILTON O.
JOHNSON, NORMAN E.
JOHNSON, RAYMOND
JOHNSON, SELDON G.
JOHNSTON, JIM C.
JONES, K.Y.
JONES, WALLACE
JORGENSEN, E.R.

- K -
KAMERY, DARRELL
KAMPF, ALFRED N.
KEIS, DONALD W.
KELLY, THOMAS J.
KEMP, WILLIAM R.
KEMPSTER, WILLIAM A.
KERR, A.H.
KERSHAW, OLAND J.
KIEHNE, RUDY A.
KILBOURNE, CHARLES R.
KILGORE,
KIMBAL, THOMAS E.
KIMBERLIN, ORVILLE T.
KINKADE, Jr., JOHN
KINSEY, HAROLD N.
KLAVE, KENNETH
KLEPPIN, ROBERT E.
KNIGHT, HERCHEL
KOERNER, FREDRICK
KOHNTOPP, LEROY J.
KOMMERSTAD, EARL L.
KRAYNAK, GEORGE S.
KRUM, NEVIN D.
KRYSAN, DONALD F.
KUGLE, PAUL W.
KUHLOW, FRANK
KUHNS, DAVE

- L -
LA MORGE, FRANK W.
LACKEY, GLEN F.
LACY, HAROLD M.
LAIZURE, T. ROBERT
LAMB, GALE V.
LAMBERT, L.C.
LAMOREAUX, DENNIS
LAND, WERNER J.
LANDRY, BEATRICE
LANSDALE, HAROLD
LATHAM, WILLIE J.
LAWRENCE, KENNETH J.
LAXSON, ROBERT A.
LE BLANC, FRANCIS S.
LEATHERMAN, ROBIN R.
LEE, EDWARD L.
LEE, W.A.
LEHMAN, HAROLD M.
LEMON, HOMER H.
LILL, ALLEN
LINCOLN, ROGER M.

LOCKWOOD, BILL
LOEFFLER, ROLAND
LONGCOR, WALTER M.
LONGFELLOW,Jr, ROBERT
LONON, HOWARD L.
LOVETT, JIM. L.
LOWE, CLARENCE A.
LOWERRE, WARREN P.
LYMAN, RAYMOND
LYONS, JOHN L.

- M -
MAC GILL, JOHN
MacFARLANE, ALAN
MADSEN, HAROLD
MALECHA, LEO W,
MALLY, WARD
MALONEY, D.L.
MANN, TOM E.
MARSH, ARTHUR W.
MARSHALL, LLOYD D.
MARTIN, VERGIL E.
MARTIN, WAYNE D.
MASSEY, Jr., ROBERT
MASSICOTTE, ROBERT D.
MATLOCK, EDWARD J.
MAURER, ROBERT
MAY, WILLIAM R.
MAYER, DONALD K.
MAYVILLE, KEN.
MC ALLISTER, JAMES A.
MC BETH, RAYMOND
MC BRATNEY, RICHARD B.
MC CLASSON, SAM J.
MC CONE, H.L.
MC CORD, LLOYD
MC DOWELL, L.R.
MC FARLAND, JAMES C.
MC FARLAND, JAMES L.
MC GOVERN, RALPH L.
MC KEEHAN, Jr., ROY
MC KENZIE, EARL E.
MC LEAN, WILL
MC PHERSON, EUGENE
MC WILLIAMS, L. ROBERT
MEADOWS, JOE
MECLEWSKI, PETER P.
MENDENHALL, DICK
MICHAEL, JOHN PAUL
MICHELSEN, MIKE" L.A.
MICHLER, ALEXANDER J.
MIKESELL, RICHARD N.
MILCOVICH, STEVEN
MILLER, HAROLD L.
MILLER, GAIL R.
MILLER, W. CHAS.
MILLER, W.C.
MILLETTE, HENRY G.
MILLIMAN, LOWELL L.
MILLS, ROLAND A.
MINIERI, JOSEPH A.
MIRANDA, JOHN A.
MITCHELL, DONALD E.
MITCHELL, FRANK A.
MITCHELL, GLENN H.
MITTELSTADT, RICHARD L.
MOLSBERRY, V.L.
MONHEIT, GEORGE
MONTGOMERY, ORVILLE
MONTGOMERY, WILLIAM P.
MOODY, CHARLES E.
MOOLE, CHARLES F.
MOORE, FOSTER A.
MOORE, HOMER LEE
MOOREHOUSE, DEAN O.

MORAND, LEE J.
MORGAN, BRADY W.
MORGAN, LEO R.
MORGAN, ROY L.
MORGAN, WARNER S.
MORIN, PATRICK A.
MOROSI, ALBERT
MORRIS, ARLIE C.
MORROW, HUGH T.
MORTON, NORMAN E.
MOSHER, KENNETH H.
MOSLANDER, CLYDE C.
MOUNTZ, G.L.
MUIRHEAD, VINCENT U.
MULLENS, EDGAR V.
MUNOZ, R.I.
MURAS, CARLES J.
MURPHY, BERNARD J.
MUSCHBACKER, EMIL P.
MYCKA, WALTER J.

- N -
NAJJAR, BURNETT
NELSEN, NORMAN E.
NELSON, JOHN A.
NEPHEW, RANDAL H.
NESBETT, CLIFFTON R.
NEVIN,Jr., ROBERT S.
NEWTON, LESTER
NICHOLS, FORREST E.
NICHOLS, JAMES L.
NIEHUES, PAUL
NIELSEN, RUSSELL L.
NIEST, FRANK E.
NIXON, SIDNEY
NOLIN, CHARLES W.
NOTT, WILLIAM H.

- O -
O'BRIEN, LESLIE J.
O'BRIEN, TIMOTHY J.
O'DELL, WILLIAM H.
O'HEARN, CHARLES.
O'QUIN, HERBERT W.
OAKLAND, MICHAEL
OBERMEIR, WALTER T.
OLBERG, STIRLING M.
OLIGSCHLAEGER, JEROME
OLINGER, WILLIAM B.
OLIVER, ALFRED F.
OLIVER, ROD
ONEY, CLYDE
ORMAN, DWIGHT L.
OSBORNE, JAMES R.
OTTOWA, ERNEST E.
OWEN, ROBERT O.

- P -
PACE, J.C.
PAGE, ROLAND L.
PALKO, THEODORE J.
PALOMO, MIKE
PATTERSON, M.L.
PATTON, L.S.
PEAY, CHARLES R.
PEDERSON, DON S.
PEELER, OLLIE E.
PEISNER, HAROLD
PEREIRA, H.K.
PERKINS, J.W.
PETERSEN, RAY G.
PETERSEN, SHANNON L.
PETERSON, A.J.
PETERSON, EDWIN
PETERSON, WARNER E.

PETRE, LLOYD J.
PETTICREW, W.K.
PFUNDHELLER, CLARENCE
PIAT, STANLEY F.
PINKSTON, WILLIAM R.
PINNELL, CHARLES
PITTULLO, JEROLD
PLATT, ERNEST E.
PLESE, WILLIAM C.
POELMA, F.W. (Pat)
POHLMANN, HARRY B.
PORTER, DEAN F.
PORTER, HAROLD B.
PORTER, LOWELL E.
POTIER, PAUL J.
PREHM, JAMES K.
PRICE,Jr., WILLIAM P.
PRISK, LLOYD E.
PROTEAU, LEO A.
PRUITT, J.W.
PUISSEGUR, "BILL"
PURSER, AARON C.

- Q -
QUINN, JAY P.
QUINN, RICHARD V.

- R -
RADER, WARD A.
RAE, SAMUEL C.
RAGLE, VERL S.
RAMOS, ROLANDO
RAWLINGS, EARL F.
RAYBURN, CHARLIE W.
RAYMER, CHARLES A.
REAM, ROBERT H.
RECTOR, HOWARD N.
RECTOR, KARL B.
RECTOR, KENNETH W.
REECE, BILL D.
REITZ, HARVEY E.
RELL, ROBERT J.
REMSEN, ROBERT N.
RENNER, CLARENCE E.
REYNOLDS, TIM E.
REYNOLDS, WILLIAM E.
RHINEHART, EDWARD
RHODE, BRYANT A.
RICHTER, WILMER E.
RIDGWAY, JESSIE L.
RIGNEY, PETE
RILEE, ROBERT C.
RIMATIME, M.C. (TE)
RINEHOLT, ROBERT E.
RING, WAYNE D.
RINGLEY, GALE
ROACH, HOMER B.
ROBBINS, TOMMY R.
ROBERTS, JIM
ROBERTS, WILLIAM J.
ROBERTS, WILLIAM R.
ROBERTSON, GERALD A.
ROBINSON, FLOYD P.
ROBINSON, GEORGE F.
ROBINSON, JACK W.
ROBINSON, ROBERT F.
ROCKER, ROY H.
ROM, WILLIAM N.
ROSENBERGER, RICHARD K.
ROSS, CHARLES J.
ROUSSEAU, JOSEPH E.
ROWE, WILLIAM F.
RUDDY, OWEN R.
RUGEN, RONALD A.
RUSK, BLAINE A.

RUSSELL, LEE C.
RUSSELL, RAYMOND A.

- S -
SALY, HAROLD A.
SANTY, NOEL F.
SAUER, HOWARD
SCHACKELFORD, EARL
SCHAEFFER, R.L. (RUDY)
SCHAFER, HOWARD E.
SCHECTER, EARL L.
SCHEUBLE, ARTHUR H.
SCHIRMER, OTTO L.
SCHISSLER, RUDY W.
SCHNEIDER, PAUL J.
SCHNETSKY, ERVEN
SCHREIBER, HAROLD A.
SCHWARTZ, KARL A.
SCOTT, DENZIL G.
SCOTT, JOHN D.
SEAMAN, EDWARD A.
SELBY, WALTER
SELLS, HAROLD W.
SESSUMS, EARL A.
SETTLE, KEITH W.
SEVERSON, WILLIAM O.
SHACKELFORD, A.E.
SHAPPLEY, WILLIAM
SHARP, R.L.
SHARRETT, DELBERT E.
SHEPARD, E.O.
SHERRILL, HARLAN A.
SHOCKLEY, JOHN A.A.
SHORDT, PETER H.
SHORT, LESLIE
SHUHARTT, CHARLES
SHUMARD, LEO M.
SHUPP, WARREN E.
SHURTZ, FRED M.
SIEH, ROLAND W.
SIEMIENCZUK, JOHN
SILVEY, CHARLES R.
SIMONIS, R.P.
SIMONSEN, JENS P.
SINATRA, LORETO L.
SINCLAIR, JOHN
SINOR, JAMES E.
SISSON, WILLIS J.
SKELTON, GEORGE T.
SKINNER, EASTON C.
SKINNER, WILLIAM W.
SLIGH, ZEB D.
SMITH, BRADFORD A.
SMITH, CHARLES A.
SMITH, CHARLES D.
SMITH, DONALD L.
SMITH, HOWARD L.
SMITH, HOWARD O.
SMITH, JAMES L.
SMITH, JULIAN J.
SMITH, L.J.
SMITH, ROBERT L.
SMITH, W.M.
SMITH, WILLIAM G.
SMOOT, JUSTICE O.
SMYTH, WILLIAM W.
SORENSON, HOWARD P.
SORENSON, ROBERT C.
SOTAK, MIKE J.
SOUTHWICK, TOM A.
SOWADA, CLAUDE A.
SPASOFF, WALTER
SPOONER, EDWIN G.
STANFORD, HARVEY E.
STANLEY, JACK

STARK, GLENN H.
STARKEY, JAMES R.
STARR, RHEA
STECKER, FREDRICK
STEINHART, DON
STENGEL, KENNETH A.
STEPHENSON, GEORGE S.
STEVENSON, OSCAR EARL
STINE, CARL W.
STONE, ELBERT L.
STOREY, EUGENE
STOUT, HERMAN E.
SUINHKONEN, JOHN A.
SUMMERELL, LESTER L.
SUMMERS, GARTH E.
SWANSON, EDMUND S.
SWANSON, ELMO
SWANSON, HAROLD O.
SWEANEY, LOGAN G.
SWEENEY, HARRY W.
SWEET, PAUL F.
SWENSON, EDWARD J.
SWENSON, HILDING
SWISHER, CHESTER P.

- T -
TAYLOR, JAMES L.
TAYLOR, WYMAN L.
TERRY, CHARLES E.
TERRY, CLIFFORD R.
TERRY, THEODORE M.
THOMAS, FRANK C.
THOMAS, G.H.
THOMPSON, LUTHER N.
THRO, JOHN B.
THRUSTON, FOLTZ
TIDWELL, GEORGE B.
TIGNAC, HENRY
TODD, HAROLD R.
TOMER, HENRY A.
TOMLINSON, C.C.
TOPPER, F. EUGENE
TOTTEN, WENDELL E.
TOURTILLOTT, ALBERT F.
TOWNSEND, DAVID W.
TRANSTRUM, LARRY O.
TRAPANI, PETER G.
TRIER, HUBERT R.
TROLLINGER, C.S.
TROTTA, JOSEPH S.
TUCKER, WILLIAM H.
TUCKER,Jr., WALTER T.

- U -
ULRICH, VERNON L.
UNDERHILL, WILLIAM E.

- V -
VAN HOOSE, S.J.
VAN VLECK, MARVIN E.
VANDEVOORDE, LAWRENCE
VARNELL, LAWRENCE
VARNUM, ART.
VILCONE, R.W.
VILLARREAL, PETE
VISLAY, LOUIS T.
VOLKERS, HARVEY R.
VORE, NED E.
VOYLES, DARREN
VOYLES, HERMAN A.
VOYLES, MELVIN
VOYLES, RAYMOND
VOYLES, WAYNE
VREEKEN, FRED R.

- W -
WADDELL, DICK
WALKER, BOB L.
WALLACE, EDWARD
WALLACE, JAMES B.
WALLACE, WILLIAM
WALLER, GEORGE E.
WANTZ, JESSIE M.
WARNER, JOHN D.
WASKEY, JAMES A.
WATERS, BOB
WATSON, CHARLES F.
WATSON, D.J.
WEAVER, LAURENCE
WEBB, ALTON W.
WEBB, CHARLES
WEBB, JAMES R.
WEIS, V.F.
WELCH, FLOYD R.
WELLS, LIONEL E.
WELLS, OTTO M.
WESTERMAN, J.J."JACK"
WEVERS, FRANK
WHITEHALL, RUSSELL W.
WILCOX, A.J.
WILCOZ, G.W.
WILDER, LEONARD A.
WILES, OSCAR E.
WILLIAMS, C.B.
WILLIAMS, CARL
WILLIAMS, CARL F.
WILLIAMS, GEORGE W.
WILLIAMS, IKE
WILLIAMS, ODELL
WILLOUGHBY, EDD W.
WILSON, LEE M.
WILSON, OLIVER C.
WILSON, PAUL L.
WINBURNE, JACK C.
WITHERSPOON, JAMES E.
WITT, CHARLES D.
WITTERS, HAROLD D.
WOLCOTT, DONALD H.
WOLDRING, JAY
WOLF, JOHN J.
WOOD, GLEN S.
WOOD, HARRY C.
WOOD, PHILLIP J.
WORLEY, SHELBY C.
WOZNIAK, THEODORE J.
WRIGHT, FRANK
WRIGHT, HUGH A.
WRIGHT, OREN W.
WRIGHT, VIRGIL L.
WYATT, SAMUEL P.

- Y -
YOPP, RALPH M.
YOUNG, E.P.
YOUNG, FRED D.
YOUNG, LAVAR H.

- Z -
ZACHERY, BILLY J.
ZAGULA, MAX M.
ZAOLINO, JOSEPH
ZEALOR, MORRAY P.
ZEBER, R.L.
ZELLMER, HOWARD
ZENNER, JOSEPH W.
ZIEMAN, JOHN
ZUNIGA, ERNEST

Members That Are Known To Have "Crossed The Bar

Walter E. Richardson
(President, 1977-79)
Angelo H. Belotti
(1st VP, 1982-89)
U.S. Hearn
R.A. Sears
Anthony Stauss
Vern D. Monson
J.C. Dimond
E.W. Hall
W.K. Memdenhall Jr.
F.E. Plant
J. McClave
Paul Stewart
J. Ridway
E.A. Bailey
T.L. Peterson
W.H. Winkler Sr.
Charles W. Hall
W.F. Carter
W.C. Deppe
H.A. Lorenz
Carl E. Taca
W. Donnelson
E. Stevens
M. Gewertz
C. Schwab
V.L. Bartley
F. Larios
C.G. White
William Weese
John Hayes
W.E. Bonadurer
J.C. Luce
J.E. Britt
H. Hertel
F. Walch
D. Welch
L. Avery
C.K. Bergin
W.T. McCarry
J.M. Wilson
R.V. (Ellis) Patterson
R.F. Jay
Robert Rosenheim
W.F. Haynes
I.C. Chidester
C. Pederson
"Tony" Fontecchio
H. Cox
L. Abraham
W.H. Bradbury
J. McGinty
Butch Player
Gerald W. Stanley
G.I. Martin
Raleigh Blanchard
J.R. Robinson
W.W. Curry
E. McKowan
D. Anderson
W.C. Avery
Leo Hoffman
C.A. Bryant
R.E. Eichenhorst
C.L. Kellog
Steve J. Kusernak
John L. Perkins
Gustin Froyd
W. Anderson
O.L. Hartle
W. Mackey
F. Collins
A. Nichols
F. Thorsell

J.E. Fender
B.A. Robertson
Williamson
Delmar D. Rowley
Kenneth C. Sims
Joseph Minnitti
J.F. Graham
L. Grabil
S. Kovack
V. Lutz
Edwin J. Segner
Charles Staggs
O.W. Fleming
G.W. Wallace
Lawrence Jackman
C.C. Blumer
James D. Barr
Glenn E. Ferguson
W.E. Benedict
George Geyer
F. Holler
V. Riska
J. Rice
William Tillman
J.J. Hamsa
S.E. Ross
Francis Perry
Marion P. Hill
C. John Carlson
Paul Dudas
D.C. Raash
J. Monday
J. Mills
C. Willard
J. Slattery
Donald Tramell
P.J. Kuyper
B.R. Wheat
Milton A. Shuett
P.B. Pratt
V.M. Cottrill
J.C. Brown
J.P. Blencowe
J. Gribble
N. DeVillars
William Colina
R. Hathaway
R. Richter
Clarence "Pete" Wernick
Emil R. Dragovich
(President, 1979-82)
C. Spraw (Plankowner)
E.R. Alverson
R.D. Lane
H.E. Whitcher
Robert A. Stahl
R.L. Ambrosia
H.L. Schutz
J.C. Sarayusa
J. Howell
R. Fields
I. Russum
D. Root
J. Miller
G.G. Crum
P.J. Landry
Oliver Thompson
Walter Klaus
Lawrence K. Hollenbeck
John Narusis
J.F. Hughes
R. Wigger
R. Heller
W. Weitzel
J. Reidhar

C.F. Lutz
G.M. Davis
C.F. Reissing
Leland Neece
J.D. Layton
Paul J. Mollaun
Virgil Zoll
R.O. Williams
G. Culver
L. Rodgers
V. Fogel
D. Hannan
R. Skipper
F.E. Dodge
E.F. Rice
J.D. Sebastian
Raymond Casey
Russel M. Andrews
George B. Spakes
L. Sarbuck
D.F. Spengler
H. Holden
H. Paris
C. O'Hearn
W. Feitz
D.E. Drennon
B. Richardson
R. Workman
Edward Johnson
Vernon West
W.W. Carmack
E. Hussey
J.J. Jeppsen
H. Oliver
R. Goodell
J. Mines
B. Silvar
R.J. Kellner
L.J. Thomas
Eban Wischow
Allen Barnabei
J.R. Stanger
W.G. Langbehn
G.R. Tiedemann
Newell Culver
C. Greathouse
S. Mitchell
I. Hall
E. Nutter
W. Kivi
F. Turner
Fred R. Rodden
Lewis H. Caw
Martin Sevick
W.C. Leake
T.H. Crawford
H. Godchaux
J. North
N. Bailey
L. Morand
M. Kovich
H. Kodus
R.A. Roe
Fredrick Ratzel
H.B. Mattox
P.D. Boyce
E.T.B. Glenn
W.R. Harris
C. Regelman
C. Benson
R. Edwards
J. Patton
F. Haberlein
J.J. Korbus
C.L. Wentworth

Harry J. Sheffler
J.D. Judy
Merl Tree
G.G. Waldrope
W.O. Moreland
H. Keller
C. Anderson
W. Bierschwale
G. Ondrick
Walter Klaus
J.B. Odom
Hank Whitcher
William T. Hanley
B.E. Epperson
B.A. Strait
H. Dressler
D. Walker
D. Edwards
C. Henkel
L.A. Lawrence
J. McGovern
D. Root
L. Smith
Robert G. Smith, MD
(1st VP, 1979-82
R. Bitting (Plankowner)
R.E. Cronin
H.M. Perry
Peter Trapani
William Hagerman
V.N. Anderson
J.D. Pendleton
R.N. Dinkel
A.N. Wiggs
Robert Beaman
O. Hankins
O. Rumore
P. Koteski
K.K. Hettiger
M. Schrieker
Virgil Caudill
Harlan C. Eisnagle
Francis O. Pudas
F.E. Pomeroy
L. Garlinger
R.W. Smithwick
L. DeVan
Leo Sylliansen
J. Parker
M. Southern
O.J. Hickman
F.J. Skiftness
Russel Sherk
Herbert Kuntz
R.H. Remmer
R.B. Pickett
E.J. Zinda
T. Wolfe
A. Johnson
J. Delton
C. Noland
C. Stansbury
J.T. Hilton
J.D. Stewart
Harley Shirley
James S. Brawley
Elmer U. Caldwell
Troy A. King
H.D. Matthews
W.A. Miller
R. Ruby
R. Arsenault
G. Will
E.L. Johnson
E.H. Holt

G.E. Tate
Ira "Bill" Pennell
Walter S. Anderson
R.G. Sproul
Lyle Steelman
J.L. Williams
John Shindle
John Starkey
R. Hettinger
F. Deluhery
M. Robinson
W. McKim
R. Worth
John E. Kozoil
R.L. Jennings
P.H. McVanus
W.H. Schuh
W.H. Huber
B. Thompson
W. Watkins
G. Haynes
F. Daeley
G. Bule
J. Miller
Gus Orsal
George W. Allanson
M. Jordan
E.O. Newton
J.W. Osbourne
P.P. Kusnerak
E. Frost
W. Temples
H. Schreiber
N. Kaschak
W.K. Clark
T. Moore
F.C. Peterson
E.G. Gilbertson
Cecil V. Harper
O.C. McGuffee
T.L. Boterf
J.E. McKelvey
D. Hamilton
H. Teklinski
E. Ballard
A. Meredith
J. Crawley
D.R. Nichols
Harold Gaylord
Virgil L. Reed
Anthony D. Vaccaro
William Gouture
H.L. Shannon
D. Pratt
A. Hooker
S. McCord
Robert Bolish
L. Wahrmund
D.W. Hardin
A.F. Rudman
Luther Haskins
Robert A. Winston
J.L. Faughn
B.S. Chatfield
E. Gambill
B.W. Moss
Wilson Weeks
William L. Tucker
E. Dessert
N. Poohar
W.A. Stephens
Harold A. Schreiber

INDEX

— A —
Admiralty Islands   11, 37, 45
Alcock, Harold B.   4
Anderson, W.S.   22, 58
Andrews, Rex William   4, 49
Anguar Islands   11, 37
Apamama   11, 25, 68
Arkansas   46

— B —
Bails, Robert   58
Baird, Lt   45
Barnes, Vernon   45
Batchelle, James H.   62, 63
Berry, Lou   41, 42
Betio Island   11, 25
Bingham, D.C.   13
Bitting, Russell J.   14, 15
Blimling, Donald H.   58
Boise   46
Bone, Freddie R.   4, 32, 34, 59
Breadman, James   49
Brier, Claire R.   4
Bryan, G.S.   13
Bryan Y3/C   58
Buckner Bay   49, 52

— C —
Canty, Dr.   50
Carlson, Colonel   11, 25
Carte, Nick   15
Cedillo, Luis Z.   4
Cedillo, Zamor   49
Chambers, C.H.   4, 49
Chase, William H.   14, 25, 26, 27, 28, 34
Clark, F.H.   13
Coleman, F.H.   57
Columbia   46
Connally, Admiral   11
Conner, Glenn H.   56
Connolly, Admiral   28, 29
Consill, J.A.   49
Conwill, J.A.   4
Cotter, Mike   62
Craft, Horace D.   50
Craven, T.T.   13
Cripes, Kenneth,   4
Crow, Ensign   20
Crow, Howard D.   4, 58
Crowe, Ensign   67
Culver, Newl G.   23

— D —
David, Justin Joseph   47, 49
Davis, L.P.   13
Decker, B.W.   13
Denver   12, 46
Deyo, M.L.   12
Dibb, Lawrence E.   33, 41, 57
Dunn, Robert A.   4

— E —
Eck, L.A.   64
Efate Island   10, 25, 68
Egen, 1/C   15

Eniwetok   11, 32, 64, 68
Epperson, Buck   45
Eresman, Arthur   63
Espiritu Santo   10
Evans, Buck   41
Evans, Charles E.   4

— F —
Fiji Islands   10, 22, 68
Forselles, Charles   16, 18, 33
Fox, James E.   15
Fox, Nathan   61
French, Lt.   26

— G —
Gabrielson, Harry   43, 59, 62
Gartes, Eugene Webster   49
Gates, Eugene W.   4
Gilbert Islands   10, 13, 27
Ginn, James B.   4
Gist, I.W.   48
Gist, James William   4, 49
Glassford, W.A.   13
Glumack, Raymond G.   90
Godwin, D.C.   13, 65
Goldman, Commander   59
Goldstein, Morris   4, 41
Goodell, Robert H.   44
Gore, Lt.   64
Guam   13, 30, 48, 62, 64, 69

— H —
Hadley, H.W.   58
Haligas, William   34, 50, 59
Hallman, Ralph   15
Halsey, Admiral   12, 45
Halvis, John   49, 50
Hansen, Bob   22
Hargrove, Roy Petty   4, 49
Harrington, James D.   4
Hathcox, William M   4
Hawaiian Islands   10, 11, 27
Hill, Admiral   25, 26
Hill, H.W.   11
Hill, Harry W.   25
Hill, Lawrence Loman   4, 49
Hilton, Carl C.   4
Hoffman, Charles J.   4
Honolulu   28, 32, 46, 57, 62
Houle, Bob   25
Howel, James W.   33
Hughes, Charles Evans   9, 15
Hydinger, "Punch"   50

— I —
Idaho   46
Indianapolis   11, 27

— J —
Jacobs, Richard   64
Jendrziczyk, Erwin   64
Johnson, Harry D.   26
Johnson, Indiana   17
Johnson, John W.   45

Johnson, Johnny   40
Johnson, Leroy A.   4
Jones, C.H.   13
Jones, Hilary P.   9
Jurovich, Robert   63

— K —
Keihne, Rudy   20
Kelly, John   45
Kendrick, Stonewall J.   4
Kerama Retto   47, 69
Kester, Robert E.   4
Kimberly, V.A.   13
Kimmel, H.E.   57
Kincaid, Admiral   11, 45
Kinsey, Harold N.   21
Klemann, J.V.   13
Klimcak, J.T.   57
Koerner, Fred   64
Korr, Ed   45
Kukon, Thomas E.   4
Kwajalein   11, 28, 29, 64, 68
Kyushu   52

— L —
Lamb, Fargust E.   4
Land, Arnold Leon   4, 49
Land, John   20
Langford, Leslie G.   4, 49
Lanning, Harold M.   4
Leyte Gulf   4, 11, 12, 33, 37, 38, 39, 41, 43, 45, 46, 61, 69
Logan, G.C.   13
Longtin, F.J.   62
Louisville   46
Lowe, Clarence A.   64
Lowerre, Warren   59
Lowery, Warren   45
Lucas, Jack S.   4
Lutz, C.S.   58
Lutz, Carroll F.   4
Luzon   12

— M —
Mackay   20
Mangold, Jack E.   4
Manly, Pete C.   4
Manning, Lt.   66
Marianas Islands   29, 52, 53, 59
Markshausen, Robert T.   4
Marshall Islands   11
Mason   59
Mathews, Harrison D.   33
McBeth, R.A.   64
McClellan, Harold   49
McCutcheon, Warren   4, 56, 64, 67
McKee, E.W.   13
McPherson, R.A.   25
McVeigh, Francis   44
Medaris, Jack Edward   4, 49
Midway   10, 64, 68
Milligan, Lloyd T.   4
Minitti, Joe   58

Minneapolis   12, 46
Mitchell, William (Billy)   14
Mitscher, Marc   48, 50
Montgomery, Wlm. P.   41
Morgan, Leo   96
Moore, Homer   58
Morris, R.   13
Morris, Robert   64
Morton, Norman   56, 65
Mosher, Richard   51
Mountz, G.L. "Salty"   61
Moyce, Harry   15
Murphy, Lt.   58
Mycka, Walter J.   2, 6, 8, 10, 18, 21, 23, 24, 56, 64, 70

— N —
Nashville   46
Nelson, John A.   42, 43
New Caledonia   44, 64
New Guinea   26
New Hebrides   10, 25, 63, 68
Newman, James "Windy"   64
Newman, Victor D.   4
Nimitz, Admiral   33, 34
Niss, Rudolph R.   4
Noel, William Orville   4, 49
Nopen, Irwin G.   4
Normandy   4, 29

— O —
Obermeier, Walt   64
O'Dell, Bill   68
Okinawa   4, 12, 44, 46, 47, 48, 49, 50, 51, 52, 53, 58, 61, 69
Oldberg, Stirling M.   22
Oldendorf, J.B.   11
O'Quin, Hollis   59
O'Rourke, Henery J.   4, 42
Overstreet, Rufus M., Jr.   4

— P —
Palau Islands   11, 37, 64
Parker, Jack D.   34
Parks, James A., Jr.   57
Peacock, "J." "R."   4
Pearl Harbor   4, 9, 11, 12, 13, 15, 22, 24, 25, 28, 32, 34, 35, 56, 57
Peay, Charles R.   25, 28, 29
Pelelieu   11
Peterson, R.A.   25
Peterson, W.E. "Pete"   15
Philippine Islands   37, 43, 61, 69
Poole, Oscar Ezra   33
Porter, Representative   15
Porterfield   40
Porterfield, L.B.   13
Portland   46
Preston, C.F.   13, 14
Proctor.   23
Prue, George E.   64
Puckett, H.W.   57

— Q —

Quinn, J.P.   64

— R —

Randall, Nelson H.   57
Ray, H.J.   13, 28, 34
Rector, Howard   65
Ricketts, Claude   62, 63
Riley, Layton F.   4
Riley, Shipmate   41
Roi Atoll   28, 29
Ross, Steve   64
Russell Jr., Lee   44
Rutherford, "Red"   67
Ryckman, Lisa Levitt   64
Ryman, Gordon Odell   4, 43

— S —

Saipan   4, 11, 29, 30,
   31, 32, 33, 34, 52, 59,
   64, 68
San Bernardino Strait   12, 45
Schmitt, Aloysius H.   19
Scott, Harold Arie   4, 49
Seagraves, Edward H.   4
Segraves, Edward
   Herbert   49
Sellers, D.F.   13
Short, Leslie Vernon   65
Sinatra, Loreto L.   43
Sitler, C.M.   32
Smith, "Howling Mad"   11
Smith, Julian J.   25, 64
Smith, "Snuffy"   32

Solomon Islands   10,
   11, 25, 35, 64
Sprague, Admiral   45
Staggs, Charles   57
Starr Jr., Rhea   64
Stillwell, General   53
Sturgeon, Raymond W.   4
Swanson, Ed   19, 20, 60, 61

— T —

Tarawa   10, 25, 26, 27,
   63, 64, 68
Taussig, J.K.   13
Taylor, Lieutenant   21
Texas   46, 49
Thau, Melvin   4
Thomas, Glenn C.   4
Thro, J.B.   57
Todd, M.M.   41
Tuscaloosa   46, 49

— U —

USS Alabama   14
USS Arizona   8, 9, 16, 22,
   23, 63
USS Benham   58
USS Biloxi   11, 69
USS Boggs   58
USS Bountiful AH 9   44
USS California   9, 11,
   17, 46, 58
USS Colorado   14, 46, 50
USS Comfort   13, 47, 48, 69
USS Cummings   58

USS Curtiss   58
USS Dewey   58
USS Downs   20
USS Helena   58
USS Luce   12, 46
USS Massachusetts   23
USS Mississippi   46, 69
USS Monongahela   64
USS Mount Hood   36, 37
USS Neosho   57
USS Nevada   9, 15, 17, 23,
   46, 49, 58, 63
USS New Mexico   46, 69
USS Oglala   58
USS Oklahoma   8, 16, 18,
   19, 20, 21, 23, 57, 58,
   63, 66
USS Pathfinder   64
USS Pennsylvania   9, 11,
   12, 46, 58
USS Phelps   58
USS Phoenix   58
USS Randolph   65
USS Sangamon   25
USS Shaw   20, 58
USS Solace   58
USS Tennessee   9, 10, 12,
   16, 22, 24, 26, 28, 46,
   58, 64, 67
USS Saufley   68
USS Wasp   69
USS West Virginia   8, 9, 12,
   14, 16, 22, 24, 46, 49,
   50, 58, 63

— V —

Van Hoose, Stan J.   63
Vann, Tompkins M.B.   62
Voyles, Hollice L.   4
Vreeken, Fred R.   2, 14,
   28, 29, 30, 32, 45,
   49, 51

— W —

Walch, Francis J.   20, 21
Walt, George   15
Welch, F.R.   27
Welch, Floyd R.   22
Whaley, F.C.   25
Whims, Howard   61
White, Clyde Tennyson   4, 49
Whitley   61
Willet, Cotton   50
Williams, F.   15
Williams, Vernon R.   4
Wilsey, H.F.   57
Wilson   61
Wilson, Captain   58
Wilson, J.D.   13
Wilson, J.W.   48
Wilson, John L.   61
Woodridge, Robert M.   4
Woolridge, R.N.   32

— Y —

Young, Lavar   64

— Z —

Zoller, Vernon   4

Company 39-21, Oct. 11, 1939, U.S.N.T.S. San Diego, CA. All of the men pictured were sent to the USS Maryland or USS California in October 1939. Leo R. Morgan is second row from the bottom, ninth position from the left. (Courtesy of Leo R. Morgan)

www.ingramcontent.com/pod-product-compliance
Lightning Source LLC
Jackson TN
JSHW051656231224
75956JS00006B/41